Celestine Sibley

Reporter

Celestine Sibley

Reporter

EDITED BY *Richard L. Eldredge*

Hill Street Press **d** *Athens, Georgia*

A HILL STREET PRESS BOOK

Published in the United States of America by Hill Street Press LLC
191 East Broad Street, Suite 209   Athens, Georgia 30601-2848 USA
706-613-7200
info@hillstreetpress.com   www.hillstreetpress.com

Certain selections in this book have been reprinted by arrangement with the
Atlanta Journal-Constitution.

Cover photograph courtesy of the *Atlanta Journal-Constitution*. / All other
photographs appearing in this book are from the Celestine Sibley papers at the
Special Collections Department, Robert W. Woodruff Library, Emory
University. Reprinted by arrangement with the Estate of Celestine Sibley.

Text design by Betty Palmer McDaniel.

Printed in the United States of America.

Library of Congress Cataloging-in-Publication Data

Sibley, Celestine.
    Celestine Sibley: reporter / edited by Richard L. Eldredge.
        p.   cm.
    Includes biographical references.
    ISBN 1-58818-043-3 (alk. paper)
        I. Eldredge, Richard L., 1964– II. Title.
    PS3569.I256 A6 2001
    814'.54—dc21   2001016770

ISBN # 1-892514-043-3

10   9   8   7   6   5   4   3   2   1

First printing

Being a reporter is one of the noblest things you can do in life. Letting the people know. It's really a holy cause. Time after time after time, in the middle of corruption and disgrace and bad politics, I've seen people come through and do for people. I write about someone in trouble and someone else rallies to help them. Through reporting, things can change.

—Celestine Sibley, April 1, 1999

CONTENTS

Chapter 2: On Assignment

Chapter 3: Breaking News

Chapter 4: The Hollywood Years

Chapter 5: In Court

Chapter 6: Politics

FOREWORD

Though my grandmother resisted the appellation of legend for herself, her life, most definitely, was full of legends. There was Anjette Lyles, who poisoned a couple of husbands, a mother-in-law, and a child for insurance money. There was the son who tried to take over his deceased father's title as governor of Georgia by gun force. There was the evil man who was sentenced to the electric chair as punishment for murdering a cow thief and the star witness against the villain, a one-eyed fortune-telling witch. There was the airplane full of many of Atlanta's most prominent arts patrons which crashed just outside of Paris. Equally sad was the young United States president who was shot and the sound of the "deep-voiced" church bells ringing for him in downtown Atlanta. There was the great black family who raised up the meek and gave them a mighty voice, a family which would live up to the dignity of its name—King.

All those legends became the fairytales of my brother's and my childhood. They were the heroes and heroines, villains and saints, saviors and sinners who filled lazy hot summer days spent drifting back and forth on the porch swing at Sweet Apple and the cold winter nights in front of the hearth. They were with us each trip to the grocery store, every car trip, and each time we drove by a courthouse. They were the everyday, the norm, the expected in our childhood.

"Everybody talked to mama when they wouldn't talk to anyone else at the paper," my mother, Mary Little-Vance, told me.

My grandmother was riding with her in the car one day in 1980 when the radio announced that the boiler at the Bowen Homes housing project day care had exploded. My grandmother asked to be dropped off so that she could catch the bus to the scene. It was on the bus that she'd get the best story from the parents rushing to see if their children were okay.

"There was a lot of criticism at Bowen Homes about the electronic media pushing parents around," my mother told me. "Your grandmother had a lot of respect for others' privacy and she didn't take it lightly. She didn't exploit people for a story—she just got the best damn story. In her reporting in the legislature, she didn't report who was sleeping with whom—although she knew where all these bodies were buried. She just didn't think *that* was the story.

"Her professional life was so amazing and her instincts were so on it. When it came to a story, she didn't have the problem of the *woman instinct*—guilt over leaving her children. If anything, she would have felt guilty about not covering a good story."

Still, a lot of times, my mother told me, "we were so bad, she couldn't get a babysitter so she'd have to take us. When Old Eugene Talmadge was on his death bed and wouldn't see anyone, the governor's aides told him, 'There's a woman reporter out here with two little babies who are driving her crazy.' His response: 'Well, send Miss Sibley in.'"

Through the stories which her former colleague Rich Eldredge has so thoughtfully and knowledgeably selected for this book, just as in the columns for which she was so well known in her later years, Celestine Sibley springs, once again, to life. Looking back now, I know that many of the people and events on which my grandmother reported were nothing short of miraculous. As my own mother reminds me, I should be and am thankful to be the descendent and namesake of such a legend as Celestine Sibley.

If we follow her example—the way she lived, the way she related with her fellow human beings—then we will know the stuff of which legends are made. And maybe, just maybe, we will be able to see a little bit more clearly, as she did, that legends are being made every day.

Sibley Fleming

INTRODUCTION

Each year, thousands of schoolchildren tour the *Atlanta Journal-Constitution* offices in the downtown section of the city. Until her death in 1999, Celestine Sibley, the building's undisputed "queen of our news shop" (as she was once dubbed by *Constitution* publisher Ralph McGill) was the tour's star attraction. She would pause from the column she was usually toiling over in her office and enthusiastically greet the youngsters as they peered in the open door at her seated at *Constitution* editor Henry Grady's century-old rolltop desk.

Like other reporters on the eighth floor, Sibley suffered when, invariably, some of the children appeared bored by the field trip to her hallowed workplace. "We used to have this city editor by the name of Lee Rogers," she once recalled as a tour group of kids tromped through the newsroom, "who would give the children a real show when they came through. He would stick a press card in his hat and start yelling 'Stop the presses! Get me President Roosevelt on the phone!' You could say he had some flair for theater."

Sibley could also spot the press-predisposed children on the tour. They were the ones who stood transfixed and bug-eyed as they watched the massive presses roll downstairs. One or two in each group would inhale the pungent metallic scent of the ink and it would travel to their bloodstream and take up permanent residence. The afflicted were easy to detect—they were the ones already imagining their by-line on the front pages whirling on the machines before them, the ones who didn't mind the ink smears on their hands as they clutched their complimentary copy of that morning's *Constitution* final. Sibley was one of them.

Growing up in 1930s Mobile, Alabama, she was one of the most energetic reporters at Murphy High School's *Hi Times* newspaper. The school paper's faculty adviser Anita Wagner was a former campus corespondent for the *Atlanta Constitution*. At age 15, when the *Mobile Press,* the town's daily newspaper, phoned the high school, looking for Saturday help, Sibley readily volunteered for the non-paying position. When she graduated from Murphy in 1933, the newspaper which billed itself as "Easy To Read and Worth Reading" hired her full-time. Starting salary: seven dollars a week. "She wrote rings around me," former Mobile colleague Dorothy Pitts told the *Mobile Register* in 1999. "She was so good, so enthusiastic."

"I had a happy childhood in Mobile and then I got to work on the paper and that was such a good experience," Sibley reflected in an April 1999 interview.

Because of the newspaper's relatively small staff, Sibley got to pen everything from film reviews (she predicted early on that Bing Crosby was a flash in the pan) to murder trials. By the ripe old age of 19, she was already skilled in interviewing convicted murderers in their jail cells. In 1934, she may have been among the first to report on what would later be termed "global warming." Articles detailing the flights of Amelia Earhart, the kidnapping of Charles Lindbergh, Jr. and the daring escapes of gangster Pretty Boy Floyd regularly surrounded Sibley's often uncredited contributions to the *Press* front page.

In 1936, she followed her new husband and fellow *Press* reporter Jim Little to the nearby *Pensacola News and Journal.* Again, because of the papers' tiny staffs, Sibley covered all aspects of local news, including health stories. When the seaside community opened its modern sanitarium for tuberculosis patients, she reported on it. She also covered the creation of a maternity home for women who didn't have the cash for a hospital stay (the house charged $5 per patient).

In 1941, she again followed her husband Jim, this time to Atlanta when he landed a job with the Associated Press there. The Pensacola paper agreed to let her go—reluctantly. Due to report at the *Atlanta Constitution* on Monday to begin her new $35-a-week job, her Pensacola bosses kept her nose to the typewriter keys until late Saturday afternoon. Finally she tied a baby bed to the back of the car and packed her mother, Muv, and her small children, Jimmy and Susan, inside for the seven-hour trip to Atlanta. Her timing proved impeccable. Minutes later, at 6:30 Saturday night, a gunman showed up outside the *News-Journal* building and opened fire on his ex-wife, wounding the woman and killing her friend. He then turned the gun on himself.

When Sibley arrived for work at the *Atlanta Constitution* on July 21, 1941, the city was in the midst of a heatwave and a garbage strike. Georgia Governor Eugene Talmadge took to the airwaves of radio station WSB to warn his "fellow countrymen" against Edwin R. Embree's new book *Brown America* which advocated "the co-mingling of the races, using the same parks, the same hotels, the same restaurants and the same schools. We revolt at the thought!" Atlanta Mayor Roy LeCraw was attempting to navigate his way to his car without stepping on a dead dog, a by-product of the trash strike. The city's minor league baseball team, the Atlanta Crackers, inched closer to the Southern League championship, beating the Nashville Vols 6 to 4 in a tight 10-inning game.

In the pages of the *Constitution*, editor Ralph McGill was eloquently railing against communism and Nazism on the editorial page. Davison's department store was hawking mink coats for $69. On the funny pages, flatfoot Dick Tracy was hot on the trail of gangster Little Face Finny.

Sibley hit the streets of her new hometown with dyspeptic veteran *Constitution* reporter Frank Drake (an ulcer sufferer, he carried a thermos of milk and antacid tablets with him) who was instructed to show her the ropes. Even then, she noted the city's nervous habit of using jackhammers to dig up Atlanta's past in favor of erecting something new.

From the start, she loved the *Constitution*, its rickety building and the town to which she was being introduced. Sibley was initially assigned to the federal beat but, being new on staff, she covered a wide range of stories.

"From the day I arrived in Atlanta I knew it was where I belonged," she observed in 1999. "I looked around at the big city and I just loved it. Mobile is one of those old Southern cities that doesn't have the affection and warmth to a newcomer that Atlanta has. You meet people in Atlanta and they remember you and they speak to you on the street. Muv moved up here with me and she had always loved Atlanta. The day after we arrived, she put on her hat and went out to see the Cyclorama. She loved Atlanta and I guess I was influenced by that."

On December 7, less than six months into her new position, Pearl Harbor was bombed, dramatically altering the landscape of the newspaper. As able-bodied males rushed to join the military, Sibley found herself named the paper's first female assistant city editor. "I had to learn everything in case our city editor had to go and fight," she explained 56 years later.

She bristled at the notion—suggested to her by an overly admiring younger reporter in 1997—that she was a trailblazer for women in a workplace traditionally dominated by men. "I was no such thing," she said. "We had no choice. There was a war on, the country was at stake and we had a paper to get out. People were concerned about the future of the country and they were worried about their loved ones. They needed news. I didn't much aspire to the job. You had to spend too much time reading other people's stories instead of going out and writing your own."

"Celestine was a great feminist," argues longtime friend and former *Newsweek* Atlanta bureau chief William A. Emerson, Jr. "There weren't a lot of women in the entire country doing what she was doing. There were women in the newsroom but most were relegated to covering fashion or society happenings."

"If she owned white gloves, they were probably boxing gloves," says Lee Walburn, a former *AJC* colleague, now *Atlanta* magazine's editor-in-chief. "There was an incredible toughness to her. She didn't need Tony Robbins screaming 'You can do it!' in her ear. She just did it."

Echoes Emerson: "At that time, very few women covered the big scale things that get you on the front page, but Celestine was a person who never never pushed herself forward. If she had made the pitch, she could have written anywhere. Her ego never got in the way of getting the story. That was always her primary goal."

"Because of the war, we were in demand," explains former *Constitution* colleague Doris Lockerman, who in 1948 was named the newspaper's first female associate editor by Ralph McGill. "It was us and the old guys who weren't allowed to sign up. Our editor Ralph McGill was a very liberal man and there was no suppression of women at the *Constitution* in any way. We were given many opportunities. It was a real departure for Southern journalism. However, we also happened to be responsible and very qualified people."

Like other females in America's newsrooms at the time, Sibley was frequently called upon for "sob sister" duties—the art of female reporters commiserating with women in dire straits, frequently murder suspects, coaxing them to open themselves up emotionally and then turning the result into a tear-stained yarn for the next day's edition. Sibley was once sent to the Fulton County jail to interview the so-called Madam X, an unidentified robbery suspect. Evelyn Kobert—on deadline, Sibley got the shamed unemployed clerical worker to reveal her name—was accused of holding up an Alabama Street liquor store with a cap gun. Attempting to make her getaway with $62 in cash while being shot at by the store clerk, Kobert ran straight into two Atlanta police officers. Unlike many of her fellow sob sisters, Sibley managed to get the facts for the front-page story without degrading her subject.

By the late 1940s, Sibley had become equally nimble in the courtroom. Sibley was such a frequent figure at high-profile murder trials, her *Constitution* colleagues had crowned her "the murder queen."

"She was fascinated by murder," says Walburn. "*Murder She Wrote* could have been modeled on her."

In June, 1947, Sibley even succeeded in getting a convicted murderer, Floyd Woodward, freed from his Fulton Tower prison cell. The reporter had first encountered the former "Bunco Ring King" gambler years earlier after he attempted suicide shortly after his conviction. Woodward always maintained that he shot the victim in self-defense. Sibley began looking into the case and, more importantly, began writing about the police and political corruption she was unearthing. Woodward's account of the shooting turned out to be accurate.

The parole board unanimously agreed with her findings and released Woodward. The soft-spoken white-haired prisoner was so grateful to Sibley, he orchestrated his release on "*Constitution* time" (after the *Atlanta Journal*'s deadline) and gave Sibley an exclusive on board the airplane winging him home to California.

She later won the national Pall Mall Big Story award (and a $500 cash prize) for her efforts. The cigarette manufacturer dramatized the story on its weekly TV program. The nicotine-free, vertically blessed Sibley was played by a chain-smoking, petite actress whose character was referred to onscreen as "Sib."

By the late 1970s, even after she settled full-time into the less hectic role of newspaper columnist, Sibley's insatiable curiosity regarding what drives people to kill continued unabated. During her career, in between assignments, she turned out six murder mysteries.

It should be noted that in the middle of life's worst moments, the individuals who assume the task of reporting on those moments oftentimes rely on their macabre senses of humor as they boil events down for mass consumption by readers. Some reporters use dark humor as a safety mechanism, a method of making Olympic Park and abortion clinic bombings, madmen daytraders on shooting sprees and the premature deaths of British princesses a little more bearable. Such was the case at the *Atlanta Journal-Constitution* on October 3, 1995.

All morning, reporters feverishly prepared stories with one eye on CNN and the Associated Press wires as the Simpson verdict was readied in Los Angeles. Someone playfully suggested a wager on the outcome of the drawn-out, dicey case. A new staffer volunteered to take up the dollar bills and record the names of bettors with their selected verdict. As he stuffed bills into an interoffice envelope, the staffer heard a voice behind him. "What are you up to, child?" Sibley inquired casually as she glanced up at the TV screen overhead. The red-faced reporter admitted the exercise in bad taste to the veteran columnist. "I'll be right back," Sibley said. A minute later, she returned with a dollar bill and the instructions, "Put me down for a 'Guilty.'"

In 1997, Sibley fed her fascination about the Sara Tokars murder case and what allegedly drove the accused Fred Tokars, Sara's husband and Atlanta businessman, to hire two men to kill his wife in front of the couple's two small boys. Sibley showed up in court to catch first-hand some of the headline-making testimony. She sat next to her friend and then-*AJC* police reporter R. Robin McDonald who was covering the trial for her eventual book, *Secrets Never Lie: The Death of Sara Tokars.*

"I knew she was having trouble hearing some of the testimony, so as I took my notes I made sure the words were large enough and legible enough for her to follow along," recalls McDonald. "At one point she leaned over and whispered in my ear, 'You take good notes!'" During a break in the case, Sibley went over and warmly greeted old friend and Tokars defense attorney Bobby Lee Cook who had celebrated his 70th birthday during the case.

With her admiration for the courtroom's Shakespearean theatrics, Sibley had been a natural to send to Hollywood to cover the movie-making capitol in the early 1950s. For five years, she contributed celebrity pieces to the Sunday *Atlanta Journal and Constitution* magazine.

"She got access to a Hollywood Who's Who of the period," says friend and 20-year *AJC* colleague film critic Eleanor Ringel Gillespie. "The only star missing was Lassie. What makes her pieces unique from the other celebrity journalism of the time is that she never assumes the role of Hollywood expert. There's always that 'I'm Celestine from the South here in Hollywood' tone to them. She was so struck by what she was seeing and wrote from that perspective. She was acutely aware of her audience back home and never condescended to those readers. In today's celebrity journalism, there is such a tendency to showcase yourself as the writer. In her pieces, she used herself only as a guide for the reader. The results are enchanting and priceless."

From 1958 to 1978, Sibley covered the Georgia General Assembly for the *Constitution* and the *Journal-Constitution*. The annual 40-day task became one of her favorite assignments. In 1959 she wrote: "In the mornings when I stand on Broad Street hopping from one foot to the other in nervous anxiety that the buses to the Capitol have surely stopped running, the sense of expectancy and excitement starts. What will they do today? What wonderful, terrible things will be said? The sessions of the General Assembly are never boring to me. Sometimes incomprehensible, yes. Sometimes maddening, irritating, bewildering, sure. But as people are interesting, as politics is engrossing, the General Assembly is both."

Lawmakers returned the sentiment a few weeks before her death in 1999 when they named the press gallery in the Capitol for her.

"While it can't be said about a lot of reporters, politicians had great admiration for her," reflects former Atlanta Mayor Sam Massell. "In her legislature reporting, her fairness came through. If she had a bias, it didn't show in her stories. She loved the political process and she loved explaining it to people in a way they could relate to."

According to Bill Emerson, Sibley excelled at so many facets of reporting because of an unwavering attraction to people in all walks of life. "She was like Dickens," says Emerson. "She lived in a weird world. Taxi drivers, policemen, legislators, street people and con artists all loved her equally. And they all had equal occupancy in her daily life."

"Along with the *Atlanta Journal*'s Margaret Shannon, Celestine was considered the best female reporter in town," says Doris Lockerman. "When she walked in, people knew a reporter was in the room. She was capable beyond anybody else."

By the 1980s, Sibley had become chiefly identified as the South's most cherished newspaper columnist. Recent transplants to the ever-expanding city of Atlanta and its suburbs hadn't been privy to her work on journalism's front lines.

"I think she sometimes felt confined in that role of revered columnist," says her editor Amanda Miller. "In her later years, there were fewer opportunities to get her hands dirty. She didn't get to go to Coweta County and cover murder trials anymore. She loved the gore of all that!"

"She's best remembered now as a columnist but in my opinion, she was a better reporter," says Lockerman. "She got the facts but there was discernment and wit in her work as well. And judging by how many people who still ask if I knew her or worked with her when I was at the *Constitution,* I can say without hesitation that Celestine Sibley and her work are far from forgotten."

From 1930 to 1999, Sibley had spent the bulk of her waking hours in a newsroom, surrounded by similarly afflicted adrenaline addicts with body clocks all ticking toward the same daily deadline. When she arrived at the *Constitution*'s offices in 1941, the windows were clouded over from the steady stream of cigarette smoke in the air. Reporters were prone to keeping bottles of whiskey in their bottom desk drawers. In 1999, employees with a fondness for nicotine were graciously asked to exit through the newspaper's "Drugs Don't Work Here"-stickered front doors and engage in their habit down Marietta Street in front of the Federal Reserve building. Manual typewriters, glue pots, carbon paper, interoffice memos, switchboard operators, teletypes, potentially lethal copy spikes and copy carriers had been jettisoned in favor of "cut and paste" buttons on computer keyboards, printers, spellcheck, the internet, voice mail and e-mail. In lieu of copy boys dashing through the newsroom with a hot story, Sibley could electronically send her stories to her editor's computer desktop without shifting a muscle in her office chair. The only elements to remain consistent were the long hours, demanding editors, the foodstuffs requiring explanatory signage in the *AJC*'s downstairs "Deadline Diner," the eternal mystery of what would next qualify as "breaking news" and Celestine Sibley's writing style. "Soul is what set her apart from the others," says Bill Emerson.

"Technically she was a solid reporter—very detail-oriented, a good ear for a quote and her copy came quickly and cleanly. But she also had the ability to get to the spiritual aspects of a story. She was a great dramatist. She was a fascinating damn woman and as far as I'm concerned, practically unparalleled in her field."

In 1999, Sibley more modestly summarized her nearly 60-year reporting career in Atlanta saying, "I've covered the courthouses in the city, the capitol and Grady Hospital and I've really become friends with basic Atlantans. There were celebrities along the way, of course, but my mother was funny about that. Movie stars would come to town and I would cover them or I would interview generals or something. She wasn't particularly impressed. But when I interviewed Mr. Hastings from the Hastings Seed Co.—oh, she was so impressed! She said, 'Oh, what was he like? What did he look like? What did he say?' She had always ordered her seeds from the Hastings people, you see."

When it was suggested that she had become as readily identified with Atlanta as Coca-Cola, Sibley laughed and said, "And the Ku Klux Klan and *Gone With the Wind,* right? It's just that I've lived here longer than anybody else!

"If it's true, I'm pleased, of course. I recently did a television thing and the people there asked me what I liked about Atlanta. I couldn't think of a real good answer for them. I know they wanted me to say the things we have, like the Braves and the symphony. I like those things but, for me, its really about the people. I've been able to cover everything for the paper. I've covered *everything*. Along the way, I've met a lot of people—people you don't get to meet if you're married to an insurance salesman and live in Morningside."

Chapter One

Cub Reporter

Overleaf: This profile accompanied Sibley's 1936 marriage announcement in the *Mobile Press-Register.*

As these early stories from the Mobile Press *demonstrate, Sibley's attention to detail and her ability to capture the individual rhythms of an interview subject's voice were already firmly in place in 1934. She was 19 years old.*

The Mobile Press

Young Baldwin Hunter Gives Blood to Aid Boy

April 13, 1934

Thirteen-year-old Ford Cooke is still flat on his back in the orthopedic ward of the Mobile infirmary from the bone ailment which has kept him almost helpless for the last eight months, but today a little color has crept into his cheeks, a little hope into his blue eyes and in his heart there is brightly burning a little flame of gratitude to a youth who came from the backwoods near Bay Minette last night to give his own blood to make it possible for Ford to travel the road back to health.

W.C. Hoffman, 20, a youth who Ford says, "makes his living hunting and fishing around Bay Minette where I live," came to Mobile Thursday night to offer gratis his own strong, red blood to the little neighbor boy who recently underwent his third operation for the painful bone disease, osteomylitis.

"He's the kindest thing," Ford declared Friday, his eyes brightening as he talked of the blood transfusion young Hoffman made possible.

"I'm already feeling pretty good and I reckon now that I've got more blood in my veins I'll get better right along.

Good Fishing Weather

"It's good fishing weather, though to have to be in bed like this," he added a little wistfully, taking in the sunshine which made bright splashes of light on his white counterpane.

Ford has been in the Rotary Club's orthopedic ward at the infirmary for many months. Before he joined the little group of white-faced boys and girls there, he was confined at Providence infirmary where he underwent two other operations.

"I reckon it will be at least four months before I can leave the infirmary," he explained, "and after that it might be a couple before I can even get around with crutches. I don't really mind being here so much but it's mighty good weather for farming."

Homesick For Pete

Ford is a real farm lad. His parents, Mr. and Mrs. E.B. Cook, have a place nine miles out of Bay Minette and Ford is desperately homesick for his pets, "Rip" and "Ranger," half-police and half-hound hunting dogs. He even feels a pang of nostalgia for the pig, which he had to feed, and the chickens, whose eggs he had such hard times finding.

However, the blood transfusion made possible Thursday night by young Hoffman has given the little boy new hope. He has even started studying up on his lessons so he can enter the seventh grade next year.

"It was a mighty fine thing for him to do," Ford declared, "and I want to thank him more as soon as I'm out of here."

The Mobile Press

Breadwinner Held in Jail, Family of Eight Hungers

May 16, 1934

Thirty-five miles north of Mobile, in a 40-acre stretch of pine woods, a three-room shanty bakes in the sun and its occupants, a tired, ill, old woman, a young mother, and six children, ranging in age from 14 to four years, wonder where their next meal is coming from.

Up one flight of stairs in the county jail, a lanky sunburned man peers wistfully through iron bars and waits patiently for the turnkey's call that there is mail for him. He is Levoyd Sullivan, convicted of slaying his 16-year-old brother, Ed Sullivan. He has been waiting almost two weeks for word from home.

No Way To Get In

"I know they can't get in to see me, because they don't have no way of going anywheres," Sullivan explained, "but I can't figure out why they don't write to me unless they're in the same fix I'm in—no stamps or paper. My mother hasn't been well in a long time, and I heard that since my father's death she's been worse. I don't know what'll become of them all unless I can get out."

Sullivan was convicted of murder in the shooting of his younger brother by a circuit court jury Saturday, and was sentenced to ten years in the penitentiary. His attorney, Norvelle R. Leigh, III, is seeking a new trial in the case.

Can't Make $1,000 Bond

"My lawyer's got my bond down to $1,000," Sullivan went on in the same monotonous, hopeless tone, "but I can't get nobody to go it for me. If I could get out and do a little work to be sure my folks were provided for I wouldn't care.

" 'Course, being in jail for something you didn't do—and the Lord knows I didn't kill Ed!—is hard enough, but I wouldn't mind it if I just knowed my wife and little boy and my mother and brothers and sisters were all right."

Sullivan has seen none of his people since before his trial. His wife, with whom he lived at the home of his parents near Shady Grove chapel, a small community a few miles from Mount Vernon, went up to Washington county to stay with her grandmother for a while, but Sullivan fears that she and the baby have returned to his mother's home and he knows they are suffering for lack of food.

Generations Stay On Spot

Asked if he could get work if he were permitted bail, Sullivan replied positively, "Yes'm. We've got some turpentine on our 40 acres that I could work and I'm sure I could sell it or take it out in trade at the store."

Sullivan was born 24 years ago on the same 40-acre tract where he has spent his life. His father, Ed Sullivan, Sr., whose funeral he was permitted to attend in the custody of officers the day before his trial last week, was also born there.

"Them 40 acres was my grandpa's," Sullivan explained, "and we all have always lived on it. The house ain't much—just a big room, a little one and the kitchen—but it's all right."

Left School at 14

He went for four years to Shady Grove school, the small school where his 16-year-old brother, Ed, was a pupil at the time of his death. At the age of 14 years, he left school to take up truck driving and since then he has worked steadily.

"There never was a very long time when I didn't have some kind of work to do. I used to cut cross ties in the river swamp and haul logs and lumber. The trees on our place are right ready for chipping now and there's a good two days' work there."

In reply to a question as to his wife's reaction to his conviction and 10-year sentence, Sullivan said quietly, "I don't know. She may not even know how much time I got, though I did write her a letter Sunday. You see, I haven't seen any of them. Victor Byrd come in to see me the other day and said he would go see them and talk to them. He's going to try to get me bond, but I don't much reckon he'll be able to. He's a poor man just like me. He's as sorry as he can be about the way his cousin testified against me."

As the conversation turned to the subject of his four-year-old son, George Cooper, a wave of homesickness swept over the lanky woodsman and he said chokily, "He's a good little kid. I'm sending him to Sunday school regular and he's going to grow up and stay out of trouble."

The Mobile Press

Grandpop's Memory Right; Weather Growing Warmer

June 5, 1934

The next time grandpop takes a look at the weather and declares that he doesn't know what the world is coming to because in his day summers were never so hot and winters were never so mild, don't smile knowingly and say the old boy's memory is getting tricky. He's right!

At least, he's partially right. In grandpop's day back in the nineteenth century, the winters were more severe and the summers perhaps a shade milder because—as Smithsonian Institute statistics, corroborated by figures at the local weather bureau show—it is getting warmer.

Rise Perceptible

Since this new century started there has been a perceptible rise in temperature, records show. Particularly since 1906 has the thermometer shown an upward trend. Prior to 1906, for 34 years the average temperature was 67.1. The 27 years since 1906, to date, have averaged 68 degrees—an increase of nine-hundredths.

An increase of nine-hundredths of a degree to the layman might not seem great enough for consideration but to statisticians at the weather bureau it is difference enough to be of importance, considering that it is an average figure. There is never a great difference in mean figures, they say, pointing to the fact that between the highest and lowest mean temperatures on record there is only a difference of five degrees. The lowest was reached in grandpop's day back in 1885, when the year averaged 64.8 and the highest year on record was 1911, with an average of 69.8.

Low In Years Gone By

The cold days that grandpop is remembering when he remarks the difference in weather were most likely in 1879, when the mercury hovered below freezing for five consecutive days; 1886, when it took a plunge to 11 degrees and lay low for seven consecutive days, and 1899, when it descended to one degree below zero.

Those years were responsible for the low average of his day, officials of the weather bureau say. However, the rise in temperature is not confined to Mobile alone, for every other locality in the country shows a similar rise for the last 30 or 40 years, it is said.

Attachés at the weather bureau do not pretend to be able to attach any particular significance to the change, nor are they able to attribute it to any phenomenon.

Harry Armstrong, acting meteorologist in the absence of Frank T. Cole, meteorologist in charge, advanced the theory that the weather moves in cycles similar to the cycle system so popular with movie producers. He pointed out that in the latter part of the nineteenth century the weather was probably revolving in a cold cycle and now is apparently moving in a heat cycle.

However, he admitted that those who prate of sun spots and the like probably have just as authoritative a theory and anybody might be right. Anyway, grandpop has the satisfaction of knowing he is.

Tracking Sibley's career at the Pensacola News-Journal *proves tricky. Her new husband Jim Little was the entire reportorial staff of the* Pensacola Journal, *the city's morning newspaper. Sibley served in the same capacity for the afternoon* Pensacola News. *While the daily* Journal's *have been archived on microfilm, the* News *editions weren't saved by the newspaper. Only the newspapers' combined Sunday editions containing Sibley's work are extant. Further complicating matters, by-lines in small city newspapers were not then commonplace (it's possible that the newspapers didn't want to call attention to their minuscule staffs).*

The advantage, as Sibley later pointed out, of being one of only a few people on a newspaper staff is that it automatically guarantees one a wide range of assignments, including an occasional stint as art critic.

Pensacola News-Journal

Maternity Home Now Filling Its Purpose but Officials Have Hopes That It Can Do More

August 8, 1937

"And I leaned over her crib and said, 'Why you little dickens, what do you mean by arriving here on Christmas Day and interrupting my celebration? I ought to paddle you but I believe I'll name you instead. They couldn't call you Santa Claus or Christmas Tree so they ought to call you Merry.'

"Just then the mother piped up and said, 'Why, I think Merry is a real cute name—yes, that's what we'll call her!' And Merry it was. She was a precious baby, too, one of our nicest. You heard about the lovely Christmas layette that came addressed, 'To the

Christmas Baby,' didn't you? Well, when it came we weren't looking for any arrivals but Merry surprised everybody and was born
at midnight, just in time to claim it."

It is a jolly, gray-haired nurse talking, one of the four capable,
motherly persons on duty at the Maternity Home out on 14th
Avenue, and the story she tells is one of countless little anecdotes,
some laugh-provoking, some heart-breaking, that form the warp
and woof of life in the home.

Pay Their Way

The nurses, following the example of their superintendent, kindly
Mrs. Margaret Pfeiffer, wouldn't pry for anything but they feel
sure there is a story of boundless sympathy and generosity back
of the gaily wrapped package which some anonymous donor addressed to "the Christmas Baby." Just as they feel ache around
their hearts when a widowed county mother, breaking her back
over a washtub, saves enough from her earnings to feed the little
ones around her skirts and to make a weekly down payment on
the one that is on the way.

The Maternity House charges $5 for the four or five days' care
it gives mothers and their babies and practically all of its patients
contrive to pay that price. Some few are real charity patients,
some have a little money but not enough for the more expensive
care at a hospital and a great many, like the widowed mother,
put 25 or 50 cents a week in the hands of Mrs. Pfeiffer while
they are still able to work so when their babies come they will
be paid for.

Founded Three Years Ago

The Maternity House was founded three years ago through the
efforts of P.M. Blount and Mrs. Adele Owens. Started as a FERA

project, it has since come to depend almost solely on private donations and the $5 fee paid by patients. Federal agencies help out
where they can, supplying WPA commodities such as prunes and
potatoes when they are available, and National Youth Administration youngsters to help with the sweeping and dusting, to mow
the lawn and wield a paint brush now and then. Mrs. Pfeiffer has
three assistants, Mrs. Sue Wilson, Mrs. Elizabeth Peake and Mrs.
Daley Harrison, all graduate nurses, who, under the WPA regulations, work five days a week each.

Since the organizers of the institution took over the old-fashioned white house at 1706 North 14th Avenue and transformed
it first to a four-bed and then to a six-bed maternity hospital, it
has attracted the attention of a surprising number of charitable
individuals and groups. Church circles work on layettes and tray
clothes, badly needed instruments have been purchased, furnish-
ings have been donated, and cash contributions revive a sagging
budget once in a while.

But workers at the home take a great deal of pride in the fact
that it is largely self-supporting. With 19 mothers to take care of
an average of four days each last month, Mrs. Pfeiffer feels justi-
fiably proud of a grocery bill that amounted to only $30.50. And
there isn't a complaint to be heard in the home.

Beds For Six Patients

"Of course," points out Mrs. Pfeiffer, "that doesn't allow much
variety in the menu but we provide plenty of fresh vegetables,
fruits and cereals, and since they only stay four or five days each,
they don't have to think of the monotony. The cook, Carrie, who
takes her meals here, too, is the only one that is bothered by the
sameness."

The home has beds for six patients and would like to accom-
modate more if there was room. Mothers normally arrive on the

day the baby is expected and remain for four days after he has arrived. County mothers are given an additional day for the same price in consideration of the difficulties of transportation.

Any physician who wants to may send his patients to the Maternity Home for confinement and the home has a staff of physicians who have volunteered for duty in charity cases or in cases where no doctor has been retained by the family.

Mrs. Pfeiffer and the physicians work with a board of directors headed by Mr. Blount and including as members Harry Lurton and Mrs. E.S. Northup.

Ambulances Free

All the ambulance owners in the city have offered the use of their vehicles for transportation of city patients to the house, charging a nominal fee for patients outside the city limits.

Pleased as they are with the progress of the home, those working with it think wistfully of improvements and additions for the future. Scrupulously clean as soap and water and disinfectant can make it and as well-equipped as limited funds allow, the home to the trained nurses who keep it still needs many things—a rolling stretcher that really rolls without requiring the combined services of doctor, nurse and father to get it to the delivery room, a settee for the reception hall where nervous fathers may wait and keep out of the doctor's way, curtains for the hall and a reading lamp, an additional instrument or two.

But the superintendent won't permit her staff to take the deficiencies seriously because, as she points out, "The home is fulfilling the purpose for which it was established, to take care of those who can't afford care elsewhere and to cut down on the appalling maternity death rate which statistics show exists in this state. Of course, we hope to grow and to cope with the problem more effectively."

Pensacola News-Journal

Screwy Abstractions of Surrealist Supply Good Laugh, but They Make You Wonder What They Mean

January 9, 1938

A doll's head floating in a puddle of gray lava with a tree denuded by fuzzy worms and a couple of bashed-in volcanoes in the background . . .

Screwy?

Well, your guess is as good as mine. All I know is that in some circles they call it Art—and it was as such that I viewed it around at the Pensacola federal art gallery the other day.

That particular opus is called *Tentative Preface to Extinction* and if you think you can look and laugh and pass on by, that's all you know about the Surrealists. You'll certainly look and you'll undoubtedly laugh—maybe a little self-consciously at first, looking quickly over your shoulder to be sure that nobody is putting you down as an unlettered, unappreciative boor—but before leaving the gallery you'll be taking a second and maybe a third look at the darned thing to figure out what it's all about. What do they mean *Tentative Preface to Extinction?* Again, your guess is as good as mine.

Mae West in Facade

But *Tentative Preface to Extinction,* found just inside the gallery door, is only the beginning, folks, only the beginning. On your left you'll find all through next week *Facade,* a neat enough front wall to a house of the fretwork era with absolutely nothing behind it except an out-sized man standing, a cadaverous-looking man sitting and way out in the back about where the kitchen would be if the artist had been painting a house there is a strange, black-clad woman with a figure like Mae West.

It's so crazy, so unexpected, this whole WPA exhibit of surrealism and abstraction you'll move dizzily from one to another of approximately 40 canvases on exhibition and refuse to believe your own eyes when you see something that looks like something you've seen before. For instance, there's a little number at the far end of the gallery with a dejected-looking individual sitting on a piece of red sewerage pipe in the foreground, a stretch of blue water behind him with a piece of statuary afloat in it, and a group of learned gentlemen in academic attire lined up under the head of a stuffed horse on his left. I saw that much before I caught the most astonishing thing in the picture: a bandage on the horse's head.

There probably are other things to be catalogued in the picture but I couldn't go on when I saw that bandage. Could a stuffed horse have a headache by any chance?

Real Salmagundi

Then there's the one called *The Changing Scene*. There are enough things on that piece of canvas to keep children busy on all the rainy days from now to doom's day: a window with an old-fashioned horsehair sofa, the head of a bed and a bit of curtain showing through one pane, the little red school house through another, miscellaneous walls and fields and roads and rocks and rills looming up everywhere with a rural route mail box, a pot-bellied stove, a rose-splashed rag rug with a tree growing out of it, a church, a railroad and freight house, pulleys and chains and fields of new corn all cropping out all over the thing. Strangely enough, when you back off and look at it, though, *The Changing Room* is kind of pretty. Reminds you of a nice colored jigsaw puzzle in which all the pieces fit but the picture doesn't match.

Nostalgia is another one to look at but not to understand—a rear view of a nude man staring unhappily at a navy blue sea while a dark hand holds a red rose in the top corner and a signboard advertising hotdogs for a nickel right under it.

Titles Add To Puzzle

Perhaps you've noticed that with the possible exception of *Tentative Preface to Extinction* there's nothing so complicated about the titles of the pictures. Well, don't be misled. You'll find one called *Chicken Coop* and one called *Smokestacks,* one called *Land and Sea* and one called *Fishing Port*—and it won't tell you a thing. The ones which simply say *Composition* or *Abstraction No. 17* are really the simplest because they prepare you for a brilliant splash of cubes and circles and don't keep you looking for chickens where chickens don't exist.

The really slick thing about the whole exhibit is that it invites you to take your hair down and honestly look at the pictures. You don't have to spend any time thinking of understanding things to say about the pictures because everybody knows that you don't understand them. You don't even have to know a watercolor from an oil or Picasso from pineapple custard to have fun looking at them.

They are challenging and, believe it or not, skillfully and seriously painted by artists, who, for the most part, know their business—no matter what you think Junior and Sister could do with crayons!

In an era of pagers and cell phones, a feature story on the new president of Western Union appears insignificant. In 1941, with the United States less than six months away from war, the visit was big news. Albert Nathaniel Williams' trip to Atlanta even warranted a favorable editorial published in the July 25, 1941 Atlanta Constitution. *The Williams story played on page 27 of a 28-page newspaper. It marks Celestine Sibley's first by-line in the* Constitution.

Western Union Head Appears Here on Tour

July 25, 1941

The only difference between running a railroad and running a telegraph company is that the railroad moves people and freight and the telegraph company moves words.

"And that," concludes Albert Nathaniel Williams, 53-year-old former Denver railroad rodman who recently resigned the presidency of the Lehigh Valley Railway to become president of Western Union, "is almost no difference at all."

In Atlanta yesterday, his first stop on a swing around the country to get acquainted with Western Union personnel, Williams shook hands with several hundred Western Union employees, inspecting plant facilities, including the new reperforator plant which is to go into service September 1, and was guest of honor at a luncheon given by C.H. Carroll, general manager at the Atlanta Athletic Club at 12:30 o'clock.

Traveling in a special car on the Southern Railroad, Williams, accompanied by three Western Union vice presidents, made Atlanta his first stop on his first official inspection tour because of its importance "telegraphically," he said.

"We in Western Union are aware of the importance of the city of Atlanta," the president told a group of business and professional men with whom he lunched.

"Probably few of you know of the important position that Atlanta occupies in the telegraph field. It is the principal office of this entire southern section of the country.

"The Southern division headquarters of the Western Union are in Atlanta and from these headquarters are directed all of the telegraph activities south of the Mason and Dixon line and east of the Mississippi river."

President Williams and Vice Presidents W.C. Titley of the plant department, E.R. Shute of the traffic department, B.D.Barnett of the communications department, left last night for Birmingham. They will go through Texas to the Pacific coast.

Williams, who boasts that he has done "practically every job on the railroad," including climbing an icy pole in freezing weather to get railroad telegraph lines open, is tackling his new job with confidence.

Right now defense activity is stepping up business for Western Union.

"A large number of our employees are on active duty in the Army and Navy and members of my official staff are directing the defense communication board's activities in both the telegraph and cable. We have no admirals or generals in the Western Union but we do have commanders and regular colonels and Kentucky colonels."

Atlantans Cling to Belief Son in RAF Is Safe

August 1, 1941

Traditionally, the Irish are the people steeped in mysticism, the believers in "luck" and hunches, the possessors of prescience denied less favored folk.

But two British-born Atlantans, clinging steadfastly to the belief that their aviator son is still alive when all official reports would indicate otherwise, may present World War II's most remarkable example of presagement, of an inner sight or of just plain faith and courage.

Those two are Mr. and Mrs. Alfred Jepson of Doraville, whose son, handsome blond James Alton Jepson, 30, the first American aviator to arrive in England under the RAF empire training program, has been reported missing for six months.

Six months ago, Alfred Jepson was called from his desk in the textile division of the Atlanta quartermaster depot to receive a cablegram from the British War Department advising him that his son had been reported missing after a mine-laying flight over the channel.

Since then they and their daughter-in-law, Mrs. Catherine Jepson, of Decatur, have had letters of sympathy from England's Queen Elizabeth, from the squadron commander, from the first lady-in-waiting, Lady Harding, and a personal visit with Lord and Lady Halifax during their visit to Atlanta. All these assurances of sympathy the Jepsons have received gratefully, but with no sense of finality.

"Jimmy is not lost," these cheerful, unemotional parents insist. "We're never felt that he was lost. He may be injured somewhere, he may be a prisoner in some foreign country—but some day, somehow, he will come back to us."

The Jepsons, sturdy, sensible Britons, would be the first to deny that their comforting conviction that their son will return has anything to do with Irishy mysticism twaddle.

"We don't believe in that stuff," says Mrs. Jepson, scornfully. "We're members of the Episcopal church, just as Jimmy was. We pray to God our son is safe."

But again and again that staunch comforting knowledge the

Jepsons possess goes back to a series of unexplainable and thoroughly mystifying events.

There is the number that has played such an important part in Jimmy's life—the number 11.

He was born December 11, 1911.

He enlisted in the Royal Canadian Air Force April 11, 1940.

He sailed from Canada November 11, 1940.

He was reported missing February 11, 1941.

And if he is not found in the meantime, he will be declared officially dead August 11, 1941.

He Promised

But the chain of events goes back further than that, even beyond that Christmas night, 1940, when Jimmy in the middle of the family's Yuletide celebration, remarked prophetically: "Well, next Christmas I'll be in the war—maybe over Berlin or London."

Then there was his phenomenal luck since childhood.

"He was always lucky," the father recalled. "He was always in and out of trouble and he could talk himself out of practically anything. I told his mother if the Germans had him as a prisoner it wouldn't be long till he talked himself free. He had a good knowledge of German, you know."

Yes, trouble slid off young Jimmy Jepson like water off a duck's back. He watched a British cruiser dock in Savannah one day from the roof of the YMCA building and in his absorption stepped through a skylight and fell three stories.

"Hardly hurt him at all," mused Mr. Jepson. "Broke a little bone in his back but nothing serious."

But the most important link in the chain of mystical events was supplied by a young Jepson cousin, a teenage hero-worshipping girl, was delighted with her handsome aviator cousin from America and enjoyed his visits at her home during his leave.

"He liked her too," Mr. Jepson said. "He took a fancy to her and promised her he'd keep in touch with her. Three months after he was reported missing she received a telephone call at the shop where she worked. A man's voice in a strange foreign accent, said, 'Jimmy's safe.'"

The girl was bewildered and asked, "Jimmy who?" "Jimmy Jepson," the voice replied.

The girl reported the telephone call to the War Department and a few weeks ago Mrs. Jepson received a letter from Queen Elizabeth assuring her of her sympathy and promising her that the British government was redoubling its efforts to find Sergeant-Observer Jepson.

Barking of Dog Saves Boy, 2, from Death

August 16, 1941

The devotion of a nondescript dog named Club Foot and the skill and quick thinking of an older brother are responsible for two-year-old Louie Goodwin being safe at his home on Cascade Road today.

Louie was lost. He had been lost for an hour and a half when his big brother, 16-year-old Everett Goodwin, found his little bare-foot tracks, leading to Utoy Creek, a mile away.

"I started following them as fast as I could and then I heard Club Foot barking and I started running," Everett related yesterday. "When I got there Louie was floating in the creek and Club Foot was running up and down the bank barking as hard as he could."

Everett plunged into the creek up to his waist, carried his little brother to the shore and started giving him artificial respiration.

"He was unconscious but I got some of the water out of him

and could tell he was breathing so I stopped and took him home as fast as I could," Everett explained.

Everett learned the technique of administering artificial respiration from his teacher, Mrs. C. M. Mitchell, at Cascade Grammar School, in a Junior Red Cross life-saving course two years ago.

"I never used it before, but I'm mighty glad I remembered how," grinned Everett yesterday.

Louie, a slender, blue-eyed little boy with a mop of pale gold curls has a spirit of adventure.

"He's the sixth one I've raised," sighed his mother, Mrs. Goodwin yesterday, "and he's the first one I've had to chase all the time. I blame part of it on that dog."

But the Goodwins are glad that Club Foot was with his young master Tuesday.

'Baby Doll,' 2, Has Head Set on Hollywood

August 17, 1941

"Baby Doll" is headed for Hollywood.

She says so herself. Ask her what she is going to be and she tosses copper-colored—really copper-colored curls—topped by a blue taffeta bow, and says, "An actress in Hollywood."

She's only two years old—a chubby, brown-eyed two-year-old with the poise of a Temple—and she has ambition. But then her mother's friends have always said Baby Doll had a "photogenic" mind.

For instance, she can tell you who freed the slaves, who crossed the Delaware and what Mae West and Greta Garbo said and she has been photographed so many times she evinces little or no interest in the experience, except to sometimes express an embarrassing (to her mother) preference for another photographer.

Real Name

"Baby Doll" was christened Jill Feldser, daughter of Mr. and Mrs. Sam Feldser, who live at Kimball House, but, as her mother explains, everybody calls her "Baby Doll." She was two in June and she remembers everything, but everything she hears. "I guess you'd call it a photogenic mind," smiles Mrs. Feldser.

"I don't know what else it is. She picks up some of the strangest things sometimes—and I don't know where she gets them."

But Mrs. Feldser does know where Jill gets her miscellaneous assortment of facts about American history. Her mother has a series of questions written down on a piece of paper and at the promise of an all-day sucker or a trip to one of the bigger department stores, Baby Doll will pitch in and tell you who made the first flag, who invented the electric light, how many states there are in the United States, the name of the president, and wind up by singing you a dozen or so nursery rhymes.

Talks For Lollipop

She'll run through the whole thing without a trace of self-consciousness, jabbing experimentally at your typewriter all the time and then she'll ask you if she can take your pencil "bye-bye" and depart triumphantly in the direction of the promised all-day sucker.

Mrs. Feldser has been in communication with a Hollywood director, Vincent Sherman, and she plans some day soon to take Baby Doll to the film capital for a fling at fame. Jill's mother doesn't feel that she is too hopeful for her daughter's future because she has a fair gauge of Baby Doll's appeal from the reaction of the hometown folks.

Just as an example, Mrs. Feldser jotted down some of her experiences, which she calls "A Day With Baby Doll."

"I'm afraid I'll have gray hair before I'm 25," the mother wrote. "We live in a hotel and naturally Baby Doll has to have her meals and fresh air. Well, I dress her and take her down.

Public Favorite

"In the lobby she is grabbed—five packages of gum in one hand and three in her pocket. Finally we escape and get outside. We walk three steps and a woman spies Baby Doll and looks at her, raves over her. 'What's her name, how old, etc.' Then we walk on again. Then someone grabs me from the back. Must see her face. Her face is like a doll, etc. Then we get on Peachtree. Baby Doll looks in a shop window. Door opens. Someone grabs her in, shows her to everyone in the store. After 15 or 20 minutes I get out.

"I can't put a sign on her not to look at her, can I? I start one or two hours early to get there on time. One lady wanted to adopt her with tears in her eyes. Why don't I take her to Hollywood?"

And that, as Baby Doll herself said, is just where she's headed.

Chapter Two

On Assignment

Overleaf: Sibley meeting Bobby Driscoll, the child star of Walt Disney's 1946 film *Song of the South,* during a preview screening in Hollywood.

In October of 1946, Constitution *editor Ralph McGill pried open the paper's notoriously tight pursestrings to send Sibley and* Constitution *film editor Paul Jones to Hollywood to see an advance screening of Walt Disney's* Song of the South. *The innovative film combining animation and live action was based on the Uncle Remus stories of former* Constitution *editor Joel Chandler Harris.*

Sibley clicked with the folksy Oscar-winning director and later covered the Atlanta premiere of the film. During visits to Hollywood in the 1950s in her capacity as silver screen correspondent for the Atlanta Journal and Constitution Sunday Magazine, *Sibley interviewed Disney numerous times. The filmmaker even invited Sibley to screen a rough cut of his animal documentary* The Living Desert *to gauge her reaction.*

True to his word in the following article, Disney lacked the nerve to actually sit through the Atlanta premiere at the Fox Theatre with the audience. He preferred to pace in his room across the street at the Georgian Terrace.

Disney Suffers, Waits for <u>Uncle Remus</u> Test

October 3, 1946

Hollywood—Walt Disney, nine times Academy Award winner, sat in his office at Burbank and chewed his fingernails in a frenzy of artistic nervousness while the first delegation of Georgians previewed what his press agents now call his "most far-reaching venture," the tales of Uncle Remus in *Song of the South.*

"I want to know what Atlantans think of it," the dark-haired, lanky Disney insisted, lounging forward in the blonde mahogany and plate glass room which is his office, "but please don't ask me to see it with you. I can't stand it. I suffer too much. It's a failing of mine. Once somebody coughed at a preview of *Fantasia* and I was sick. I knew they didn't like it. And once there was a laugh at the wrong place in another one of my pictures and I thought I'd go crazy. I knew it was a terrible flop. When Uncle Remus is previewed in Atlanta I know I'll spend all my time in the men's room suffering."

The film, being heralded in beautiful double-truck magazine advertisements throughout the country as *Song of the South* but still affectionately referred to by Disney and his associates as *Uncle Remus*, will be given a world premiere at the Fox Theater in Atlanta Nov. 12.

"Perce Pearce, the associate producer, hit upon the name *Song of the South* as having the most box office appeal," Disney explained, "But I was brought up on Uncle Remus stories in Missouri and I will always think of the picture as being his story, although his name is mentioned only secondarily. We think *Song of the South* is a good title and our tests have proved it has appeal. Do you know that the word *South* has tremendous pulling power in all sections of the country? Even in part of the North where, not so familiar with the stories of Uncle Remus, they still flock to see anything with *South* in it."

The story of the tar baby, hilariously presented by the human Uncle Remus, James Baskett, in *Song of the South*, with the aid of inspired Disney animated characters, is perhaps Disney's favorite.

The one-time "boy wonder" of Hollywood, known familiarly as "Walt" to even the lowliest of his 6,000 employees, admitted he had a difficult time choosing which of the Joel Chandler Harris stories to retell in his film. He called upon such Southerners as George Stallings, of Savannah, and Bob Cormack, former Atlanta newspapermen, and Dalton Reymond, who wrote the original story, based upon Uncle Remus tales, for assistance. He also received research from Mr. and Mrs. Wilbur Kurtz and made full use of Selznick's *Gone With the Wind* file for background information.

"We swap around and borrow out here in a fine neighborly fashion," Disney said. "But I'm especially proud of the help given us by the Harris family."

Among the many books scattered around on the low tables and chairs in Disney's office suite is an old and dog-eared volume of Uncle Remus with the signature of the author pasted on the flyleaf and this additional inscription beneath it, "He would have liked Walt Disney immensely. So do I—Joel Chandler Harris, Jr." Disney said the book was presented by Harris' son to him in 1940 when he went to Atlanta immediately before work was started on the film.

The four Atlanta newspaper reporters who previewed *Song of the South* this afternoon followed precisely the "audience reaction graph" which a branch of the Gallup Poll had already prepared on the film. The graph, based on the reactions of four different audiences, showed that a strictly Southern audience recruited from various Southern clubs in California surpassed all others in enjoyment of the movie. Other audiences included a "Disney audience," "a non-Disney audience" and an "average audience."

Atlantans Hail **Song**'s Artistry, Disney Puts 'Tough Audience' in His Pocket

November 3, 1946

A Fox Theatre audience of admittedly prejudiced people—the friends, neighbors, children and grandchildren of Joel Chandler

Harris—took Walt Disney and a constellation of Hollywood stars to its heart last night, swapping for the artistry that is *Song of the South* their tears, laughter and sincere appreciation.

They liked what Disney did with their Uncle Remus, the Brer Rabbit they were bred and brought up on—and they showed it by their laughter, by greeting each new character with a spontaneous burst of applause that swept the house from the gallery to the orchestra pit.

From the moment the house lights dimmed, the music rose, the curtains parted and the film foreword began—"Out of the humble cabins, out of the singing heart of the South"—Disney had "that tough" Atlanta audience in his pocket.

Previously the youthful Hollywood producer and many-times winner of the Academy Award had confessed to the audience he was so nervous he had "started on my other hand," demonstrating with a finger-biting exhibition. In the breezy warm-up stage show which preceded the picture, Disney charmed the audience by greeting it with a "How are you-all?" in the voice of Mickey Mouse, the character he habitually "voices." Pressed with questions by Vox Poppers Parks Johnson and Warren Hull, he said he liked the picture himself, but had not allowed his young daughters to see it because he was terrified they would apply their severest criticism—"that's corny, Dad."

The audience hastily reassured him on that point—and it was the same audience the lanky, unassuming producer had said was "Wonderful . . . I hope."

Deep sighs and appreciative long-drawn *Ahs* greeted the scene in which the Little Boy, his parents and his nurse rode through the Georgia countryside to the plantation home of the Little Boy's grandmother. A ripple of recognition ran over the audience as Hattie McDaniel, who will ever be identified locally as "Mammy" of *Gone With the Wind* fame, briskly took charge of her role as Sis Tempy, the Little Boy's nurse. When the youthful father (Eric Rolf) was identified as "an Atlanta newspaperman" someone murmured, "That was Mr. Harris himself."

Almost immediately after Glenn Leedy, the sprightly little colored boy who is the playfellow and frog-hunting companion of the Little Boy, appeared on the screen he drew a roar of laughter from the audience with the lines: "Uncle Remus, you is the best story-teller in the whole 'N'united States of Gawgia!"

As the picture gathered pace and the animated characters appeared, one by one, the applause rose and fell. The first glimpse of the combination of animation and live action brought an ovation. Uncle Remus walked through a watercolor countryside, singing and talking with moles, butterflies, bluebirds, bees and hummingbirds.

Long before the picture began, the audience was seated, with standees filling up the area in the back of the theater. Organ music, with selections ranging from the "Desert Song" to the latest Disney melodies, was played and then Parks Johnson and Warren Hull took over the stage with their radio show, *Vox Pop*. Atlantans co-starred on the show, first Joel Chandler Harris, Jr. known locally as Jake Harris, and two six-year-olds, Sarah Aldredge and Janet Farris, who were picked from the Uncle Remus Memorial Association float in the Armistice Day parade, to tell their favorite Uncle Remus stories on the air.

Harris and Radio Showman Parks Johnson reminisced humorously of their childhood days in the West End when they were members of rival gangs, fighting as West End Sluggers. Harris recalled his father's days as editor of the *Atlanta Constitution* and said, "As a matter of fact, Dad didn't tell us the Uncle Remus stories. I reckon he wrote them. I used to see him writing a lot and then I'd deliver his manuscript to the *Constitution*. But to us, he was just a regular Dad who grew some trees in the backyard so he could use their limbs occasionally."

Johnson and Hull staged a hilarious show preceding the premiere of the motion picture by calling on the audience for participation in a string-chewing contest, and a balloon-busting contest. They introduced a roster of Disney stars, Cliff Edwards, the Ukulele Ike of *Ziegfeld Follies* fame who voiced Jiminy Cricket in *Pinnochio* and the voice of Pluto and Goofy.

The young RKO stars, Bill Williams and Barbara Hale, his bride of four months, participated in the stunts by choosing a couple from the audience to assist them in the balloon-busting, which was done by hugging. Gifts were distributed to all the participants, including the West Coast honeymoon couple, who were flown to Atlanta for the premiere as their reward for performance on a radio show. Disney and Harris, the announcers said, declined their gifts and the Lipton Company, sponsors of the program, will present an equivalent check to the Junior League for its charities.

Disney thanked both the Junior League and the Uncle Remus Memorial Association for their part in staging the premiere. James Baskett, the Negro actor who portrayed Uncle Remus did not attend the premiere. Mayor Hartsfield praised his acting and his interpretation of the sensitive role.

"It was a great job," said the mayor, and the house roared with applause.

Later, Disney paid tribute to Baskett, with another resounding acclaim from the audience, then thanked Atlanta for its unheard-of hospitality and kindness. "The reception has been wonderful, and I have thanked so many folks I am getting monotonous. You have been unbelievably generous."

Will Help Correct Airport 'Typo':
UDC Protests War Name to Mayor

May 26, 1948

The Daughters of the Confederacy didn't exactly declare war but they let Mayor Hartsfield know that what he designates that unpleasantness back in the '60s can be a fighting matter, suh!

The question of whether it was a Civil War or a War Between the States is "not by any means academic; it was the question that brought war in the first place!"

With that ominous warning, Atlanta Chapter, United Daughters of the Confederacy, holding aloft the dusty banner of the Lost Cause and suppressing with lady-like restraint their rebel yells, Tuesday afternoon called upon Mayor Hartsfield to wipe the cursed words, *Civil War*, from the mural in the Airport's new terminals and substitute the words *War Between the States*.

"We're sure it was an oversight and we'll all be glad to go and help the mayor make the change," concluded the President, Mrs. Frank Davenport.

The Chapter unanimously adopted a resolution, offered by Mrs. Forrest Kibler and seconded by Mrs. Q.L. Palmer, Chairman of the War Between the States Committee.

"We of the UDC want it designated by the name to which is attached the least aura of bitterness," Mrs. Kibler's resolution stated. "That seems to us a reasonable request, and one, certainly, which has been widely heeded. . . . The War was not fought in a spirit of civil insurrection, to overthrow an existing government, but in a spirit of independence by men who were convinced of their right to establish a government of their own, separate from the original Union. From that point of view, it is manifestly a war between two schools of thought, two groups of States. It was in

1899 while in Washington, D.C., in attendance at the DAR Congress, that Mrs. W.G. Raoul, member of Atlanta Chapter, UDC, introduced the resolution that the term *War Between the States* be the correct one in alluding to the struggle of the '60s.

"For 50 years the Daughters of the Confederacy have striven to this end and their guiding motto has been, 'Loyalty to the Truth of Confederate History.' I move that the Atlanta Chapter go on record as protesting the caption of Civil War under the Cyclorama scene in the Airport in Atlanta and that a letter of protest be sent the Hon. William B. Hartsfield, mayor of Atlanta, asking that the words *Civil War* be removed and the words *War Between the States* be substituted."

'Old Belle' Was Tendered on Account: Grady Regrets Losing Goat Deal

August 24, 1947

Grady Hospital's administrative forces had to admit Saturday they weren't on their toes.

Several weeks ago they were offered a milk goat in exchange for saving a woman's life but their acceptance was so slow coming the goat donor, W.B. Miller, reported Saturday he had withdrawn his offer.

"Too bad," hospital administrators said sadly. "We just couldn't make up our minds whether to turn the goat over to the business office (accounts payable) or over to the dietary department."

Goat owner Miller took the appearance of a reporter and a photographer at his asphalt-can residence near Adamsville as a belated show of interest on the hospital's part and he was genuinely regretful.

"Now I'm just as sorry as I can be I didn't hold that goat for the Grady," Miller declared. "I sold her for $10—and she was worth three times the price. As good a milker as you ever saw—five quarts a day if she was fed right."

Old Belle, the milk goat, was the first payment Mr. Miller had to make on what he felt was a long-standing account at Grady Hospital.

"The Grady saved my wife's life," he said, "and there's hardly a one of my people who haven't been there for one thing or another. I was there myself once—my wife was there three times—and nearly all my brothers and my sisters and their children have been treated there. Yes, sir, offering them Old Belle was little enough to do. And if they're still interested, well I'm going to see if I can't get my hands on another good milker for them."

Miller and his wife, Lula, live on a rutted red slope off Fairburn Road in a three-room house built entirely of asphalt cans cut, straightened out and nailed to a framework of timbers from trees felled on the site.

"Paid five cents a piece for the asphalt cans," Mr. Miller explained, "and me and my brother did all the work ourselves. Only leaks in two places."

Although the little structure, now seven years old, has dirt floors, it is wired for electricity and by pulling a string the householder turns on a light, a radio and an electric fan. The clean-swept yard is bright with beds of flowers and a well down the hill and an asphalt can outhouse provide plumbing facilities.

A well-fed cow and a mule occupy stalls in the garden and a cat and a dog share space under the stove. There are animals a-plenty but Mr. Miller is still sad over the untimely sale of Belle.

"Slick as a butter mold, she was," he sighed. "Woulda been a fine hospital goat."

'Re-Kidnap' of Girl, 6, Hair-Raising

May 28, 1948

Six-year-old Linda Gale Brooks, who was reported "kidnapped" by her mother May 16, has been "re-kidnapped" by her father—and if anybody thinks that's a hectic life for a little girl, they ought to hear what happened to her mothers, Nos. 1 and 2!

Mrs. Clara Haynes Brooks, mother of the little girl and first wife of Platt Everett Brooks, told it to Sheriff's Deputy W.M. Eason Thursday when he served her with a court order restraining her from again "kidnapping" her daughter.

The first Mrs. Brooks, who admitted to swooping up the little girl in front of her father's College Park home and taking her to Florida, told the officer Brooks and the second Mrs. Brooks returned the call the other afternoon. They drove down to her home near Orlando, Fla., swooped up little Linda Gale, who was again playing in the yard and started to drive off with her.

Mrs. Brooks said she ran out of the house and leaped on the moving car, resisting all efforts to dislodge her. Unable to pull or push her off the car, her ex-husband then set out to drive her off, Mrs. Brooks told the deputy, speeding down the road at the rate of 60 miles an hour.

"I was scared to get off then so I just reached in and grabbed his second wife's hair and held on for dear life!" the deputy quoted Mrs. Brooks as saying.

Her grip held until Brooks drove into the Orlando police station where the law sided with the child's father. Brooks brought Linda Gale back to Atlanta and the first Mrs. Brooks followed later . . . by public carrier.

Hearing on the restraining order is set for 9:30 A.M., June 7, before Judge Bond Almand.

Wails, Tales and the Jail: It's a Quiet Night, Said the Matron . . . the Girl Sobbed On

August 1, 1948

Quiet night, the police matron said.

Nothing much going on. Rare for a Friday night but she wasn't complaining. The quieter, the better.

Twilight was beginning to soften the outlines of the buildings outside the barred windows and the rosy blush of a just-lighted neon sign glowed in the distance. Geneva, the Negro maid, swept the corridor and sang softly as she worked.

"I was way down yonder all by myself . . ."

"Request card! I gotta a request card!" somebody bawled at the other end of the corridor.

Policewoman Frances Lykes, matron for the night, grinned wryly and picked up a pencil and paper. "Somebody wants to make bond," she explained over her shoulder as she hurried down the corridor. "You have to let them send a request card down to the station's lieutenant's office."

Geneva put down her broom and walked slowly down the other end of the corridor. In a second she was back.

"Mrs. Lykes," she panted, "girl down there say somebody she love upstairs. She say she gotta little white pill and she gonna swallow it!"

Keys in hand, Mrs. Lykes was down the corridor in a flash. A slender, big-eyed girl sat on a bunk, her hands clenched, her head raised defiantly. A cheap brown satin dress clung to her slender figure. She wore dirty white sandals.

"Now what's your trouble?" the matron asked casually, dropping down beside her.

"Oh, I'm sick and I'm in love," the girl moaned and then as an afterthought, "I'm in jail!"

"When did you come in?" Mrs. Lykes wanted to know.

"This morning. My husband—he's an old man, 46 years old—he wanted revenge and he had us arrested. He practically give me to this boy and me and the children was getting along so good with him—and then he had us arrested, my husband did. They got the boy upstairs."

Quietly Mrs. Lykes took her hand and opened it. She had a screw in it. The matron pocketed the screw and looked in the girl's other hand. She searched the tumbled bunk and asked a few more questions. Satisfied that the girl had swallowed nothing and had nothing to swallow, she left her.

"Suppose she was like me," put in a voice from the cell next door. "She's just charged with adultery—but they got me for larceny!"

She rose from the bunk and came closer to the door, barefoot and clad in her slip. "My girlfriend lent me a nightgown and two bedjackets to take to Grady when my baby was born. That was only four weeks ago—and here she's arrested me for stealing them. Can y'magine?"

Whatever the matron would have said was drowned out by the ringing of the bell in the front corridor and a hoarse voice from the bullpen repeating in a singsong monotone: "Mrs. Lykes, Mrs. Lykes, Mrs. Lykes!"

"Mamie's waking up and wants to call her boyfriend to get her out," Mrs. Lykes said briefly and started toward the ringing bell but was halted by the would-be suicide.

"You didn't get everything," the girl called triumphantly and popped something in her mouth. In a second Mrs. Lykes was at her side, her hands pressing her throat. "Spit it out," she ordered. "Spit it out."

"Oh, stop it," whimpered the girl. "You're hurting me!"

"If I have to send you to Grady it's going to hurt worse," said the matron grimly.

The girl raised her head curiously. "What'll they do?"

"You'll see," said Mrs. Lykes. "Did you ever have your stomach pumped out?" The girl became suddenly docile. She leaned over the toilet in the corner and spit a washer the size of a quarter into it.

"Fish it out and hand it here," said Mrs. Lykes wearily. Sniffling, the girl obeyed. Mrs. Lykes studied the screw and the washer curiously for a moment and then her face lighted up with recognition. "She took them off the toilet," she pronounced. "Guess I'd better put you in the slicker before you eat up the rest of the plumbing," she said.

The "slicker" is a shallow cell that is absolutely bare. It opens on the corridor but has no outside windows, no bunk, no toilet, nothing but clean yellow tile walls and iron bars. The girl slumped over on the floor and Mrs. Lykes hurried to the front door.

"New customer," she announced and a battered old derelict greeted her enthusiastically. "Hi, darling! Long time no see!"

"Unh huh," the matron said cheerfully. "Been about a week. How are you, Tessie?"

Tessie grinned toothlessly and reeled with obvious familiarity into the little office. Automatically the policewoman's hands moved over her frumpy frame. The placket of Tessie's dress was open, revealing an area of dirty rayon and an area of dirty skin. Satisfied that she had neither knife or gun, Mrs. Lykes opened her cheap patent leather pocketbook and pulled its contents out on the desk. A fine powder covered the desk. The matron sighed in annoyance but Tessie's voice was raised high in reproach.

"Darling! Watch whatch doing! That's my snuff!" Grabbing a dirty handkerchief she started raking the snuff back into a little box. "Just a'wasting my snuff," she said tearfully. "Don't care nothing 'bout me. Just a-wasting. . . ."

Mrs. Lykes handed Geneva the keys and smiled at Tessie. "Go on with Geneva now and behave yourself. You can take your snuff with you but I'll keep the rest of your stuff."

The old woman waddled off, revealing a fresh white bandage on the back of her gray head. Mrs. Lykes counted the woman's money and made an entry beside her name on the ledger: 64 cents. Slowly she returned the things to the black bag, a rayon slip, a bottle of hair tonic, a box of talcum powder, coin purse, billfold, switchblade knife.

Before she could finish locking up Tessie's bag and washing her hands, the bell was ringing again. Lora Lee, 18-years-old, was slim and redheaded and very drunk. She wore an elaborately draped, tight black dress, four strands of pearls and fancy dangling earrings, but her bare legs were dirty and her scuffed play shoes had a hole in them.

"I gotta bad break!" screamed Lora Lee. "I don't care if you send me to the Big Rock! I don't care if I rot in jail . . . I got a bad break!" Her voice trailed off in a stream of profanity.

The bell rang. A 14-year-old boy with a bundle of clothes and six comic books stood there. "I'm back, Mrs. Lykes. They told me I was only supposed to stay one night over there at the 'Y.' You got any ideas?"

The occupant of the "slicker" was screaming that she had swallowed a bobby pin and "It's killing me." Lora Lee was turning the air purple with shouted obscenities. Three Mexican girls, held by immigration authorities for illegal entry were jabbering softly in Spanish to an interpreter. Mrs. Lykes reached through the bars and patted the boy's shoulder. "Wait outside a minute, son. We'll figure something out."

Between putting Lora Lee in the other "slicker" to shut her up and removing the bobby pins from the would-be suicide's head she worried about the boy.

"Father's a habitual drunkard," she explained. "They came in here on a fruit truck and the father was so drunk the kid had to drive. He got 30 days in court yesterday and I sent the boy to the 'Y' for the night. He doesn't seem to have any relatives anywhere, though."

Somehow she found time to make a few phone calls. The juvenile home would take the boy, if detectives would deliver him there. In the "slicker" Lora Lee's language got worse and then stopped entirely. She went to sleep on the floor, one skinny little hand folded under her cheek, a look of childlike peace on her gaunt face.

Somehow the matron found time to talk with the suicide and find that she was pretending about the bobby pin—that all she wanted was attention and assurance that she'd have a chance to tell her story in court. She returned to her cell, talking dreamily of her "desperate love" for the man upstairs and how she ought to put up her hair so she'd look nice for him in court on the morrow.

Tessie had a "spell" and hit her head on the floor. Her cellmates put her shoes and her dress on her, lecturing her severely about drinking "alkyhaul" when she has "the sugar diabetes and the high blood," and an officer came to take her to Grady for treatment.

The Mexicans asked for their prayer books. Another police-woman from the Detective Bureau dropped by on her supper hour with hamburgers and a carton of hot coffee.

Mrs. Lykes sat down long enough to take a sip of the coffee. "Awfully quiet tonight," she assured her sister officer. "Awfully quiet for Friday."

When Sibley moved to Atlanta in the summer of 1941, the hoopla surrounding the publication of Gone With the Wind *and the film's Atlanta premiere in 1939 had only partially diminished. Margaret Mitchell, who had served as a reporter for the* Atlanta Journal *in the 1920s, was by then a bona fide worldwide celebrity and spent much of her time christening battleships, giving speeches and raising money for war bonds. She never missed an Atlanta Press Club meeting though and Sibley became friends with both "Peggy" and her husband John R. Marsh. Since Sibley knew the traditionally private couple, she was the reporter sent to keep vigil at Grady Hospital after Mitchell was struck by a car as she crossed Atlanta's Peachtree Street.*

Margaret Mitchell 'Definitely Better' in Fight against Death

August 13, 1949

Game, fighting Margaret Mitchell Marsh, like the heroine of her own *Gone With the Wind,* was apparently set to conquer desperate odds against death at Grady Hospital last night.

Her husband, John R. Marsh, Georgia Power Company executive, reported that her condition was "definitely better" for the first time since she was rushed to the hospital 24 hours earlier with critical injuries when she was struck by a car.

"I'm greatly encouraged by her condition," Marsh said. "She is definitely better, although she is still not fully conscious. She is no longer under the oxygen tent and the nurses tell me that she responds to some extent when they speak to her."

The author's husband, a semi-invalid himself since he suffered a critical heart attack three years ago, said he was resting at the home of his physician, Dr. W.C. Waters, and waiting for the moment when Miss Mitchell would regain consciousness.

He quoted attending physicians as saying Miss Mitchell was in a condition of "extreme shock" and they would attempt to make no X-rays until she is better. She is able to move her arms and legs, but the extent of her head injuries has not been fully determined. She is believed to have suffered a basal skull fracture and possible concussion of the brain.

The world-famous author was struck down and dragged 15 feet by an automobile driven by Hugh D. Gravitt, 29, of 220 Gresham St. N.W. in front of the Peachtree Art Theater near Thirteenth Street. She became frightened when she saw the car driven by Gravitt coming toward them, Marsh told police and turned back toward the curb. Gravitt, booked for drunken driving, said he "would have missed her if she had not run back."

Throughout the day Grady Hospital was besieged by telephone calls from all parts of the United States and visits from scores of Georgians who anxiously awaited word of the beloved little author's condition.

To these friends and admirers of his wife, John Marsh last night issued this statement: "We're terribly grateful for their kindness. When we took Peggy to the hospital there was a spontaneous show of affection and sympathy from our friends and from some people who were strangers to me but who seemed to feel that they knew Peggy. We are thankful to them all."

Grady Hospital reported it was receiving the greatest number of calls since the Winecoff fire disaster. Many of them were from faraway cities and from people who did not know the little author personally, but felt that they knew her through her famous novel. Scores of friends and fans visited the hospital, but went away when they learned the gravity of her condition would prevent even members of her family from seeing her.

Supt. Frank Wilson designated Mrs. Louise Durden, Grady

Hospital public relations director, to handle the calls on Miss Mitchell and set aside a small room nearby for her friends and relatives. She is confined to Room 302. Flowers arriving for her were not placed in her room because of her serious condition.

As a newspaper reporter seeking a story and later as a friend of the underprivileged, Miss Mitchell was a frequent visitor to Grady Hospital. She wrote many human interest stories about the sprawling charity hospital and after the phenomenal success of her novel she regularly made generous contributions to the work of the hospital.

Scores of people who have received financial help from the famous writer were among those who called. Quietly and unobtrusively, she has made substantial contributions to nearly every charity in Atlanta as well as to many individuals whose needs she knows.

A Negro waiter who had served her many times stood in a hospital corridor and cried unashamedly when a nurse told him Miss Mitchell was "too sick to see you."

Several times during the day Miss Mitchell recovered consciousness to the extent of answering when her name was called but at no time was she fully conscious, doctors said.

She is attended by three specialists. They remained at her side most of the day and night and had breakfast served to them in her room. They asked that their names not be published and one of them said he would be "busy operating" and would not be able to receive calls for information.

Asked if he meant he intended to operate on Miss Mitchell, the physician declined to answer.

The lively author, whose age was listed on hospital records as 43 years, is easily one of Georgia's most widely known and loved citizens. She refused to go to Hollywood for any of the fanfare attendant on the filming of her book but continued to move with naturalness and freedom among the people with whom she has always worked and played. Until the recent illness of her husband she never missed a meeting of the Georgia Press Association. She is a member of the Atlanta Women's Press Club and frequently drops by newspaper offices to visit with old friends.

During the war she worked tirelessly for the Red Cross and the Civilian Defense. She christened two cruisers named *Atlanta* and sparked a campaign to raise funds to build the second one after the first one was sunk.

"When I was a child," she frequently told bond-buying audiences, "I heard the older people tell how the ladies of the Confederacy gave their jewelry to fight the war and I always regretted that I hadn't been there to give my locket. Now we women of Atlanta have our chance to give again."

She was an ardent movie fan and was on her way with her husband to see *A Canterbury Tale* at the time of the accident. Every time *Gone With the Wind* plays a return engagement in Atlanta Miss Mitchell and her husband try to see it. Recently she related that they missed it at the Tenth Street Theater because they were unable to get seats. The manager heard that the creator of Scarlett had been turned away from seeing her own picture and the last time he exhibited the film he telephoned Miss Mitchell in advance and invited her and her husband to come as his guests.

The picture just completed an engagement at the Rhodes Theater.

Miss Mitchell is a great favorite with prisoners at Atlanta Penitentiary where she has talked many times.

In his cell at City Jail, Gravitt maintained that he would not have hit Miss Mitchell if she had remained in the middle of the street beside her husband. He seemed greatly concerned over her condition and declared that he was "praying that she will live."

Peggy Is Getting Mad—Beginning to Fight

August 14, 1949

The thing that physicians and her friends all over the world were hoping for, happened yesterday: Margaret Mitchell began to fight.

Heralding it as a sign that her still critical condition was taking a turn for the better, physicians at Grady Hospital announced that the famous little author had practically regained consciousness and was "getting mad."

"When Peggy gets mad, it's a good sign," declared a physician and a family friend. "The chances for her recovery look better today than we thought they would when she was brought in here Thursday night."

Miss Mitchell recognized members of her family and protested at being fed intravenously. She complained of the pain in her legs and arms and asked her sister-in-law, Mrs. Stephens Mitchell, and her private nurse to remove the tube from her arm, through which a saline solution was being administered.

"I told her she had some pretty flowers," Mrs. Mitchell reported, "and she said, 'Yes, they're pretty but I need some yellow ones.' There are some yellow roses in her room and I realized she wasn't quite rational but it was a great relief to have her able to recognize us and to talk at all."

For the first 36 hours following the automobile accident Thursday night in which she was struck down and dragged 15 feet along Peachtree Street, Miss Mitchell was never fully conscious.

The full extent of her injuries cannot be determined until she is strong enough to be X-rayed, physicians said, but she is believed to have suffered a basal skull fracture, concussion of the brain and possible internal injuries. Her arms and legs, although badly bruised, were not broken, as first feared, members of her family said. Her temperature ranged around 104 most of Friday but was down a degree or two yesterday and appeared to be stabilized.

President Truman wired Miss Mitchell yesterday: "Hope you are better soon." His telegram was one of hundreds which poured in from all parts of the world where *Gone With the Wind* first won friends for the little author and where her own generosity later cemented many friendships overseas. During the war Miss Mitchell sent hundreds of food and clothing packages to starving people in Europe and the Far East. Her book, with its account of the sufferings endured by Georgians during the War Between the States, brought courage to people in war-torn countries everywhere and Miss Mitchell said she could not turn a deaf ear to appeals from starving families who felt that they knew her personally through her *GWTW* characters.

While her husband, John R. Marsh, an executive of Georgia Power Company, rested at the home of his physician awaiting the time when she should be fully conscious and he would be with her, Miss Mitchell's friends mobilized to handle telephone queries and visitors.

Grady Hospital would have had to place two additional telephone operators on duty to handle the calls, Supt. Frank Wilson said, but the author's friends systematically undertook the job. Dividing the days and nights up into four-hour shifts, one or two close friends of the Marshes were present at the hospital all day and all night to give out what information was available.

Countless people called and left messages but only one or two bunches of flowers were allowed in the room. The others were distributed to the other patients in Grady and some were taken to St. Joseph's Hospital and placed in the chapel, where the Sisters of Mercy were praying for Miss Mitchell's recovery.

Meanwhile, Hugh D. Gravitt, 29, was released from city jail

under $5,450 bond on a charge of driving while drunk. Gravitt, a taxi driver who was operating a private machine at the time, said he struck Miss Mitchell when she started back to the curb. Gravitt's bond was signed by a bonding company.

Margaret Mitchell Rites Listed Tomorrow at 10; Aid for Grady Requested

August 17, 1949

Death came to Margaret Mitchell at noon yesterday—but even death did not end the beloved little author's generosity and philanthropy.

Instead of sending flowers to her funeral, which has been tentatively set for 10 A.M. tomorrow at Spring Hill, the friends of Margaret Mitchell will send money to Grady Memorial Hospital to be spent for the treatment of others.

That announcement was made by members of her family last night as a nation and citizens throughout the world went into mourning for the gallant little woman who gave the world its greatest story of Confederate courage—*Gone With the Wind*.

"Peggy never wanted flowers for herself," a member of the family said. "Her friends will want to send her flowers, we know, but we feel that perhaps Peggy would like it better if they brought medical service for people who need it. Any gifts can go to Grady Memorial Hospital in memory of Margaret Mitchell."

Meanwhile, Mayor Hartsfield declared official mourning for the author, who died from injuries received last Thursday night when she was struck by an automobile on Peachtree Street—a thoroughfare that became known around the world through the pages of her book.

Flags at Five Points, atop the City Hall and at the Cyclorama will be flown at half-mast until after the funeral, the Mayor said. He asked that Atlantans pause for a moment of silent prayer at 10 A.M., the hour set for the funeral. Funeral services will be private, attended by members of the immediate family and close friends. Admission will be by card.

John Marsh, Georgia Power Company executive and husband of Margaret Mitchell, received the news of her death at the home of his physician, Dr. W.C. Waters, about half an hour after it was known at the hospital. Her brother, Stephens Mitchell, and Dr. Waters telephoned the house and asked members of the household to keep the news from Marsh until they were there to tell him because of his delicate heart condition.

He received the news "remarkably well," his physicians announced, but changed his plans to visit the funeral home where the body was taken and went to their apartment on Piedmont Avenue instead. He authorized an autopsy to determine the immediate cause of death, and the body was returned to Grady about mid-afternoon.

Frank Wilson, Superintendent of the hospital, said the exact cause of death might not be known for several days but added, "According to my best information, Miss Mitchell died from massive brain injuries."

A preliminary autopsy report yesterday afternoon showed Miss Mitchell suffered contusions of the brain, Wilson added.

News that the little author was dead spread through the hospital like wild fire within a few minutes. Stephens Mitchell said he and Mrs. Mitchell were with her when doctors announced the decision to operate after a sudden sinking spell at 11 A.M.

The proposed operation on the brain would have been to relieve pressure there, according to Wilson.

One of the three doctors in attendance walked into the room

and said, "We'll have to do it quick," Mr. Mitchell reported. He said they immediately began to prepare his sister for the operation and he walked from the room and returned to the small office on the first floor where friends and members of the press were keeping a 24-hour vigil.

"I had just sat down when Carrie Lou (Mrs. Mitchell) came and told me she was gone," he added.

Mrs. Mitchell left the hospital and Mr. Mitchell and Dr. Waters conferred briefly with the other three attending physicians before going to inform the author's husband.

There were no signs of weeping in the hospital corridors but other patients who were ambulatory and members of the staff gathered in little groups, talking in hushed tones. Friends of the author, who had inaugurated a telephone service to keep her fans and admirers informed of her condition, continued to sit by the telephone, although there was an almost immediate cessation of telephone calls.

"They must know," declared Marguerite Steedman, also an Atlanta author, who was in charge of the desk when death came. "The phone has stopped ringing."

Close friends of the light-hearted little writer did not give noticeable signs of their grief.

"I have only the happiest memories of Peggy," declared Mrs. Athos Menaboni, writer and wife of the famous bird painter. "I intend to keep them uppermost in my mind right now."

She recalled that when her husband's mother and sisters came from Italy, their one desire was to meet the author of *Gone With the Wind,* which they had read in Italian.

"We called Peggy and she invited them to tea and went down and dug up a copy of the book in Italian and gave them that along with a letter and some Confederate money," Mrs. Menaboni went on. "I'll always remember her that way—merry and full of fun and always thinking of other people."

"I was with Peggy when she met Mr. Latham (Harold Latham, of MacMillan, who was later to publish her book)," declared Marguerite Steedman. "She said, 'Marguerite, haven't you a book you're working on?' and then she took me in her car and made me get the book and show it to him." (Miss Steedman's book was later published.)

Mrs. Mary Clifton, teacher at Spring Street School, was in charge of the telephone for most of the afternoon. She took from her bag a letter from Miss Mitchell thanking the children for singing carols at her apartment during her husband's illness. The letter referred to a chain which one of the children lost in the apartment at the time, and Miss Clifton said it was returned by the author "beautifully wrapped."

"She always sent me money to be used in sending two of the children with the school patrol to Washington," Mrs. Clifton added, "and she always said if there were others who were qualified to go and didn't have the money, she would send that, too."

Frank Wilson, Grady Superintendent, roamed the halls dejectedly following the death of his most famous patient. He knew her well and had previously mentioned that she frequently came in the hospital and made contributions for the use of charity patients. Asked the extent of her generosities following her death, he said, "That's something she knows and I know. She wouldn't want it talked about."

Dorine Cullen, 17-year-old high school girl, appeared at the hospital shortly after noon clutching a copy of *Gone With the Wind* and a small autographed pamphlet which Peggy had given her.

"I know I can't see her," began the young girl apologetically, "but I thought I could talk to some of her friends and ask about her."

"She's dead, honey," somebody murmured, and the girl's eyes filled with tears.

She found a chair in a nearby office and sat there, fingering the little pamphlet and dabbing at her eyes.

Included in the pamphlet was Harold Latham's account of his efforts to persuade Margaret Mitchell to let him see the book after Atlantans had told him she was writing one.

"Finally it was my good fortune to meet Peggy Mitchell," he wrote. "She proved to be a diminutive person with a very lively sense of humor and a proficiency in the art of conversation rarely encountered these days." He said she was "known to have a critical mind, an impatience with shams, an eager curiosity and a striking ability to get at the root of things."

He was greatly impressed with her, he wrote, but was unable to persuade her to let him see her book until the day he checked out of his hotel for California. He said he received a telephone call that she was in the lobby and he went down to find "a tiny woman sitting on a divan and beside her the biggest manuscript I have ever seen, towering in two stacks almost up to her shoulders."

Later Peggy told him she got the idea of the book from childhood trips with her mother about Atlanta to places which still bore the marks of the War Between the States.

She said she had no love of school and her mother was attempting to impress upon her the importance of an education. Her mother, he quoted the author as saying, pointed out the homes of people who had the ability and the willpower to rise above the wreckage, and she pointed out others where families had sunk "because they had no resources within themselves to aid them in surviving this catastrophe."

Miss Mitchell said herself that if her novel had a theme it was that of "survival"—the story of "Georgians who did come through and Georgians who didn't."

The following was co-written by Sibley and Harold Martin.

Margaret Mitchell Buried: Beautiful Rites Honor South's First Lady

August 19, 1949

On a hill overlooking the city whose story she made immortal, Margaret Mitchell Marsh was buried yesterday in the beautiful ritual of the Episcopal Church.

Only a few of the millions who in all lands mourned her passing were present on the sunny slope in Oakland Cemetery as Dean Raimundo de Ovies, rector-emeritus of the Cathedral of St. Philip, scattered upon the ground a handful of the red Georgia earth that Peggy Mitchell loved, and pronounced the solemn and beautiful words:

"Unto Almighty God we commend the soul of our sister departed, Margaret, and we commit her body to the ground: earth to earth, ashes to ashes, dust to dust . . ."

The people standing by, hushed and still in the heat of a sun that came and went through drifting mists, were few but as varied as the characters who made up her city, who marched through the pages of her great book; they were white and black, rich and poor, wise and foolish. They were her friends—the people she had loved, and who had loved her, and as the service ended with the benediction, they seemed hesitant to leave the green mound where the tiny vault of white and silver lay under its blanket of white flowers.

Finally, the dean approached the grave and pronounced a final prayer, an extemporaneous blessing and farewell that came not from the book but from the heart. Only then did the people begin to leave, filing slowly past the grave into which the vault, bearing one white carnation, had by now been lowered.

The grave lay in the Mitchell family plot, where Margaret's mother, father and little brother also sleep. From it, through tall oaks and magnolias, the skyline of Atlanta, the city whose story had never been told until she told it, could be seen towering in the sun.

The services at Spring Hill Chapel had been as brief and as beautiful as those at the grave side. The hour of the service was at 10, but long before then those who held cards had gathered in the pews while the organist softly played Schumann's "At Evening," Handel's "Largo," "Crossing the Bar," and the triumphant paean from the Episcopal hymnal, "The Strife is O'er."

There were few flowers at the family's request, but at the left of the silvery casket, before the American flag, was one wreath that would have deeply touched the heart of the one it honored. It was of white roses and cockscombs and golden marigolds, simple flowers grown behind the walls of Federal Prison, picked by the prisoners Wednesday morning in the rain and fashioned into a wreath by the hands of the men who loved Margaret Mitchell for her sympathy and understanding. The 2,100 men whose love these flowers represented had already sent their contribution to Grady Hospital, as the family had asked, but by special request through the prison chaplain they had asked to do this one small extra thing, as a tribute to the little lady who often had come to talk to them, not as outcasts, but as men no different in their hearts from those who walked the free world.

There was not the sound of a breath or a cough or a shuffling foot in the little chapel as the rich, deep voice of the white-haired dean began the reading of the service.

"I am the resurrection and the life, saith the Lord; he that believeth in me, though he were dead, yet shall he live; and whosoever liveth and believeth in me shall never die. . . . We brought nothing into this world and it is certain we can carry nothing out. The Lord gave, and the Lord hath taken away: blessed be the name of the Lord."

And then the reading of the 27th Psalm, and of Romans 8:14 and the prayer: "Remember thy servant, Margaret; O Lord, according to the favour which thou bearest unto thy people; and grant that, increasing in knowledge and love of thee, she may go from strength to strength, in the life of perfect service, in thy heavenly kingdom; through Jesus Christ our Lord, who liveth and reigneth with thee and the Holy Ghost ever one God, world without end."

To which the dean appended these words extemporaneously: "Bless, oh God, thy servant, Margaret, who made the long-since dead live for us again. We pray Thee that she who brought the past into our present, may take all her pleasant present into a glorious future that shall be forever more, through Christ our Lord. Amen."

At the right of the casket as the dean pronounced these words hung the flag of the Confederacy, symbol and memento of those "long since dead," who lived again and will live forever in the pages of *Gone With the Wind*.

As the benediction ended there was still no sound until, far down at the front, a small boy broke into the unashamed sobbing of a grieving child. Thus the multiple grief of the world found voice in the crying of a little boy as the flower-blanketed casket moved slowly through a mourning city to a hill where Margaret Mitchell sleeps.

Like any streetwise reporter, Sibley winced when she returned from covering a murder trial in the winter of 1950 and Constitution city editor Luke Greene introduced her next assignment by saying, "This is right down your alley." In her absence, both the Constitution and its rival Journal had published many mournful stories concerning the untimely expiration of Alice, the sole elephant at Grant Zoo. The Journal already had a new elephant fund going. Sibley's assignment: get the Constitution a bigger, better elephant—and get it first.

After coming up with a grand total of $7.82 after a week of fund-raising, Sibley opted to seek the support of Coca-Cola multimillionaire and animal lover Asa Griggs Candler Jr.

Not coincidentally, Candler was suffering a spell of negative publicity at the time. (As owner of the Westview Cemetery, he had pushed for a modernization of the property which included the removal of ancient tombstones. Atlanta citizens reacted by taking the matter to court.) He readily agreed to financially assist the effort. Before Sibley and Candler were through, the Constitution's "I Would Like to Select Coca II" contest involved six local youngsters, a trip to Boston on Candler's private jet, a meet-and-greet with Vice President Alben W. Barkley and national media attention.

On to New Hampshire for Coca II: Boston Warms to Elephant Hunt; Veep Heartens Young Georgians

March 30, 1950

Boston, Mass.—A covey of weary, happy airborne young elephant hunters from Georgia nestled in the chill, age-darkened towers of historic Boston last night and they were well content.

They had:

1. Met and captivated one of the nation's premiere elephant

trainers—Vice President Alben W. Barkley himself.

2. Booed Gen. William Tecumseh Sherman and his horse, drooled over the U.S. Mint, laid hands on a bonafide "Yankee" with an accent and stood in wordless awe before the great marble memorial to Abraham Lincoln.

And in the process the six young winners of the Constitution's "I Would Like to Select Coca II" contest, five of whom had never been in an airplane, met and conquered modern air travel like veterans.

The sextet from Georgia reached out and took the notoriously complacent city of Boston to their warm young hearts last night before Pilots B.A. Hawkins and E.W. Hightower had even set down the 12-passenger Lockheed Lodestar of Asa Candler, Jr. at Boston's Logan International Field.

"Geeminee," squeaked Henry Ramsey, tilting his hat on the back of his head, and pressing his freckled nose against the window. "Look at the lights. And boats, boy, look at the boats."

"Ohhh," breathed Carolyn Bowen, of Augusta. "The prettiest lights."

At the old Parker House Hotel, where they had reservations, they were greeted by a member of the staff who asked graciously, "Is this the Candler Patty?"

"The what?" echoed the youngsters and gathered round.

"The Candler Patty," repeated the hotel official.

"He said Patty," chirped one young Georgian. "Talk some more," urged another. "What do you mean, Patty?" demanded another. The hotel man hastily retreated behind the desk and found bell boys to dispatch them to their rooms.

Eight-year-old Johanna Wendt, of Commerce, was the first to unpack and for a good reason—she had a new pair of patent leather slippers to wear. Gently rubbing their mirrored surfaces,

Johanna wondered aloud if she should wear them to dinner. "It's not raining," she said. "So I wouldn't get them wet."

"Oh, sure, wear 'em," advised older Jeannine Hart, of Atlanta. "You're in Boston, aren't you."

If Mr. Tanner, operator of Tanner's station grill, of Commerce, reads this, Johanna would like him to look for the new patent leather pocketbook and red gloves which the teachers and children of Davis School gave her as a going-away gift. She thinks she left them in his place but she is worried. The red suit which was the gift of friends in Commerce is the brightest thing in Boston, however, and Johanna is wearing it.

Thursday, the youngsters will leave Boston at 9 A.M. for a sightseeing trip before going to Nashua, N.H. to pick out Coca II at Benson's Wild Animal Farm.

With stars in their eyes and whiffs of clouds still clinging to their ears, the six young Georgians had earlier carried their hunt for an elephant into the heart of the city where the elephant is said to be as extinct as the dodo—Washington, D.C.

They took their problem straight to Vice President Alben Barkley himself.

"Do you think we will find an elephant in Washington, Mr. Vice President?" asked Johanna, plucking the Veep's sleeve anxiously.

"Elephants? In Washington?" boomed the Veep delightedly. "My dear, you'll find white elephants only."

But the four other elephant hunters already had temporarily sidetracked the elephant hunt for the autograph hunt and were pressing pencils and pads into the Veep's hand.

And the fifth one, 10-year-old GMA Cadet Bobby Hardwick, already known to the party as "Sarge," had his eyes fixed above the Veep's head and his lips puckered in a low approving whistle at the glittering Thomas Jefferson chandelier of gold and Bohemian crystal.

The Veep received the Georgia elephant hunters—Bobby, Johanna, Jeannine, Carolyn Bowen, Dick Cossitt and Henry Ramsey—and their host, Candler, in the historic Vice President's office in the Capitol.

The Veep stepped out of the Senate Chamber to greet his former schoolmate, Candler, with whom he attended Emory at Oxford from 1896 to 1899, and to chat with the young Georgians.

Previously the youngsters visited the Vice President's office in the Senate Office Building—"his working office," as his secretary, Miss Laura Barron, explained—and they all sat in the Veep's chair and examined his collection of Henry Clay etchings, as well as a photograph of the beauteous Veepess. They rode to the Capitol by Senate subway train.

New Englanders Gasp at 'Celebrities': Young Georgia Elephant Shoppers Buy 3,000-Lb. 'Baby Girl' in N.H.

March 31, 1950

Nashua, N.H.—Here at the "strangest farm on earth," the Benson Wild Animal Farm, six Georgia children completed the most momentous bit of shopping of their short lives. They bought a 1½-ton hunk of baby elephant for the Grant Park Zoo.

The seven-year-old Siamese elephant, up to now called "Nedjt" by her Indian trainer but soon to be rechristened Coca II, endeared herself to the emissaries of 700,000 Georgia children almost immediately. She reached out a tentative pinkish gray trunk to them and as eight-year-old Johanna Wendt, the baby of the party, solemnly explained: "Smiled at us the nicest you ever saw."

From that moment on there was little choice to be made between the young elephant and her four stablemates.

Their choice made, their thoughts turned homeward. Candler

said his plane would put them down at Atlanta Municipal Airport at 5 P.M. today.

The decision of the children was unanimous. GMA Cadet Bobby Hardwick, the last to make up his mind, finally announced his choice by pointing to the vivacious lass, around which other members of the party were gathered. Concurring were Johanna, Jeannine Hart, Carolyn Bowen of Augusta; Henry Ramsey and Richard Cossitt.

"The children have made an excellent choice," pronounced Parks Director George I. Simons. "I have never seen a finer elephant."

Asa Candler Jr., who flew the children on the shopping expedition on his private plane and who is helping them to pay for their elephant, stood in the background and declined to have a hand in the choice.

"It's your elephant, Sarge," he grinned at young Hardwick. "Get together on your decision."

Meanwhile, New England was turning out to welcome the young Georgians and their host. Mayor Hugh Gregg, of Nashua, arrived to conduct them on a tour of the bright, sunswept textile town and to invite them to dinner.

Representatives from newspapers and wire services here in Boston and nearby Manchester gathered in the gabled barn to await the dramatic moment when the youngsters would decide on their elephant. Paramount Newsreel recorded the event on film and radio and television crews stood by to record the news to be rebroadcast on the Mutual Network at 10:15 P.M. Friday.

"Goo-ood grief," commented Henry Ramsey of the blue eyes and rumpled blond hair. "This makes us whatcha-call-'ems cele . . . cel . . . oh well, you know."

"Celebrities," finished off Dick Cossitt, competently. "I guess we're the funniest looking elephant hunters they ever saw around here."

The young elephant hunters, well-fortified with clam chowder and history picked up along the road from an inspired sight-seeing guide, were in truth the starriest-eyed expedition to make a safari into the tidy wilds of New England.

They came to Nashua from Boston by chartered bus along the road traveled by Paul Revere. Rolling along the sunlit New England countryside where patches of snow still lingered in the shadow of red barns and trim houses. They relived the tense moments which precipitated the Revolutionary War. They stopped at Lexington and gamboled over "the rude bridge which arched the flood." They paused before the homes of Hawthorne, Louisa May Alcott, Longfellow and Ralph Waldo Emerson. Early in the morning, with a chill wind whipping across Haymarket Square, they visited Old South meeting house and the graves of Revere, John Hancock and Mary Goose, author of the Mother Goose rhymes.

Today they are invited to be special guests at a joint session of both houses of the Legislature of the Commonwealth of Massachusetts and Gov. Paul Dever.

Bands, Oratory and Peanuts: Coca II Gets Heroine's Welcome in Atlanta

April 9, 1950

With bands playing, flags flying and hundreds of children to cheer her, Georgia's newest elephant, Coca II, has set up housekeeping at Grant Park Zoo.

The seven-year-old elephant swung joyfully out of her heated van into Springtime's most perfect weather yesterday afternoon, pausing under a dogwood tree at Grant Park to wink a coy eye at Mayor Hartsfield and to acknowledge a burst of applause from friends all over Georgia.

She now is at home at Grant Park Zoo—the most fêted elephant in the United States.

Welcoming Coca II, the elephant bought for the zoo through the *Atlanta Constitution* fund, was a genuine community project. A big bustling city intent on pre-Easter affairs cheerfully paused in the midst of Saturday's business to extend a warm welcome to one of the peculiar treasures of childhood—an elephant.

Police chief Herbert Jenkins donned his colorful Shriner's regalia and rode in a motorcycle for the first time in many years to head the parade. The Mayor was there to welcome the elephant with a pretty speech. The First Lady of the State and her two sons, Bobby and Gene Talmadge, greeted her in front of the *Constitution* Building and offered Coca II her first taste of Georgia peanuts.

There was music and marching and United States Marines. The West End Elementary School band rode in a bus borrowed for the occasion from J.C. Steinmetz's dogwood tours. Fort McPherson, taking a neighborly interest in the doings, sent over the famed Third Army Band to march in the parade and to play a lively concert later for the throngs enjoying their first Spring outing at Grant Park.

Mike Benton, President of the Southeastern Fair Association and dean of Atlanta parade marshals, took charge of the hastily assembled procession. He served as grand marshal with Rich Paul to assist him and provided last-minute decorations for all the cars of officials who rode in the parade.

The Shriners, those effervescent fun-makers, appeared with their famed Yaarab Mounted Patrol with clowns and zany automobiles with their degree teams and a genuine, circusy steam calliope. Six roistering Georgia Tech tumblers bedecked as clowns, capered in the parade and convulsed onlookers with their stunts.

All officialdom was there. Dr. M.D. Collins, State Superintendent of Education, appeared for all the Georgia school children who contributed to the elephant fund and who wrote letters to the *Constitution* contest. He rode in the famous white Auburn which Austin Abbott has driven in more than 300 Atlanta parades. Sheriff A.B. "Bud" Foster and Jack Lovelady, two Shriners who helped raise funds for the elephant at an amateur show, were in the triumphal procession.

The American Legion's nationally known locomotive, manned by members of Fulton Voiture 127, Forty and Eight, puffed and clanged realistically down the parade route and all the way out to Grant Park.

Asa Candler Jr., heaviest contributor to the elephant fund and donor of the first Coca to the Grant Park Zoo, rode in the parade with four of the youngsters who were his guests on an elephant-buying hunt in Nashua, N.H. He and the four—Bobby Hardwick, Jeannine Hart, Richard Cossitt and Henry Ramsey— beamed happily at Grant Park when a young bystander glimpsed Coca II and piped: "That's a PURTY elephant!"

There were only two brief touches of formality about the entire reception—one at the *Constitution* where young Gene Talmadge shyly offered Coca peanuts and one at Grant Park when the Mayor received the elephant.

Dr. H.F. McMurray, personal physician to the elephant, who rode here from Benson Wild Animal Farm in Nashua, N.H., to attend to her, presented an official greeting to the people of Georgia from Mayor Hugh Gregg, of Nashua.

"We are very happy to have you, Coca II," said Mayor Hartsfield, "and we greatly appreciate the expression of friendship from your former townspeople in Nashua."

Editor Ralph McGill, of the *Constitution,* accompanied Mrs. Talmadge and her young sons to greet Coca and presented Asa Candler to the throng gathered in front of the newspaper office.

Coca II, seven years old and a ton and a half in weight, was bought at a cost of $5,000—all of which was contributed through the *Constitution* elephant fund. She was brought to this country from Siam and has been part of a four-elephant act at the Benson farm. Trainer Johnny Dilbeck immediately took charge of her from the four attendants who made the trip to Atlanta with her.

'Madam X' in Holdup Tells Her Name, Story

February 20, 1959

"Madam X," the mystery woman held as a robbery suspect, Thursday admitted she is Mrs. Evelyn Kobert of 86 Fifth Street, NW, an unemployed clerical worker, police said.

Told that her picture would be furnished to newspapers and television stations in an effort to have her identity established, the slight, middle-aged woman took a pen and wrote the name and address on the back of an enlarged police photograph.

Speaking softly and hesitantly, she described purchasing a single-shot cap pistol in a drug store and then walking around until she found a whiskey store on Alabama Street, SW, that "looked like it would be easy to rob," Lt. R.F. Jordan said.

Asked about family connections, she said her parents are dead and that she has no children. She said she has two sisters, but hastened to add: "I don't want them involved."

Earlier, in an interview in her cell, Mrs. Kobert said: "What I did was terrible. I wouldn't have believed I'd ever do anything like that. But sometimes you get desperate. I'm willing to work—any kind of work! But do you think anybody will hire me? I walked the streets and asked. To save carfare I telephoned. After you're 30 nobody wants you, unless you're beautiful or a snappy dresser. I got down to my last dollar and I had no place to go . . . no roof over my head . . . no food. I thought I'd get a little money to tide me over and when I found work I'd repay it."

Tears welled up in her slate-gray eyes and she shook her head impatiently and wiped them away with a lace-edged handkerchief.

"I'm through feeling sorry for myself! I'll take my punishment for what I did."

Asked if she had a husband or children, she shook her head violently. Asked where she was from she said shortly, "Not from here. Not until recently." Asked if she had any kind of job experience, she said, "I worked once. Not lately. But I'll say this, I can work. I'm not afraid of work."

The incongruity of the name, "Madam X," on this plain, aging woman shivering in a jail blanket struck even her as a bit of ironic humor. In the movies, "Madam X" was a glamorous spy. In the Atlanta city jail she is a tired and frightened and bitterly unhappy woman who has tried, probably out of personal fastidiousness and an eagerness to please, to keep herself looking nice. There was polish on her fingernails, the remains of lipstick on her mouth and she kept her head covered in the thin silk scarf she was wearing at the time of her arrest because "they took my comb away and my hair is a sight."

She keeps going over and over in her mind the horror of the moment when she pulled her toy pistol on Morris Weisman, proprietor of the liquor store, and got $62.

"I've never been as scared of anything in my life. After I started running and he was shooting at me it wasn't half as bad as standing there holding him up." Her sad mouth lifted in a smile. "When I used to read of crimes like that I always said, 'If I ever pulled anything like that, they'd catch me right away.' Well, they did."

Patrolmen G.E. Wallace and A.C. Potts happened to be driving by the liquor store as the clerk shot five times at the fleeing woman. They followed and picked her up a block and a half away near Whitehall Street.

"They took my fingerprints," she remarked listlessly. "That won't help them any. I've never been fingerprinted before. I was never in jail before and I never had a job that required it."

As for interested friends or somebody who might help her, she shrugged the question off.

"I'm not going to embarrass or hurt anybody else," she said.

It's a Scream: That Uproar? What It Was Was Beatles

August 19, 1965

What it was was not baseball.

What it was was the Beatles.

That commotion at Atlanta Stadium Wednesday night was 30-odd thousand teen-age children and a few assorted parents giving the British mophead musicians a tumultuous welcome.

For a brief half hour John, Paul, George and Ringo twisted and shuffled, snorted and yodeled from center field of the beautiful new stadium, climaxing a day which saw several hundred teenagers shrilling and clawing at the entrance to the ball park as early as 9 A.M.

The limber-legged, bushy-headed Britishers tripped across the ball diamond at 9:39 P.M. while a cordon of Atlanta policemen, who had been stolidly facing the crowds for more than two hours, held the audience of writhing, squealing teen-agers in their seats.

From time to time a few of the bleeding madras-clad audience slipped from their seats and headed for the field only to be turned back by the police officers who circulated in the stands.

Although first-aid stations were operating there were few casualties beyond a sore throat or two.

After the performance, two teen-age girls who broke from the stands and raced across the field to the stage which their idols already had vacated were pulled down bodily by police and in the midst of the thrashing, flailing arms and legs hauled to an exit ramp.

The audience, which came from all over the United States, was admitted to the stadium starting at 6 P.M. and sat peacefully munching doughnuts, hot dogs, fried chicken and pop corn and watching a Piper Club airplane play around overhead towing a sign which said, "WPLO—It's What's Happening, Baby."

Hundreds of the youngsters were ornamented with giant badges which read "I Love Paul" or George or Ringo or John as the case might be.

E.M. Hendrix, operator of a souvenir concession who follows the Beatles about, said that in Atlanta Paul was the heavy seller.

The program on stage opened with an Atlanta team of musicians called the Vibrations playing for a fashion show which was narrated by a Britisher and drew applause when the narrator threw in comments like, "Ringo loves this one."

Throughout the crowd there were signs identifying fan clubs and one big placard which said simply, "We Luv You Beatles."

Mayor Ivan Allen, who already had presented a key to the city to the Beatles at a late afternoon press conference, took the field to declare the boys to be "honorary Atlantans."

"The Beatles and the Braves are both in first place where they are and in our hearts," the mayor said to a resounding round of cheers and applause from the stands.

He tried to get in a plug for courtesy and good behavior, urging the fans to stay in their seats, but was almost drowned out by one cheering section.

The Beatles themselves were almost drowned out—but enthusiastically.

One 13-year-old girl who stuffed cotton in her ears and calmly told her Atlanta host that she was going to the concert "not to listen but to scream," set the pattern for thousands of them.

They flung themselves into the air, trembling, jerking, squealing and flailing their arms about. Many burst into tears.

A peculiar brand of clapping which involved a way of weaving fingers reminiscent of Hawaiian dancers, swept the stands in the warmup portion of the program when a great number of skinny young people, variously labeled dancers, headhunters and musicians, engaged in grasshopper-like gyrations on the stage.

This form of audience participation reached its zenith when the Beatles took the stage and played a number called "Dizzy Miss Lizzie."

(Other numbers readily recognized by teen-agers—although unintelligible to most adults—included "Twist and Shout," "She's a Woman," "I Feel Fine," "Ticket To Ride" and their latest movie hit, "Help!")

The concert was punctuated by cries of "Yeah, yeah, yeah," with some incitement from electric signs which urged, "Everybody Yeah!"

The Beatles were sped out of the stadium in three Cadillacs and whisked to the Atlanta Airport and their charter plane for a trip to Houston, Texas, next stop on their current American tour.

Meanwhile, back at the stadium in a first-aid station, two teenage girls were being treated for hysterics. One of them reclined on a bed sobbing, "I don't want them to go. I don't want them to leave. I love them."

On the soles of her tennis shoes she had inscribed, "Beatles," in case you didn't know who "them" were.

Another female walking from the stadium with her boyfriend was heard saying, "Crawford, if you were a girl, you'd understand."

Hundreds Fill Church to Bid McGill Good-bye

February 6, 1969

The red clay soil of the Southland he loved received the body of Ralph Emerson McGill Wednesday afternoon.

Before a throng of mourners which included the former vice president of the United States and a Negro Boy Scout troop from a nearby mission church, the 70-year-old *Constitution* publisher was laid to rest in Westview Cemetery shortly before 4 P.M.

A simple graveside service followed the rites attended by an overflow crowd at All Saints Episcopal church and a procession through predominantly Negro sections of the city where school-children lined the sidewalks and housewives and laborers paused in their work and stood with tears in their eyes to watch the hearse go by.

Former Vice President Hubert H. Humphrey, whose campaign for President *Constitution* Publisher McGill strongly supported, and Mrs. Humphrey attended both services, standing close behind Mr. McGill's son and widow at the graveside. They were accompanied by the Mayor and Mrs. Ivan Allen.

"I am the resurrection and the life, saith the Lord; he that believeth in Me, though he were dead, yet shall he live; and whosoever liveth and believeth in Me shall never die," intoned the Rev. Frank Ross as the coffin of the famous editor was borne down the aisle of the church.

All Saints, the red stone church at the corner of North Avenue and West Peachtree, is the church where Mr. Gill was married to his second wife, the former Dr. Mary Lynn Morgan, two years ago. It was filled to capacity with mourners standing along the walls and overflowing to the vestibule and the sidewalk.

The rector, Mr. Ross, read from the Episcopal service for the burial of the dead, closing with a passage from Romans: "For I am persuaded that neither death, nor life, nor angels, nor principalities, nor powers, nor things present, nor things to come, nor height, nor depth, nor any other creature, shall be able to separate us from the love of God, which is in Christ Jesus, our Lord."

The Rev. Samuel Williams, Negro chairman of the Community Relations Commission and pastor of the Friendship Baptist church, gave the eulogy, quoting from Mr. McGill's column which appeared Tuesday after his death from a heart attack Monday night.

"'You may be assured . . . that the freedom of choice plan is, in fact, neither real freedom, nor a choice. It is discrimination,'" read Mr. Williams. And then he added: "His final words to us! And how true to his spirit.

"Ralph McGill has been for more than 20 years pleading with us to listen. He never lost the faith that we would eventually hear, even though we seemed to be so deaf to his constant pleading with us to act justly. He lived among us as our teacher loving us as Jesus taught us all to do, yet shocking us, chiding us, goading us as Socrates did his beloved Athens.

"He never tired trying to teach us what it means to be a civilized community, for the qualities of such a community were clear to him. They are Truth, Beauty, Peace, Adventure, Art, Justice and Love.

"Ralph McGill was in his person the exemplification of these qualities . . . In the cultivation of these qualities, McGill was of the conviction that, by means of these, civilization would triumph over barbarism and the long hard struggle toward establishing of justice in the community could be achieved.

Cause of Justice

"Working hard always, he had the faith to believe that justice would eventually rule in his dear Southland. He died before its coming, but if and when it does come, he will be one of the inescapable causes for its having come."

A few sentences later the dark-skinned minister closed by repeating Mr. McGill's admonition, "Listen, please!"

The Rev. Walter Smith, curate at All Saints, assisted in both the church and the graveside services, praying for the editor and his family and the community he left.

As the church began filing more than an hour before the service, the organist, Gregory Colson, played selections by Bach, Handel and Brahms.

But the hymns sung by the congregation were two old-fashioned ones which the Presbyterian-reared Ralph McGill might have sung in the country churches of his childhood—"O God our help in ages past, our hope for years to come" and "A mighty fortress is our God, a bulwark never failing."

Join Us in Song

Mourners throughout the church, from the *Constitution* staffers who gathered on the left to the former Vice President and Mrs. Humphrey to Jewish rabbis, business and civic leaders and political figures, joined in singing.

Humphrey and his wife, Muriel, shared a hymn book and sang the old words and toward the back a shabby white man who wore neither coat nor tie but a look of grief on his face sang, too.

Although the family had requested that in lieu of flowers donations be sent to found a Ralph McGill Memorial at Atlanta University, the chancel held many flowers. A cross of white blossoms was attached to the pulpit. The coffin went undecked to the grave but was followed by two vans of flowers sent by friends from all parts of the world.

Through Slum Areas

The route of the procession was through an old section of town, part of which has been reduced to slums, some of which is a middle-class Negro neighborhood similar to that where the editor-publisher was stricken with a heart attack on the eve of his 71st birthday.

Children of Agnes Jones Elementary School on Fair Street, largely a Negro school, lined the sidewalk outside the school and waited to see the funeral procession go by. A garbage truck moved over to the side to give way to the hearse while its driver watched with grave eyes.

One of the motorcycle police officers escorting the procession stopped at the gate to Westview and stood with his white helmet over his heart waiting for the funeral cars to go by.

At the cemetery the Rev. George G. Kinney, inner city minister of the Hope Lutheran church, what he called a "a store-front mission church," brought Troop 584, Negro Boy Scouts.

Wearing their uniforms and looking solemn, the little boys stood in a straight line a few paces from the grave, waiting to say good-bye to a man who had fought for their rights long before they were born.

"They have no official reason to be here," the young minister said. "They just wanted to come."

Pallbearers for the celebrated author-editor were long-time friends and associates: Henry Troutman Sr., Atlanta attorney; John Griffin, chairman of the Southern Regional Education Board; Harry Ashmore, former editor of the *Little Rock* (Ark.) *Gazette,* now director of a California foundation; James M. Cox, chairman of the board of Atlanta Newspapers Inc.; Eugene Patterson, former editor of the *Constitution,* now with the *Washington Post;* and *Constitution* staffers Reg Murphy and Harold Martin.

Out-of-town newspaper and television friends who came to attend the funeral included: Dan Mahoney, president of the *Dayton News* and Mrs. Mahoney; Greg Favre, managing editor, Chuck Glovers, business manager, Robert Sherman, vice-president and Ryan Sanders, chief photographer, all of the *Dayton News;* Howard Kleinberg, managing editor, Clark Ashe, associate editor and Jack Kazewitz, editorial page editor of the *Miami News;* Sander Vanocur of the National Broadcasting Company; Tom Winship and Charles Whipple of the *Boston Globe;* Bill Sexton of Publishers Hall Syndicate; Ann Landers, syndicated columnist and John Segenthaler of the *Nashville Tennessean.*

Student Editor

Mark McCrackin, associate editor of the Vanderbilt *Hustler*, a position Mr. McGill held in his student days there, also came to Atlanta to attend the funeral.

Among the hundreds of telegrams which poured into Mrs. McGill and Jack Tarver expressing sympathy was a touching one from an old neighbor. Mrs. Frances Hargis McCrorey of 1275 Briarcliff Road, N.E. wired: "It was my privilege to know Ralph 58 years. He lived next door when I was four years old in Tennessee. His mother once told my mother, 'I've never had to whip that boy. God made him good the day he was born.'"

On the evening of February 20, 1974, Constitution *editor Reg Murphy was abducted from his Emory University neighborhood home. Meanwhile, in Hillsborough, Calif., the Symbionese Liberation Army was demanding an additional four million dollars from the parents of kidnap victim Patricia Hearst. In a tape recording sent to the* Constitution *the following day, Murphy told his colleagues that the kidnappers, "The American Revolutionary Army, as I understand it, feels that the American news media have been far too leftist and too liberal. They intend to do something about that. That's the cause for my abduction."*

The paper was caught in the bizarre position of its editor being the top story of the day. "It was as surreal then as it seems today," says Jim Minter, who served as Murphy's managing editor and later delivered the ransom money to his boss' kidnappers. Sibley was initially sent to write a scene piece at Murphy's home.

During the next news cycle, Sibley, like much of the staff, waited as Minter drove off with a parcel of money. She later wrote that her old boss Ralph McGill considered all good managing editors to be

"S.O.B.s" *but she wondered if, in Minter, the* Constitution *didn't have a hero on its hands.*

Today, Minter clears up any misconceptions. "McGill was right and Celestine was wrong. I was an SOB. It's in the job description." Murphy was released unharmed.

At Home: A Wife and Friends Must Wait and Wait

February 22, 1974

A wood fire burns brightly on the hearth. Yellow daffodils are a jaunty bouquet on the table by the window. It is a golden room, a comfortable and serene-looking room—but all serenity and comfort fled when its owner, Reg Murphy, picked up his jacket and followed a man out the door.

Now a slim, brown-eyed woman in rumpled slacks and sweater and in her stocking feet wanders like a forlorn ghost through the room, smiling gently at her children and those who came to comfort her and jumping expectantly every time the telephone rings.

Virginia Rawls Murphy, white-faced and sleepless since her husband left, was the one who tried to comfort her parents and his parents all through a dragging and seemingly hopeless vigil Thursday. She glanced out the window often at more than a hundred television, radio and newspaper reporters and worried constantly that they might be uncomfortable and that she was unable to give them the story they were waiting for.

"I wish they didn't have to stay," Mrs. Murphy said. "I wish we could make them comfortable. They are in the same business Reg is in and he might have been out there with them."

Friends hung a bedspread over the arch separating the

Murphy's living room from the den, hoping that the kidnapped editor's wife would get some sleep when she stopped walking around the house and huddled under an old-fashioned quilt on a sofa near the telephone. For the first eight or 10 hours, Virginia Murphy insisted on answering all telephone calls herself, believing that she might be able to speak to Reg or that his captors would feel easier talking to her than to one of the many male friends who stood by ready to help. Finally, weariness began to take its toll, and a doctor friend persuaded her to take a tranquilizer after she first made sure it would not put her to sleep.

The editor's parents, Mr. and Mrs. John Murphy of Gainesville, heard the news of their son's kidnapping over the radio at 6 A.M. Thursday when they arose to go to work, Mr. Murphy to the store he operates and Mrs. Murphy to the school where she teaches first grade.

Virginia notified her parents, and they arrived later in the morning from their home in Williamstown, in Pike County, where white-haired Roy Rawls has a cattle farm.

On his way into the house, Rawls made a brief statement to newsmen saying that his son-in-law's family was a close-knit one and appealing to the kidnappers for Murphy's safe return.

Later, Rawls worried that he should not have said anything, fearful that any words of his might be misconstrued or might be used against his son-in-law.

Throughout the long day, the two families waited, watched the traffic jam in front of the house and listened for the telephone. Friends and neighbors poured through the front door and the back door throughout the day bringing a bountiful supply of baked dishes, salads, cookies, cakes and fried chicken. In the end, it was the visitors rather than the family who ate the food.

One neighbor went home and brought back a giant-sized cof-

fee pot, and the Rawlses and the Murphys drank coffee throughout the day, touching very little food. They listened to the news
bulletins on the radio and television and tried valiantly to divert
one another by talking of matters other than the kidnapping.

A vacant house next door to the Murphy home was rented by
one group of newsmen as a headquarters. Others brought up
trailers and parked them in the driveway, apparently planning to
stay in for the night. Less fortunate ones brought out plastic bags
to cover their camera equipment and their heads when a slow rain
started falling late Thursday afternoon.

The Rev. Robert McMullen, pastor of the Emory Presbyterian
Church which the Murphys attend, was one of the first people
to arrive at the house after news of the kidnapping became
known. He returned Thursday afternoon to sit with the family
and to offer them comfort wherever possible.

The late afternoon traffic in front of the house creeped by as
sightseers apparently joined the throng of homeward-bound
workers in driving slowly by the door.

The Man: He Was the One, the Drop Guy

February 23, 1974

Managing editors are not heroes. Everybody knows that.

The late celebrated editor-publisher Ralph McGill felt it was
his duty to warn all neophyte journalists that the rules of the
trade absolutely decreed that the managing editor be "an S.O.B."

It's a fact that young aspirants in the newspaper business
learned with the who-what-when-where. It's a circumstance that
old hands accept philosophically.

But the news staff of the *Atlanta Constitution*, frazzled with
worry and waiting and a strange kind of crisis inactivity, watched

their managing editor, Jim Minter, walk out of the newsroom at 4:50 P.M. Friday, wondering with a touch of awe, if they didn't have a hero on their hands.

Minter, who looks younger than his 42 years, was scowling over his half-chewed cigar, striding purposefully toward the freight elevator, carrying a department store paper sack in his hands. He was going to change his clothes for perhaps one of the most frightening, the most crucial assignments in any newspaperman's career.

Jim Minter was on his way to take $700,000 in cash to the kidnappers of editor Reg Murphy.

The kidnappers gave Minter that assignment. In one of several telephone calls about the ransom money which they said would buy the release of Murphy, they told Minter that he was the one, the drop guy.

He would, they specified, come in an open Jeep, obviously to make it apparent from a distance that he was unaccompanied. He would wear white tennis shoes and a short-sleeved white sport shirt, clearly for the purpose of letting them see that he was unarmed. And although a bitter wind blew in from the north and the temperature was dropping fast as nightfall drew on, Minter did not protest. He complied.

Somebody went out and bought him a summery sports shirt. He got some white sneakers. The FBI produced a late model no-top yellow Jeep. Two new beige suitcases were brought in and $700,000 in $5, $10 and $20 bills, neatly wrapped in plastic, were stowed in them as casually as tuna fish sandwiches for a picnic.

And then with the ubiquitous cigar jutting from his face and the managing editor's scowl suitably in place, Jim Minter took off—up Highway 400 for a rendezvous with nobody knew what.

The *Constitution* news staff, watching, gulped.

This M.E., as they used to call them in old newspaper movies, looked like something pretty special in the way of M.E.s. If, as McGill contended, managing editors are S.O.B.s, this one—the staff knew to a man—was OUR S.O.B. He was on his way to risk his life to save a colleague.

All over the newsroom people stood around watching the clock and drinking terrible coffee out of soggy paper cups. Jim Rankin, assistant managing editor, went down to Fayetteville to sit out this assignment with Jim Minter's wife, Anne, and their two sons, Ricky, 16, and Robby, 13. Rankin had for two nights slept on a sofa in the home of Reg Murphy. Now Minter's peril seemed almost as great as Murphy's and his family needed company.

Phones rang constantly in the newsroom and there wasn't anything special to tell the staff that one ring was from Minter. But when it came everybody knew it. Faces relaxed, shoulders sagged and somebody murmured, "Minter's on the way back. The kidnappers called. They got the money and they say they'll release Reg at 9 o'clock tonight."

Minter's return was as undramatic as the return of any hero can be. He came in wearing a new blue zippered jacket, a cap with ear tabs and gloves and his first words were: "It worked."

They were followed by two others: "I'm cold."

Somebody brought him coffee and a sandwich and the story, when he got around to telling it, was almost as ludicrous as the summertime attire he donned for the life-and-death errand.

He drove the FBI Jeep to the end of Highway 400 up beyond Alpharetta, he said, made a U-turn and drove about 50 yards before he stopped and got out. A taxi cab with two people in it waited at the end of the road and he watched to see if it moved. It didn't so he unloaded the suitcases and put them by the roadside.

"Did you ever try to lift $700,000?" he asked. "It's heavy."

The money jettisoned, he drove as the kidnappers had directed, to the State Bridge-Alpharetta exit, from which he could see a car stopping at the spot where he'd dropped the money. He couldn't be sure in the light but he thought it was the taxi.

In Alpharetta he drove down Highway 19 until he felt certain he wasn't being followed and that it would not alarm the kidnappers if he stopped and used a telephone. Then he turned around and went back to Elliott's Drug Store where he asked to use the telephone. The phone was in the prescription department and he asked the clerk back there to step out and let him use it privately. The manager arrived and Minter asked him to go out.

"He said he was the manager," Minter said, "and I showed him my 1973 press card—I never got one for '74—and he went out. So I called the office and then I called home and told Anne I was in Alpharetta and I had to go back by the office."

When he left the drug store Minter sought out a clothing store, settling on Alpharetta's Discount House, where he bought a coat, cap and pair of gloves for $17.

"A lady in there noticed I was driving a Jeep in summer clothes and she said, 'You must be from the North.' A man invited me to warm by a gas heater and I did. They were watching television and they said there was going to be an announcement about Murphy. I started to wait and see it but there were so many commercials I decided to leave." Of such undramatic elements as discount clothiers and television commercials and outdated press cards the saga of risk and ransom was told—and those who heard it laughed uproariously, from relief and amusement.

Old Friends Mourn:
'Mama' King's Faith Recalled

July 3, 1974

The personal faith, strength and hope of Mrs. Martin Luther King Sr. were mirrored in the civil rights movement her son led—and one of the fruits of her "faith in action" was that her accused killer was able to "ride a bus from Ohio without having to sit in the back or eat at separate counters or drink at separate water fountains."

So Walter E. Fauntroy, black delegate to the U.S. House of Representatives from the District of Columbia, told a church filled with mourners at a memorial service for Mrs. King at Spelman College Tuesday night.

Old friends, black and white, including comedian Flip Wilson, who called himself "one of her boys," filed by the rose-colored coffin for an hour before the service started.

Earlier several thousand went to Ebenezer Baptist Church to view her body lying in state just a few feet from the church organ which she was playing when a gunman shot her to death Sunday morning.

After the memorial service her body was returned to Ebenezer for the funeral service at 11 A.M. Wednesday.

Dr. Benjamin E. Mays, president emeritus of Morehouse College, who delivered the memorial sermon, and four other speakers emphasized "Mama" King's love of God and her fellowman and her quiet strength in crisis.

Fauntroy, who served in the civil rights movement with her slain son, Dr. Martin Luther King Jr., said often the young marchers and protesters were "sustained by her strength, inspired by her faith and love."

"We just got to go on and do it," Fauntroy said "Big Mama" would tell the young civil rights workers when the going got rough.

Dr. J. Randolph Taylor, pastor of Central Presbyterian church and chairman of the Community Relations Commission of Atlanta, told of hearing of Mrs. King's death as he was standing at the door of his own church shaking hands with departing worshippers Sunday morning.

"That word," he said, "moved from church to church, home to home, heart to heart, till it gathered up this whole nation, this whole world."

As he spoke of "Daddy" King, Martin Luther King Sr., and asked, "How long, oh God, how much can one man stand?" the white-haired husband of the dead woman bobbed his head emphatically. Dr. King sat on the front row with his daughter, Mrs. Christine King Farris, his daughter-in-law, Mrs. Martin Luther King Jr., and a number of his grandchildren. Twice during the service, a white uniformed nurse brought him a paper cup full of water and several times the old minister took off his glasses and wiped his eyes.

"For those in the family and my sainted brothers, who are not here to speak," Mrs. Farris said. "Mother was a rock, a great bulwark of strength."

Shortly after Dr. Martin Luther King Jr. was slain in Memphis in 1968, his brother, the Rev. A.D. King, was found accidentally drowned at his home in Atlanta.

Pale pink, apparently the favorite color of Mrs. King, was used in her coffin, her lace dress, the blanket of carnations which covered the coffin and a special memorial program that includes the Sisters Chapel service and the funeral Wednesday.

In a note "To Our Friends," the family wrote, "When tragedy

strikes, a family turns to friends for comfort, support and prayers. The response by our friends to the loss of our beloved 'Bunch,' Mother and 'Big Mama' has done much to sustain our strength and faith in this period of mourning. We are deeply grateful to you."

The Rev. Calhoun Morris, executive director of the Martin Luther King Jr. Center for Social Change, said about 50 dignitaries had started arriving Tuesday to attend the funeral. Mrs. Gerald Ford, wife of the vice president, is expected and Stanley Scott, former Atlanta newspaperman who now serves as a special assistant to the President, is coming to represent President Nixon.

Sen. Edward M. Kennedy, D-Mass., is sending Robert Bates as his special representative. Three black congressmen and nine black mayors, including Mayor Charles Evers of Fayette, Miss., are also on the list of visiting dignitaries.

Funeral services for Edward Boykin, the church deacon who was slain with Mrs. King, are set for Friday at 2 P.M., also at Ebenezer. Both Boykin and Mrs. King are to be buried in Southview Cemetery.

Tributes to Mrs. King will be given at the funeral service by Mayor Maynard H. Jackson, the Rev. L.V. Booth, pastor of Zion Baptist church in Cincinnati; the Rev. Ralph D. Abernathy, president of the Southern Christian Leadership Conference, and the Rev. John J. Mulroy, pastor of Holy Family Church in Marietta. There will be tributes from three other speakers, a eulogy by the Rev. Sandy F. Ray, pastor of Cornerstone Baptist Church in Brooklyn, and Rev. King will deliver a statement on behalf of the family.

Chapter Three

Breaking News

Overleaf: Sibley pondering a lead at her *Atlanta Constitution* typewriter in the 1940s.

In the early morning hours of Saturday, December 7, 1946, the Winecoff Hotel in downtown Atlanta caught fire. The 15-story structure contained no sprinkler system or fire escapes. 119 people died and more than 100 were injured.

Constitution editor Ralph McGill and reporters Keeler McCartney and Harold Martin all covered the then-U.S. record hotel fire disaster. McGill managed to get inside the structure once the blaze was out and, as water dripped onto his notepad, recorded the gruesome scene in front of him. McGill wrote: "Down there on the 12th floor is a woman sitting in the window. Her arm is on the ledge. Her nails are scarlet with enamel. But where is her head? It is gone, burned away by the blowtorch heat of exploding gases generated by burning carpets, paintings, mouldings, bed clothing, chairs and other things that burn."

In what was perhaps a display of gender limitations, Sibley did not cover the fire itself (or she may have simply had the weekend off). At least one local man on the scene later recalled giving Sibley a tour of the surviving structure.

As the demand for new fire code regulations rose in the days that ensued, Sibley filed the following story as local women organized.

Women's Clubs Join Fire Fight

December 10, 1946

Determined "it shall not happen again," 200 Atlanta club women, outraged and horrified by the preventable loss of life in the Winecoff disaster, will hold a special meeting at 2 P.M. today to study city and state fire laws and launch a personal, city-wide inspection of escape facilities in other hotels, big stores and public buildings.

Mrs. Robert H. Jones, President of the Atlanta Federation of Women's Clubs, called the meeting at the insistence of "scores of our members who are thoroughly angry and shamed that such a thing could happen here."

The meeting will be held in the Blue Flame room of the Gas Company where the members will dissect the Georgia and city fire code, preparatory to learning first-hand where it should be rewritten and where it should be strengthened.

"Afterwards our 200 members will divide up into committees of three or four and make a personal inspection of all the other hotels, stores and big apartment houses in the city," Mrs. Jones declared. "We realize we are laymen without the experts' understanding or knowledge of what is needful to make a building safe. But more women gave their lives in the Winecoff fire than men and we believe it our responsibility as citizens to be informed in the future and to let the public know."

Mrs. Jones and the women who will attend the meeting will represent all the organizations in the Greater Atlanta Federation.

Meanwhile, the Civic Welfare Committee of the Atlanta Methodist Ministers' Association passed a resolution urging City authorities to take "proper and prompt action to remove at whatever cost the fire hazards which menace the lives of people in hotels and other public buildings."

"We cannot as individuals or as a City shirk this duty which now rests upon our conscience in the terrible light which glows in our memories from the Winecoff Hotel," the resolution stated.

On May 14, 1947, the body of Margaret Alston Refoule, the daughter of a prominent Atlanta family, was found strangled in Peachtree Creek. The chief suspect in the murder was the victim's husband, Paul Refoule, a French-born artist who taught at the High Museum and Oglethorpe University. While his students told Atlanta police that Refoule never left the building on the day of the murder, the

investigation uncovered an extra-marital affair between the young,
handsome Refoule and a 19-year-old female student. Fueled by
titillating newspaper headlines, Atlantans demanded action in the
case. On June 14, 1947, Refoule was arrested on morals charges.
Sibley staked out the family home and filed the following account.
Fulton County Superior Court ultimately did not pursue the morals
charge. Refoule was never charged with his wife's murder and died in
1948 of lung cancer. The case was never solved.

Parents Suffer Shock on Learning of Charge

June 15, 1947

With the arrival of Paul Refoule on a morals charge Saturday, the
household of his slain wife's family turned again to the atmosphere of deepest mourning which prevailed there a month ago
following the death of Peggy Refoule.

Close family friends and connections rallied around, and both
Mrs. Margaret Alston, mother of the mysteriously slain young
woman and Maître and Madame Robert Refoule, parents of Paul,
were said to have "gone to pieces entirely."

They received no one, retiring to their rooms while friends took
over for them downstairs, receiving telephone calls and visitors,
many of whom came to express sympathy. Members of the Atlanta French colony called intermittently during Saturday afternoon, offering their assistance as interpreters to the senior
Refoules, who were said to be experiencing great difficulty in
understanding why their son was torn from their side shortly after their arrival at Municipal Airport Friday night.

The elderly French couple, both clad in somber black, spent
the morning in company with Mrs. Alston and their grandson,

nine-year-old Jon, but retired to their room to rest during the afternoon.

Only Jon, a tanned, fair-haired youngster, said by the neighbors to be "the image of his father," appeared to be untouched by what the household regarded as the striking of a second tragedy.

The little boy, in a bathing suit, swinging home from swimming in a neighbor's pool, his trousers under his arm, and the family's ancient collie, Patty, at his side, stopped and picked up a newspaper out of the mailbox. He glanced indifferently at the headline, which quoted his father as saying, "I did not love my wife," and then turned to the comic page.

Meanwhile, the sightseers who have turned the wooded grounds around the Refoule home on Howell Mill Road into a carnival midway with their rubbernecking had apparently transferred their attention to the Alston home at 1180 Bellaire Dr. N.E. Neighbors said the traffic on the quiet street had never been so heavy, and scores of cars passed during the afternoon, slowing down while their occupants craned their necks at the square white house with its drawn curtains and closed door.

The Refoules were described as an elderly couple, moving in a quiet manner. Mrs. Refoule was dressed entirely in black, including her stockings. She wore her gray hair drawn back severely.

Saturday morning they went shopping with Mrs. Alston, accompanied by young Jon, the son of the Paul Refoules.

Mrs. Alston said the Refoules were staying at her home temporarily but that they had received numerous invitations from Mrs. Alston's friends and French groups here.

Refoule's arrest was not deliberately timed to wrest him from the arms of his aging parents so shortly after their arrival, police said. The officers insisted they had intended to take him into custody for questioning and did not anticipate in view of the French rail strike that his parents would be present when they took him.

Refoule returned to the Alston home late Saturday afternoon after he was released from bond. In the face of moral charges brought against her son-in-law and his declaration that he did not love her daughter, Mrs. Alston continued to protect him from visitors.

Her only comment was, "We don't know what to say."

In the age of CNN, it seems unfathomable that there was once a time when a single elected official could corral and control the nation's media on a major story. On August 30, 1961, Atlanta Mayor William B. Hartsfield did precisely that when Atlanta desegregated its public schools. As nine Atlanta African-American children walked into four formerly all-white schools for the first time, Hartsfield threw a party for the press gathered in the city to cover the story. "It was a stroke of genius," says former Atlanta Mayor Sam Massell of the Hartsfield maneuver. "He was very adept at being pro-active." With tongue planted firmly in cheek, Sibley filed this story from the unusual scene. The young woman Sibley quotes in the article's final paragraphs would grow up to be Charlayne Hunter-Gault, the Johannesburg bureau chief for CNN.

Press Feasts at City Hall

August 31, 1961

The phalanx of out-of-town and out-of-state reporters come to cover school desegregation, got all-out assistance from the home-folks Wednesday.

They were given in the following order: 1) the News. 2) Telephones, teletypes and typewriters on which to transmit it. 3) Side servings of Smithfield ham and hot biscuits to wash down with coffee and the ubiquitous Atlanta beverage, Coke, and other soft drinks and fruit juices. 4) An artful selling job on the charms of Atlanta, including a sightseeing trip and a party.

The center of this hospitality, which one visitor likened to a wedding feast, was the City Hall itself—the stately council chamber, converted for the nonce into clattering newsroom with 50 typewriters going at once, a police radio spouting routine signals, four direct telephones to the desegregated schools going intermittently, and radio and television men speaking richly and mellifluously into microphones.

Mayor Hartsfield, who cheerfully took credit for "brain-childing" the press center, and School Supt. John W. Letson and his deputy administrator, Dr. Rual W. Stephens, took turns presiding over the day-long party. They were in telephone communication with the principals of the four schools at the key points of the day—when the Negro transfer students arrived, after lunch and when school ended.

The telephone conversations were broadcast over a loud-speaker and before each one ended Dr. Letson invited reporters to ask any questions they wanted to ask.

"There was some suspicion about this center when it was first mentioned," chuckled its instigator, Mayor Hartsfield. "Some of the press seemed to think we were planning to give them a snow job instead of the news. Now that they see it's working they're full of compliments."

The mayor said he conceived the idea of a gigantic press center, patterned roughly on the facilities set up for covering a big political convention or campaign. Charles Rawson, the advertising executive, helped him with the details. The Coca-Cola Company set up the snack bar, the Chamber of Commerce provided members to assist the visitors, Atlanta merchants financed a cocktail party at the Biltmore Hotel, the Atlanta Transit Co. provided buses for the tour and Southern Bell and Western Union moved in the communications equipment.

"Altogether," said the Mayor, "this will cost the city about $2,000 and save these visitors a lot of confusion and inconvenience of trying to cover four widely separated schools and track down a lot of rumors."

Good Pickings

Alert reporters eager for "souf in the mouf" quotes had pretty good pickings off and on through the day.

Mayor Hartsfield was good for several. He repeatedly referred to the Biltmore cocktail party for the press as "what we in Georgia call a buttermilk party." He called would-be troublemakers "the outhouse gang" and "the two-hole toilet crowd," pegging them as "visitors" from rural areas.

In midafternoon, he took the microphone in the City Hall press headquarters to intone: "We told you we'd give you the news. Listen. Stop the press. The City Hall is being picketed."

A few reporters got up and the mayor laughingly sent them scooting for the front door by flapping his arms and crying, "Shoo!"

At police headquarters, Judge Luke Arnold began the trial of the five young would-be pickets by banning smoking in the courtroom. But, he added to the amusement of visitors, "If any of you care to chew tobacco, that will be all right."

Most reporters considered the best quote of the day came from

H.W. Kelley, principal of Northside High, who announced shortly after school opened that as opening days went, Wednesday was a "bit more normal than usual."

McGill Saluted

Constitution publisher Ralph McGill got a round of applause from the newspaper fraternity when he visited the press center briefly during the morning. Mayor Hartsfield said in other places the press "has been blamed" for "agitating" racial strife but he said if Atlanta comes through without trouble it will be "due to the magnificent cooperation of the press."

The mayor introduced McGill as a long-time fighter for "decency and law enforcement" who "knows what it is to be criticized." He said McGill "emerges today the great man of the South."

The publisher acknowledged the applause with a quick wave and smile and one sentence. "This," he said, "is what you get when you vote for Hartsfield every time he runs."

Charlayne Here

Charlayne Hunter, the young Negro girl whose admission to the University of Georgia with another Negro student, Hamilton Holmes, resulted in a short show of violence last winter, said Wednesday she was "not sorry it went that way—now that it's over."

The knowledge that desegregation could erupt into fights and strife contributed to Atlanta's long-range preparation for a peaceful changeover, Miss Hunter said.

The Negro journalism major, who plans to return to the University of Georgia this fall, is covering the Atlanta desegregation story for the Negro paper, the *Atlanta Inquirer.* She has been in closer touch than other reporters with the nine Negro transfer students, lunching with them and visiting their homes at night.

"All our talks have been in a light key," she said. "There's not much I can tell them. But when they walked up the walks to those schools this morning my heart was with them."

At the peak of a 1963 suburban Atlanta Halloween carnival on the Marietta town square, Atherton's Drugstore exploded, killing six and injuring dozens. The blast originated from a gas leak in the structure's basement. Sibley was one of five reporters on the scene. She had the difficult task of interviewing terrified parents looking for their children in the rubble and at Kennestone Hospital.

Her Son Lost, Husband Dead— Mother Keeps Tragic Vigil

November 1, 1963

Marietta—A 7 year-old boy's search for a Halloween mask to wear with his devil's suit lead a family into Atherton's Drugstore minutes before the blast that killed at least six people here Thursday night.

One of the victims was the little boy's father, Joe Ben Carter, 33, a worker at General Motors.

The child's two brothers and mother escaped with minor injuries and Terry Wayne Carter, 7, is still missing.

Mrs. Lillian Carter, 29, sat in the emergency room at Kennestone Hospital Thursday night suffering lacerations to her hands and arms and bruises about the body and anxiously searched the faces of arriving friends and relatives for some word of Terry Wayne.

"He was wearing blue jeans almost new and a dark green polo shirt . . . have you seen him?" she asked.

While relatives tearfully shook their heads, the dark-haired young mother, who had been given some sedation, maintained an appearance of superhuman control.

"I saw him walk with his daddy to the cashier place to pay for the mask," she said. "Me and the other children went on outside. They wanted masks too, but they hadn't seen anything in there that suited them and we were aiming to walk on down the street.

"My oldest (Danny, 10) went on ahead and was across the street. I had the baby (Bobby, 5), aholding him by the hand when the light changed and we stopped. There was kindly a blast and it knocked me to the cement but I was not unconscious.

"I kept aholding to the baby. The baby had a couple of scratches; and when I could get to my feet I took him across the street and left him with Danny and told them to stay right there while I went to see what happened to their Daddy and Wayne.

Was Bleeding

"I couldn't seen no one and some people come and told me I was bleeding, and an ambulance was coming and to come on and get in it."

Mrs. Carter delayed long enough to collect Bobby and Danny, who came to the hospital with her and were later dismissed and sent to the home of relatives.

Another of the victims of the blast was Mrs. Betty Carlisle, 27, cashier in the drugstore and the mother of five children.

Mrs. Carlisle who worked nights at the store, had been on duty little more than half an hour when the explosion occurred.

It happened at 6:35, according to George Kelley, one of three policemen who were severely injured as they stood on the sidewalk in front of the store. Kelley said his watch stopped at 6:35.

The three had just walked out of the store together, Kelley said from his hospital bed. "I heard a big whooshing," he said.

"When I woke up I was across the street in front of the bank and two or three guys were leaning over trying to help me. I could see smoke pouring out of the drugstore and hear a lot of people crying but I couldn't tell what had happened."

Father of 4

Kelley, 31, is father of four children. He suffered a leg injury and lacerations about the forehead. His wife, who is pregnant with the couple's fifth child, sat nearby as he spoke.

Wyndell Black, 23, another of the injured officers, said he "heard an explosion and that's the last I knew until I woke up with a great big chunk of masonry on the chest."

He said he started yelling for "somebody to come and get this rock off my chest but I couldn't make him answer me." Black is suffering from a broken pelvis and a cut on the forehead.

Only immediate relatives of the injured and the dead were admitted to the hospital, and relative quiet prevailed in the halls. But outside throngs of people seeking lost children, husbands and wives, gathered anxiously at the doors to ask Red Cross workers and hospital attendants, "Have you seen my . . . ? Is there any report on . . . ? Please give me some information."

A bright Halloween moon rode high in the sky but a chill wind sprang up and many of the people who had rushed from the supper table or from helping little children trick or treat shivered in sleeveless dress and tee shirts while they waited on the cold, concrete steps.

There were many stories of young people who had planned to be in the drug store but who, for one reason or another, were delayed in getting there. One young man in a football sweater asked anxiously about a girl named Evelyn who was not listed among the injured or the dead.

And under a tree at the edge of the hospital driveway, a teenage girl sobbed uncontrollably in the arms of an older woman.

Joe Barnett, public relations representative for Kennestone Hospital and a resident of Marietta since 1925, said the explosion was "the worst disaster in my recollection."

Farmers Stream In

Overall-clad farmers who heard the report on radios and television sets came in from the outlying communities to see if they had relatives or friends who were hurt and remained to offer their services as blood donors or stretcher bearers in the hospital.

The shock of the disaster and their personal uncertainty and anxiety kept most of the people waiting almost unnaturally quiet. There was little conversation and only occasionally the sound of someone crying.

When an ambulance would arrive with it whirling light casting a red shadow on their faces, the waiting people caught their breath and many of them clutched one another for support.

At the back door, those released from the hospital found eager relatives to receive them.

As Atlantans made their way from church on Sunday, June 3, 1962, radio reports informed them that 106 of their friends and neighbors had died in an Air France plane crash that morning outside of Paris. The group of high-profile cultural and civic leaders had been visiting France as part of a European tour sponsored by the Atlanta Art Association. Sibley arrived at the downtown Air France office (located near the Journal *and* Constitution *building) just as fearful relatives of the victims began pouring in to scan a confirmed passenger list.*

A Time for Tears: "'I'm Sorry . . .
I'm So Sorry'—That's All She Could Say"

June 4, 1962

The uncertainty, anxiety and grief of thousands of Georgians crashed like a mighty wave across the Forsyth Street offices of Air France in Atlanta Sunday.

Here the phone calls came. The pitiful, determined, hopeful ones beginning, "Are you sure my parents (or son or daughter or friend) were on board?" The very careful ones with names spelled and initials precisely enunciated . . . and the hysterical ones.

Here relatives and friends assembled, tears streaming down their faces, restlessly to and fro waiting to have bad news confirmed.

Staff Called In

Air France's staff of young people hurried from their homes to open the office shortly after 9 A.M. Their regional manager, blond Henri Lardon, who came from France six months ago to take the post, was awakened at his home on Jett Road at 8:45 A.M. by a phone call from Paris.

"They told me," he said shaking his head slowly, "the plane crashed on takeoff. The shock . . . I cannot tell you what a shock it is. Our loss is personal, too. Our friend Paul Doassans, district manager of this office, was aboard. He went to Paris beyond his duty to be with the Atlanta group and to help make the trip a success."

Married Five Months Ago

Lardon spoke from Doassans' office and as he spoke his eyes moved over a group of photographs ornamenting the walls, some of them autographed to Doassans. These included one of President Charles DeGaulle and some of Air France's officials and pilots. Doassans was married only five months ago to a young woman from Omaha and all his colleagues here flew to Nebraska for the wedding. His young widow, Marguita, was notified of his death while visiting her parents in Omaha.

All day long the weary, quietly courteous Air France staff stood at their posts, buffeted by phone calls and visitors and wave after wave of newspaper, radio and television reporters and photographers.

In the center of the storm, soft-voiced Colette Lautzenhiser, chief reservation clerk sat like a small rock, saying over and over into the phone: "I am very sorry, sir, to have to tell you, she WAS on board. . . . Madame, I am so sorry. Yes, they were on the plane."

She spoke softly and slowly in English, faster in French when speaking with one of her co-workers, and occasionally she would grip the telephone receiver so hard the knuckles on her hand would whiten and she would close her eyes with pain.

Her husband, Bill, an American Air Force man, stood by, ready to run errands and to help answer the phone. He was home on weekend leave from Shaw Air Force Base in South Carolina. Their three children, ranging in age from 22 months to four-and-a-half years, are visiting their grandparents in France.

Even while she placed and received phone calls, Mrs. Lautzenhiser was surrounded by people who came in person to check the passenger lists. Some came from tennis courts, wearing shorts and sneakers, some came from the golf course and some came from church.

Robert Gerson, young advertising man, had already learned his parents, Mr. and Mrs. Saul Gerson, were dead. A friend in France, who took them to the airport and witnessed the take-off, had telephoned him.

"I had to come—just in case there was any other news about it I could learn," he said dazedly, wiping his eyes with the back of his hand. "This was their first trip, and they had looked forward to it all their lives. They were happy as kids. Mother was 60, Dad 63. Every time we heard from them they wrote how happy they were."

P.H. Perkins, an architect whose wife was on the flight, told in the simple eloquence of deep bereavement how she had celebrated her birthday in Europe.

"I'm glad it happened at the end of the tour so she got to see the things she had always wanted to see," Perkins said softly.

While most of the passengers were seasoned travelers who had been abroad many times, a number of them were people who waited until their children were reared and their responsibilities eased up to make the trip.

"I can't believe it!" a young girl cried as she checked a list. "That woman—a friend of my mother's saved all her life for this trip."

The voice of Colette Lautzenhiser, speaking into the phone, reiterated the tragedy. "I am sorry, sir. They were on the list."

The concern of neighbors in time of trouble was shown the Air France people by their commercial neighbors downtown. Davis Brothers restaurant across the street, sent over pots of coffee and a tray of cups. A representative from Western Union dropped by to offer the use of desks and telephones for the airline workers or the overflow crowd of reporters.

Arthur Harris, French consul in Atlanta, issued a statement in behalf of the French ambassador to this country, Herve Alphand. Ambassador Alphand telephoned him from Washington as soon as he learned of the tragedy, Harris said, to express "my deepest sympathy and regret to the people of Atlanta."

Church Bell Tolls Out 46 Times—It's a Time of Prayer for All of Us

November 23, 1963

The deep-voiced bell of Atlanta's oldest Roman Catholic church, the Shrine of Immaculate Conception, tolled for eight minutes Friday afternoon, spelling out in a centuries-old manner the message downtown workers, passing pedestrians and the busy stream of expressway traffic already had.

President Kennedy was dead.

For 46 times the old bell rang—once for each year of John Kennedy's life. And to the faithful, where they heard it, it said, "Pray for him and pray for yourself, for this time comes to all."

Father Linus Tigue, the Franciscan priest who serves as assistant pastor of the church, set the bell to ringing by pushing an electrical switch and then hurried to the sanctuary to pray.

Throughout the church, bars of sunshine coming through the stained-glass window threw patches of bright light on kneeling people. There was a Negro woman in the uniform of a nurse, a wrinkled blue scarf over her head. Two women office workers with handkerchiefs hastily pinned to their heads, knelt near the back of the church. Plaid-skirted school girls from the convent next door came in, solemn-faced and perspiring in the unseasonal heat, a policeman and an old man with a walking stick knelt together.

The church was silent except for the occasional sound of a woman weeping and the sibilant rush of prayers spoken.

"Eternal rest grant unto him, O Lord, and let perpetual light shine unto him. May he rest in peace."

Father Tigue had been in the sanctuary moments earlier while the president was still alive to pray that he be spared, if possible, and that his "agony be aided." He went as soon as a friend called him with the news of the shooting and then he returned to his study in the rectory to turn on the television set.

"The people had already started coming in," he said. "I don't know how so many of them got the news so fast. But they were there when I first went in and I could hear them crying."

When the news that the president was dead had been confirmed the priest said what priests all over the world were even then, or later would be saying, the ancient prayer for the dead, beginning: "O God to whom it belongeth always to show mercy and to spare, we humbly beseech Thee for the soul of Thy servant, John, whom Thou has called out of this world, that Thou deliver him not into the hand of the enemy, nor forget him forever."

The Negro nurse walked down the steps into the sunshine, her face wet with tears.

"How could they do it to him," she asked. "How could they?"

On February 4, 1974, a group identifying itself as the Symbionese Liberation Army kidnapped Patricia Hearst, the daughter of newspaper magnate Randolph A. Hearst and his wife Catherine, an Atlanta native. Working her sources, Sibley acquired the Hearst family's home phone number and filed the following exclusive front-page story.

Mother: "I Feel So Numb Inside . . . I Can Hardly Think"

February 14, 1974

Atlanta Constitution reporter Celestine Sibley spoke Wednesday by long distance telephone with Mrs. Randolph Hearst, mother of kidnap victim Patricia Hearst and a former Atlanta resident.

Mrs. Randolph Hearst answered the telephone herself.

The voice was strong and unwavering—and you could only guess at the hope and fear and days and nights of remitting anxiety in that single, "Hello?"

It could have been the kidnappers of her daughter. Or it could have been 19-year-old Patricia herself calling home to say she was free and safe.

Instead it was a call from Atlanta, where Mrs. Hearst, the former Catherine Campbell, grew up in the 1930s. And she treated it like a call from home.

"Atlanta?" she said. "Oh, how nice! I've just heard from the kindest woman there."

The "kindest woman" is a legal secretary and law clerk named Betty Lassiter, who looked in her pantry Wednesday morning and thought of all the women over the country who could pull out enough stored-up groceries to meet the demands of Patricia's kidnappers for food for the poor.

"If you can get that food thing organized before the 19th then that's okay and it will speed up my release," Patricia said on a taped message sent to her parents.

Mrs. Lassiter, who remembered when Catherine Campbell was a pretty girl living nearby on Rumson Road, put in a call to the Hearsts' San Francisco home and suggested a food contribution campaign to start here in Atlanta, where Patricia's parents met and were married.

"She didn't tell me to go ahead with it," Mrs. Lassiter told the *Constitution,* "but she was very warm and gracious and thanked me over and over. Do you think it would work?"

The *Constitution* put the question to Mrs. Hearst herself.

"I don't know," she said. "It's hard to know what to do. It might not be a workable plan (collecting food over the country) because it wouldn't get here for such a long time. And then so many of the people it's intended for don't want it. We've had calls from people who said, 'I wouldn't eat blood money, I'd starve first.'"

Her husband, Mrs. Hearst said, is "trying to figure it all out"—how to meet the kidnappers' demand that he open two chains of stores to the poor people of the area three days a week for five weeks and let them get $70 of groceries each.

"We are afraid it will create anarchy in the stores," Mrs. Hearst said. "A man in the grocery business told my husband it will cost $300 million for five weeks and $150 million for a couple of weeks. We're just having to try and think and assess it."

And then her voice broke a little.

"I feel so numb inside," she said. "I can hardly think of anything really."

Does she sit by the telephone constantly and answer all the calls herself?

"Almost," Mrs. Hearst said. "There are other telephones in the house, but there's nothing else I want to do until we . . . hear, you know. They said we wouldn't be hearing again soon, but I hope and keep praying. We try to sleep a little and eat a little. One tries to keep up."

As if she couldn't bear any more of that conversation, Mrs. Hearst quickly returned to Betty Lassiter's call and her offer.

"Please express my thanks to her and to all the other people back home who have written to us. People have been so . . . so wonderful. The press, too. The press has been so marvelous, so grand. Everybody wants to help us, but there's nothing, nothing. . . ."

And then once more Catherine Hearst, remembered in Atlanta as "such a pretty, such a nice girl," took a sort of social grasp of the situation.

"We hope to be in Atlanta this summer. We had Patty there

last summer and Ginna, who's 24, is going to be in Sara Keenan's wedding. . . . Thank you for calling. I wouldn't want to tie up the line in case. . . . Please tell everybody to keep praying."

In the fall of 1980, Atlanta TV newscasters began their late reports, intoning: "It's 11 p.m., do you know where your children are?" The city was in the middle of its baffling "missing and murdered children" case where, at its peak, the bodies of African-American children and young men were being found almost weekly. Atlanta's inner-city population—ground zero for the story—lived in a panic while keeping close watch on their children.

On the morning of October 13, 1980, a boiler exploded at the Gate City Day Nursery in the city's Bowen Homes housing project. Four children and a teacher were killed and others were injured. When Sibley arrived on the scene with three other Constitution reporters, the parents rushing to their children couldn't be certain of the explosion's origins. Some were convinced their children had been victims of a hate crime. Two years after giving up a daily reporting deadline to concentrate on column writing, Sibley, at age 66, provided the less experienced members of the AJC staff the following lesson on how to write a breaking news story.

Twenty years later, Sibley's former AJC colleague and current Atlanta magazine editor Lee Walburn still marvels at the piece. "Listen to this," Walburn says reading a paragraph aloud. "In the middle of chaos, she was still able to capture the cadence of a Baptist preacher."

Fear Grips City's Parents as News of Blast Spreads

October 14, 1980

The MARTA bus lumbered along in the autumn sunshine, making all the stops along Bankhead Highway Monday morning, but when it reached Yates Drive the doors burst open and a dozen people hit the street running.

Fear ran with them.

They were parents or grandparents, uncles or aunts, of children who attend Gate City Day Nursery—children who might have been among the five people killed in the mid-morning explosion.

"Poor things," said Mrs. Mary Williams, president of the Bowen Homes Tenants' Association. "They didn't know. We weren't able to call everybody. I wonder why they caught the bus?"

Black women who are maids and office workers and clerks in stores, men who are laborers and truck drivers, were reflecting a panic that was general among parents all over the city of Atlanta. Day nurseries of all kinds, church "Mothers' Morning Out" groups, kindergartens got the phone call and many parents showed up to get their children early.

"They weren't afraid of an explosion," a northside teacher said. "They were just afraid. Something like this brings out the fear in everybody who has a little one who might have been a victim."

Mrs. Barbara Knox, a mother who got off the bus, holding tight to the hand of her school-age daughter, rushed to the scene because of her four-year-old niece, Cean Knox. She learned immediately from her mother-in-law, who lives in Bowen Homes, that Cean had been kept home Monday.

"You know how it is sometimes," she explained. "There be days when you just keep a child home. We lucky."

The noise of weeping lifted in the bright cool air, pouring out the open doorway of an apartment nearby. Mrs. Knox slowed her footsteps, her face suffused with sympathy.

"Trouble there," she said softly. "They got loss in that house."

The loss of four little children, fresh from coloring pictures and playing with the brightly painted toys in the schoolroom which still stood, was taken quietly by the parents who gathered at Grady hospital morgue. They went in silently, fearfully, and they came out to stand in the sunlight and lean together, weeping noiselessly. One woman put her head down on the iron banister outside the doorway and wept soundlessly for long moments before relatives led her away. Another stood on the curb, staring blindly at the street and the little group of waiting people. Tears coursed down her cheeks.

"Nothing . . . I can't say nothing," she whispered.

Members of the housing project community were more vocal. Convinced that the explosion had been a bombing, despite efforts of their leaders to tell them it was accidental, they shouted, chanted and demanded.

"We think it was a defective furnace," said Mrs. Mary Williams, president of the Bowen Homes Tenants' Association quietly. She attempted to get order and announce a meeting of the association "to get all the facts" Monday night.

"Who's going to protect us while we're attending that meeting?" a young woman demanded.

"There will be police protection," Mrs. Williams said patiently.

"Don't put me behind no closed doors!" shouted a man.

Gray-haired E.F. Swain, 58, a Baptist radio evangelist led the shouting.

"We going down to the place where the mayor is, where the mayor goes!" he cried. "Down where the jailhouse is, that's where we need to go!"

The explosion, he said, was "somebody undermining the work we're doing—a group of race-haters."

Eventually the group grew quiet and dissipated, and back in the building through an open gash where a wall had stood a few hours before, a fireman loaded a child's little red wagon with rubble and slowly hauled it away.

They were searching, another fireman explained, for any small bodies that might not have been found.

Chapter Four

The Hollywood Years

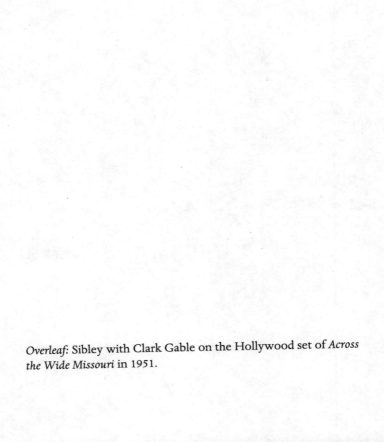

Overleaf: Sibley with Clark Gable on the Hollywood set of *Across the Wide Missouri* in 1951.

In the early 1950s, the growing popularity of television caused perspiring Hollywood studio executives to pump more and more money into print advertising in an effort to compete with the new entertainment medium. To further drum up publicity, the studios began granting access to the newspapers with which they were advertising.

Sibley would later dismiss her contributions to celebrity journalism as "puff pieces." Strictly speaking, the Hollywood stories Sibley filed from 1951 to 1955 for the Sunday Atlanta Journal and Constitution Magazine were just that—mostly positive profiles of Tinseltown's top stars pushing their latest pictures. Regardless, the inimitable Sibley style shone through each dispatch.

George Biggers, the publisher of the freshly merged Atlanta Constitution and Atlanta Journal, promised to pay her $100 a piece for each story. The single mother of three jumped at the assignment.

The times have changed so much," reflects former colleague and Atlanta Journal-Constitution film critic Eleanor Ringel Gillespie. "Today, the whole idea of coming out to Hollywood and having a studio publicist take you around is gone. The studios are spending their money elsewhere.

"Celestine's Hollywood stories are fascinating because there was this unwritten agreement where both star and reporter knew it was 'curtain up' time during the interview. But she's also savvy and she always gets what she needs. She didn't just read the press notes she was given. She did her homework."

If Gable Kisses Gardner It May Be the Year's Best Love Scene

August 5, 1951

A reporter is bound to get a hot story in a Hollywood studio overheated by Klieg lights and Gable-Gardner love scenes. This is a first in a series of exclusive reports from the movie capital by Atlanta Constitution *columnist Celestine Sibley who went to the West Coast for* The Atlanta Journal and Constitution Magazine. *Don't miss her intriguing, behind-the-scenes articles on the pictures you'll be seeing this fall.*

Clark Gable took Ava Gardner in his arms. Their lips were only inches apart. He looked at her ardently.

"Well, Dev," she said huskily, "you've won, haven't you?"

"Have I?" asked Gable softly.

She nodded tenderly. "You're a strange man . . . but quite a lot of man!"

She raised her lips. His arms closed on her.

"Hold it!" shouted a raucous voice. "She's watering!"

Miss Gardner mopped her eyes and moaned faintly. "These lights," she said, "are blinding me." A make-up woman rushed forward and did things to the actress' eyes with brushes and lotions and the director yelled wearily, "Try it again."

Gable put down his coffee cup and they moved together again with the same words, the same yearning expressions but just short of the kiss a voice yelled, "Hold it!"

They stood as they were, waiting, a mere kiss apart. Gable was saying something to her that the script didn't call for and I pushed my head around a big arc light and strained forward to hear.

"Your doughnuts," said Gable to Gardner, "are getting cold."

And that, disillusioning or not, is the way what may turn out to be one of the year's better love scenes was played in a dusty road on a hot summer's day in Hollywood.

The time: according to the script, was 1845. The place: a frontier village called Austin, Texas. The people: Gable, a rugged Texas adventurer and cattle owner who fought for annexation, and Miss Gardner, probably the most sumptuous-looking, red velvet-bodiced country newspaper woman the land has ever seen.

They were making the final scene in *Lone Star,* Metro-Goldwyn-Mayer's epic about the hullabaloo attending the addition of the Lone Star State to the Union. And, watching from Director Vincent Sherman's chair, I was worried. Not about Texas (I knew how that would turn out), but about that kiss.

Every time they went into a clinch, every time the big cameras moved up, every time Miss Gardner said, ". . . but quite a lot of man!" Clark Gable closed in for the kiss, just barely grazing the lady's lips somewhere off center. It was not, I felt, like Gable to miss. So I asked him, "Aren't you ever going to kiss her?"

"No! Ain't it murder?" shouted the big actor explosively. "They've stopped all that. You can't make money because of taxes. And you can't make the girls, even in Texas. You don't know what I go through!"

He was laughing and I laughed too, but actually, what Clark Gable is going through in the making of *Lone Star* is nobody's secret. He wants a good picture, his first really top-flight one since before the war. He wants to turn out a performance befitting his acknowledged position as the all-time "king" of Hollywood leading men—and he wants the public to be pleased. He doesn't expect to repeat Rhett Butler or *Gone With the Wind.*

"I know that's the best picture I ever made," he said soberly. "Margaret Mitchell made that possible with a superb story. We'll never have another one like *Gone With the Wind*. There's nothing the matter with the picture business that a story like that, a good story, couldn't cure."

He squatted down on the ground and stirred idly at the dust with a stick after the manner of any country man hunkered down before a crossroads store on Saturday afternoon.

"You know," he said, looking up and squinting against the sun, "Margaret Mitchell was quite a person. That was a terrible thing, that accident. I tried to express my sympathy to her husband John Marsh, but none of us could ever really say how we felt. Hit people all over the world pretty hard. A woman was here from France last week to give me an award for Rhett. They're just getting to see *Gone With the Wind* there since the war."

He was silent for a moment and director Vincent Sherman, native of Vienna, Ga., and former *Atlanta Journal* police reporter, passed and leaned over.

"Did you hear we're changing the name of this picture?" he whispered confidentially. "Going to call it *Thunder Over Georgia*."

"May it bring us luck," said Gable grinning. He chuckled to himself and chewed on a straw. "I'll never forget how I met Margaret Mitchell," he went on after a time. "We were all at the Piedmont Driving Club and I was anxious to talk to her. She had helped me so much with Rhett. But there were so many people about and so much going on. We finally went into the ladies lounge and locked the door!"

Lone Star even without the lucky Georgia locale, has something of a Rhett Butleresque quality in its hero. The dashing adventurer who says he favors annexation because he expects to get a fat contract to sell beef to the soldiers who will have to fight Mexico. "Will the public like it?" is Gable's test question.

The public, enamored of Western pictures as it repeatedly demonstrates at the box office, will find at the very least that the

picture is a super-deluxe horse opera with Lionel Barrymore playing ex-President Andrew Jackson, with politics, patriotism, and
more especially, a young person who is rapidly making herself
known in press agent parlance as "the hottest thing in Hollywood," Ava Gardner.

As Clark Gable talked to me, Miss Gardner sought refuge from
the sun and the brassy glare of the big reflectors under a shed
nearby. She looked unbelievably beautiful—fresh and warm and
natural with little make-up except vivid lipstick on her full lips—
and she was very hungry. She finished eating two big sugary
doughnuts and ordered another cup of coffee.

Earlier, Gable had said she was "getting to be a fine actress"
and was working hard. He had recalled working with her in *The
Hucksters* when she had a "don't care" attitude.

"Ha!" hooted Gardner, brushing flakes of doughnut sugar off
her full 1840s skirt. "I was so impressed by Mr. Gable I was silly!
I kept wanting to get his autograph. Forgot I was an actress and
every time he would walk on the set, I'd say, 'There's Clark Gable!'
and start acting like a bobby-soxer. Darned near wrecked me and
you can imagine what it did to my love scenes."

The girl who was "raised up in Smithfield, N.C." and attracted
her first attention by a brace of unsuccessful marriages—first to
Mickey Rooney and then to bandleader Artie Shaw—is working
very hard these days to forget what she says is her real calling: "A
home and kids."

She liked playing Helen Morgan's role in *Showboat*. Miss
Gardner was excited by the challenge it presented and pleased at
being allowed to sing even after the studio had hired somebody
to dub in the vocals. She thinks the MGM picture, *Pandora and
the Flying Dutchman,* is one of the best yet and she has high hopes
for her role as the beautiful and militant Martha in *Lone Star.*

"But I have no illusions about becoming a great American actress," she said, grimacing. "All I really want is a husband and a house and a lot of children."

At that moment director Sherman spoke and his alter ego, the assistant director, took up the cry and magnified it. "Let's go kids! Action!"

Gable and Gardner, tagged by a couple of people with combs and powder puffs, resumed their ardent, esoteric stance beneath the bright lights, the cameras and the eyes of half a hundred crewmen and extras.

"You're a strange man," murmured Gardner, "but quite a lot of man!"

Gable closed in for the kiss but until I see the movie I'm convinced it's the kiss that never really came off.

What's Wrong with Marriage? 'WOMEN!' Says Jane Russell

August 19, 1951

The sign on the door to her portable dressing room was printed in letters of a size usually reserved by super markets to advertise bargain bacon or hog jowl. It said: "JANE RUSSELL, the Original Hard John."

I asked Miss Russell what it meant and she lifted a dark eyebrow and shrugged a smooth shoulder.

"That Mitch," she said. "Robert Mitchum. He says I remind him of the meanest woman he ever knew and he's always calling me 'the Original Hard John, a ha-ard man to shave!"

"Doesn't make sense to me," I offered after a moment, fighting my way up from Miss Russell's ivory divan and a nest of sofa cushions trimmed with ivory lace flounces.

"Um-m," agreed the actress, lifting a blue-jeaned knee to her chin and showing her perfect teeth in an indulgent smile. "Not a bit of sense."

The same thing, most of Hollywood seems to agree, might be said of all the facts about Jane Russell herself. Add them all up and, like "Mitch's" nickname for her, they don't make a bit of sense.

Jane Russell is known variously as the celluloid's sultriest siren, the kind of girl whose appearance in a picture is practically excuse enough to get it banned, and as one of the community's sincerest practicing Christians. She is that paradox—a deeply religious woman who loves her husband, eschews hard liquor and . . . looks like a gorgeous sinner.

She is also holder of the odd title: "Hollywood's Most Unreleased Girl of 1951." Cinematically speaking, that is. At the time I talked to her she had been working very hard, had a starring role in five brand-new pictures, and all of them were on the shelf awaiting the propitious time for release. The five, which are now beginning to reach theaters, include *The Las Vegas Story; Montana Belle; It's Only Money,* with Groucho Marx and Frank Sinatra; *Macao; Hong Kong* and *His Kind of Woman* with Mitchum.

She was on her way over from her permanent dressing room— a suite done up in the modern manner with lots of mirrors, pale satin upholstery and touches of Chinese red in dragon lamp bases and wall hangings—to her portable dressing room on *The Las Vegas Story* set and I went with her. It was the last day of shooting on the picture and the star was both busy and happy. She would have to give a party for the crew. This detail she took care of by calling in Mitchum's secretary and ordering two cases of whiskey for the men and blouses and jewelry for the make-up women and her stand-in. She had a lot of thank-yous to make for the presents that her coworkers had brought her the day before on her 30th birthday and she was looking forward to a holiday.

"Oh, am I though!" she said exultantly. "I'll have time to really get acquainted with my new baby!"

The new baby, an adopted daughter named Tracy, was still at the hospital, but the knowledge that it was to be hers had added considerable luster to Miss Russell's day.

She talked about the baby and her husband of eight years, Bob Waterfield, the professional football player, as she changed clothes.

"We've wanted a baby for so long," she said. "I'm one of five children and I don't think any marriage is complete without children. I always wanted a houseful and Tracy is going to be the start."

She ran Harry Scott, the RKO publicist, formerly of Savannah, out of the little trailer, closed the door and started zipping out of her jeans and jacket. Confronted with the Russell figure, unconcealed and oft-banned, I could think of but one question: "How do you know you'll be a good mother?"

"I don't know, of course," she said, taking a black dress from the hand of the wardrobe woman. "I hope I'll be. I'll work at it. Robert and I know but one way to bring up a child—and that's to be as good a Christian as possible. My mother brought my brothers and me up to worship God and to live as nearly as possible by the Bible. I'll teach Tracy the same. I can't imagine making an important decision of any kind without praying over it, and I'll have that to guide me."

The dress with a boned, built-in bra hugged her figure so tight it was, I reflected, fortunate she wore very little under it. Another ounce and it would have split at the seams when she sat down to fix her face.

It didn't split and she embarked thoughtfully on one of her favorite subjects, What's Wrong with American Marriage?

"What?" I asked.

"Women," said Miss Russell briefly.

"Women," she went on smoothing her lipstick, "have become such smart alecs they've run men out of marriage. Read your Bible. God intended man to be the head of the house, second only to God. And the wife is second to her husband. But women won't have it that way. They've pushed the guy into the back seat. Man is the least thing in the home!"

Miss Russell's eyes sparkled and snapped as she took a deep breath. "I think guys are dying to be kind, sweet and chivalrous, but women have made them such docile, down-trodden creatures all they can do on their own initiative is fight back once in a while."

Jane has known her husband since high school days and she followed him around during the war, spending eight months in Georgia when he was stationed at Benning. She defers to him all decisions and, she added, grinning, "then he usually gives me my way."

"To be a woman," she went on gravely, after a moment, "is very important. A woman should be the consoler, the mother type, tempering the way, smoothing the male ego. My own mother still lives in the San Fernando Valley where we grew up. My father is dead but my brothers run a farm out there. We have a little chapel of our own where we go for prayer and services, and somebody made a little sign—a picture of a little hen surrounded by chickens. Under the picture they wrote: 'Mother Russell and Her Chicks.'

"Everybody who ever came to our house was crazy about my

mother. In high school I went with a kind of a wild crowd and every one of them that ever got into any kind of trouble always came to my mother for help first. She is a wonderful person. In my father's lifetime she was a past master at giving in—and she also had the world's happiest husband."

The director yelled and Miss Russell darted out of the dressing room. I followed and saw her get into a car. Half a roof had been cut away to give the camera room to photograph her and Brad Dexter, who played the villain. A desert roadway and passing scenery flashed on a screen behind the car, giving the illusion of fast traveling. A fan blew Miss Russell's hair and two morose-looking laborers with two-by-fours in their hands jiggled the car from side to side to make it look like it was moving.

As I slipped out a side door I noticed that Miss Russell's dress, a sleek, low-cut, form-fitting black, had its bodice outlined in little white daisies.

Shelly Winters Is Hollywood's Corn-Fed Bombshell

September 9, 1951

"You'll want to see Shelly Winters," they stated, rather than asked, in Hollywood.

"We'll try to get Winters for you," they said at not one but two studios, both Universal and Paramount.

"That's nice of you," I said politely, wondering vaguely who this Shelly Winters could be and why it was imperative that I see her. There are so many actresses in Hollywood and after five or six days all of the young ones seem of a sameness. You get the jaded impression that there hasn't been a new face since Garbo, and the present crop, with few exceptions, is uniformly beautiful, bright, businesslike . . . and indistinguishable.

Then I met Shelly Winters and ran head-on into the exception!

People tried to warn me. Looking back, it seems that everybody had something to say about her and to be perfectly truthful, not all of it was complimentary. "Screwball," said her friends firmly. "Fiend," said at least one of her enemies. "Hard to get along with as Bette Davis and not that good . . . yet," said a weary young man at a studio where she once worked. "Almost beautiful and always bombastic," said a co-worker.

And eventually, whether they were friend or foe, they invariably added: "Watch her. She's headed up. She'll probably win the Academy Award next time for that part in *A Place in the Sun*."

A Place in the Sun, which is scheduled to open in Atlanta at the Fox Theater on September 19, is Paramount's remake of Theodore Dreiser's *An American Tragedy* and one of the reasons I finally got around to seeing Miss Winters. She plays the role of Alice Tripp, one of the dreariest, most tragic females of contemporary literature—a drab factory worker about to become what the social workers call "an unwed mother." She is neither lovely nor loved, much, a character completely foreign to the picture of a blonde, bosomy siren which was the picture I was beginning to get of Miss Winters.

So I went to see her and as I approached Paramount's still photography studio a solemn, unidentified citizen gave me my last warning about her. He stood outside, lounging easily against the door.

"Going to interview Shelly?" he asked.

I nodded.

Slowly he held up his hand and deliberately he crossed his fingers. "Good luck!" he whispered.

"Will I need it?" I asked nervously, my hand on the door knob.

He smiled a tight, close-lipped smile, turned his head and said no more.

Now unnerved completely, I tripped over the doorsill and fell into the room.

"Welcome!" said a light, childish voice.

Across the room under the muzzle of a great still camera and a half a dozen bright lights sat a plumpish, curly headed blonde in a droopy-necked peasant blouse, a cheap black skirt and common-sense shoes. She was, strictly speaking, neither particularly young nor dazzlingly beautiful. Her biography gave her age as 28 and a mirror in front of her gave back the reflection of a healthy, slightly corn-fed looking young woman whose front exposure happened to be well adapted to droopy-necked peasant blouses.

"Jeez, kid, I'm sorry about the interview," she said when we were introduced by an emissary from the publicity department. "They forgot to tell me and I've got a date in ten minutes to pose for some high-style pictures for *Harper's Bazaar.* How about lunch tomorrow?"

I mentioned haltingly that I had a date for lunch the next day and she said, "Well, come on into the dressing room and talk to me while I change. And if you don't mind hanging around we'll talk between these pictures Whitey Scafer is taking for poster art."

That was the bombastic Miss Winters.

She talked, easily, lightly—still in that childishly high voice—while walloping her head of tight yellow curls with a hairbrush. She fixed her face and went out for more pictures and came back and talked more. Once she abruptly hoisted the dark skirt, grabbed a safety pin and firmly anchored the shirttail of her blouse to her girdle.

"What's that for?" I asked, flabbergasted.

"Pulls the blouse down tight in front," she said, grinning. "Look." She took a deep breath, smoothed her blouse and gave us a profile view of her chest. "Get that front line? This is poster art and I've got to look like a poster girl. It's hard enough with all the weight I had to gain for *A Place in the Sun*. George Stevens, the director, is a demon for realism. He wouldn't let me wear any decent clothes or a bit of make-up and then he made me gain weight so I'd look pregnant. Now they need glamour to advertise the picture and have I any glamour left? I ask you."

She grinned briefly and was gone again.

While she was gone the publicist told me of the fight Shelly had waged for the part in *A Place in the Sun*. She besieged director Stevens until he consented to test her for the role of Alice and then she was a miserable flop. But she kept on until he consented to give her a second chance and then she made good. It was a repeat of her first good screen role, that of a waitress in *A Double Life*. She fought for that chance and eventually made good.

The tough Miss Winters, born Shelly Schrift in St. Louis, August 18, 1923, made her first appearance on a stage in an amateur contest screeching the then-popular "Moonlight and Roses."

"The more they tried to get me off, the louder I sang," she confessed. "Finally in desperation the master of ceremonies gave me a size 14 knitted sweater that hung down to my feet."

The result may well have been Miss Winters' durable philosophy that if she worked hard enough—"and loud enough"—she'd get whatever she wanted. She has been married and divorced once and lives with her parents in a Hollywood apartment.

She wanted a straight dramatic role, the kind offered by the

Alice Tripp assignment, because she was tired of musical roles and sexy siren parts.

"I don't mind being ugly," she said candidly. "If I feel like the part is worth it. I think, I hope Alice is worth it."

As Alice she is the epitome of that homely Southern expression, "ugly as a mud fence," in at least half her scenes and uncannily appealing in spite of it.

The publicists and I left her still posing for poster art but I ran into her later at Universal, her home studio, where she was working in a picture with Frank Sinatra called *Meet Danny Wilson*. It is a return to the glamorous night club singer role and she looked glamorous that day in a smart dress and high-heeled shoes with nail polish and a new hairdo.

The same evidence of hard work was there. The day was hot but she manfully shouldered the heavy fur coat required for the role and went through the same scrap of a scene time after time. It was a tense little scene with a combination of emotions. First, she had to tell Alex Nicol, pal of Danny, played by Sinatra, that she loved him and learned that he loved her but could do nothing about it because "you are Danny's girl." Then she had to turn from him and storm from the room.

Each time she turned and walked out, I noticed that tears streamed down her face and no make-up woman had been near her. They went through the scene a total of eight or ten times and each time it was the same. Tears, real tears, coursed down her cheeks as she turned from Nicol and walked away.

Finally I asked about it. "Is she really crying? Those are not make-up department tears?"

"Shelly?" said a member of the crew. "They're her own tears, all right. Shelly's got as many faces as Lon Chaney . . . and she does it with emotions, not make-up!"

Watching Groucho and Irma
Make the Year's Funniest Movie

October 28, 1951

The luscious blonde in the low-cut dress looked at the man in the sailor suit as many other blondes have looked at men in sailor suits.

She smiled one of those slow, calculating smiles. I followed her glance and collapsed in a paroxysm of soundless mirth, the only kind permitted on a sound stage when the red "Quiet" light is winking.

The target for that smile was probably the most over-ripe sailor ever to don the Navy blue. Hash marks encased his left arm like a splint from cuff to collarbone. He wore horn-rimmed glasses and a mustache while a cigar stuck out in the middle of his face like Tybee Light rising from the sands of Savannah Beach. When he moved it was with none of the Navy's dashing "Anchors Aweigh" swagger. He loped as but one man in the world lopes. He was that man: Groucho Marx.

"Isn't he marvelous?" said the blonde in a vague, dreamy voice that any school child with a $9.98 radio would identify immediately as belonging to the dumbest girl in America—Irma of *My Friend Irma.* Or as she is officially named, Marie Wilson.

Marie Wilson and Groucho Marx were putting the finishing touches to what has every right to be one of the season's funniest comedies; a little gem which RKO Radio studios for a time considered calling *They Sell Sailors Elephants,* but which will hit local marquees under the name *A Girl in Every Port.* William Bendix is in the picture with them and for relief from comedy a handsome leading man named Don DeFore and a pair of racehorses.

Making a comedy is a slow, plodding, painful business and a line that is funny the first time you hear it has been wrung dry by the time you've heard it eight or 10 times. Production crews don't expect to be amused but on the Groucho Marx-Marie Wilson set they laugh all the time. I know why, too, because I saw the same little scrap of a scene rehearsed over and over and over again, and each time Groucho leaned over to stuff his middy blouse full of his host's cigars, I laughed harder than ever. And every time Marie Wilson widened her bright brown eyes and opened her mouth to emit a high, sweet, dumb sound everybody on the set grinned.

Groucho Marx can't stop being funny. As his radio and television fans know, his funniest lines are not in the script. He is a formidable ad lib artist. "Let's go, Captain Bligh!" he calls to the gentle, soft-spoken director. "Where's Bendix? Doesn't he work here anymore?" he demands when his partner is slow to lumber out of his plaid dressing room. "You better let Bendix go and get Lou Holtz for this part," he assures the director gravely. But even when he is kidding his co-workers and clowning, Marx somehow absorbs his lines to absolute, letter-perfect perfection and he has never been known to muff a scene.

"It's a break, working with him," said Marie Wilson over bitter coffee in her portable dressing room. (We had gotten the coffee in thick cups from an elderly man who operates a concession at the rear of the big RKO sound stage, sloshed a little canned cream in it and departed with Miss Wilson saying to him in a very Irma-ish voice: "Can I owe you for it, honey? Seeing as how we're going to get married . . . ?")

But on the subject of Groucho Marx she was not Irma-ish. "He's about as funny as anybody in the world—easily the funniest man in America, I guess. I keep hoping some of it will rub off on me. He has the most facile mind and something that is rare in show business . . . real humility."

Marie Wilson has humility too. She got her first real break in movies as the dumb blonde in *Boy Meets Girl*, and since then she has ridden to fame and "regular eating" on the coattails of the sweet simpleton. As radio's Irma she is a once-a-week visitor to half the homes of America and her two Irma pictures have been box office hits. In *A Girl In Every Port* she plays a car hop who owns a plow horse turned racer and inadvertently falls into the clutches of sailors Marx and Bendix who own the twin to her horse. She thinks it will be her best movie since *Boy Meets Girl* and she proudly exhibits the eight changes of costume which she wears in the picture—$1,200 worth of "sweet but sexy clothes."

"They have to be kind of inadvertently sexy," she explained ingeniously. "As if I don't know what I'm showing."

Miss Wilson knows what she is showing though, all the time. She knows that her charm as Irma is more than pleasant stupidity. It finds a deep, answering chord in the hearts of nearly everybody.

"Most people have a hassle anyway," she explained. "Irma is kind-hearted and loving and always in trouble. That's what most of us think about ourselves. I had a letter the other day from a woman whose little boy was worried because I was sick in the hospital. He said, 'I hope Irma gets well because she's kind to animals.'"

The actress giggled light-heartedly. "I'm that . . . anyway," she said.

With DeMille and $3,000,000 . . . It's <u>The Greatest Show on Earth</u>

January 15, 1952

For the first time since she first bellowed and kicked her way to stardom, the screen's most strident comic, Betty Hutton, has an arena big enough for her talents—the circus tent.

For the first time since he took up acting to eat, Jimmy Stewart has a role that fills his most ancient and deep-seated yearning—that of a circus clown.

Dorothy Lamour, who, you might think, would be beyond the apprenticeship stage in such subjects, took lessons in necking to get in the act. (In circus parlance "necking" is not the mild exercise routinely practiced by most young Americans but a strenuous form of neck-muscle conditioning necessary to all ladies who would swing by their teeth from the Big Top.)

Gloria Grahame sent Cecil B. DeMille gardenias in a campaign to win the coveted honor of having an elephant step in her face.

And all of this adds up, at least in title and perhaps in fact, to *The Greatest Show on Earth*—a modern-age DeMille spectacle which comes hot out of the Technicolor laboratories this month.

The title was borrowed from the late P.T. Barnum, who succeeded in convincing half the people of the world, including Cecil B. DeMille, that the circus was, in truth, the greatest show on earth. If the movie is not a close runner-up for the title of "greatest" it will be because $3,000,000 and the combined forces of Ringling Brothers and Barnum & Bailey and Cecil B. DeMille have somehow made a bobble—an eventuality Hollywood does not even consider within the realm of possibility.

The day I went by Paramount Studios in Hollywood to see Mr. DeMille was, they told me, an exceedingly lucky day for interviewers.

"C.B.," said his staff, "has just seen *Greatest Show* and he's in fine form! When C.B. makes a good picture he's a happy man!"

"C.B." was a very happy man that day. He wanted to talk about *The Greatest Show on Earth* and he had ample opportunity because practically everything in his office reminded him of the picture. The DeMille office is a sort of museum. A few things are standard items in the decor. A great silk flag with the original colonies' warning, "Don't Tread On Me," flies from the doorway. A life-size Norman Rockwell oil painting of Victor Mature wrecking the temple as Samson fills one end of the room. Around the other walls, shelves, cabinets and bulletin boards hold photographs, sketches, clippings, scraps and snippets of anything and everything having to do with the current DeMille picture—in this case, *The Greatest Show on Earth*.

My eyes were irresistibly drawn to a toy float contraption, drawn by six gray pottery elephants and decorated with other elephants and pink ribbons. "That?" chuckled Mr. DeMille, leading the way to its shelf. "Gloria Grahame sent me that. I talked to Gloria about the part of the elephant girl in the picture but she was reluctant to take it. I told her that she would have to have the elephant put his foot in her face—and it was, of course, a risk. If she took the role it was her risk. No stunt players in this picture.

"She left to think it over and in a little while she sent me this thing filled with gardenias. Very beautiful."

Gloria herself is very beautiful and they do say that the day the elephant finally lowered his paw on her face she was very scared. The old circus theory that elephants will not put their weight on anything as shaky as the human nose was small comfort to Miss Grahame. She had heard, she said, of elephants who made mistakes.

But Gloria, Mr. DeMille insisted, performed in the best circus—

and DeMille—tradition. She was a trouper and so was Betty Hutton, who went to work with trapeze artists for coaches and actually learned to fly through the air with the greatest of ease, just like Holly the circus girl she plays in the picture. In fact, the energetic Miss Hutton won DeMille's vote as "one of the three greatest feminine troupers I have directed in four decades of motion pictures." (The other two are Gloria Swanson and Barbara Stanwyck.)

James Stewart took a salary cut just to play the role of Buttons, the clown in the picture—a role in which he never removes his clown make-up to show the handsome Stewart face. "I always wanted to play a clown," Stewart drawled in that slow, shy fashion that has endeared him to feminine movie-goers the world over. "I hope I do justice to Buttons."

Charlton Heston plays the busy and heroic circus manager in *Greatest Show* and Cornel Wilde is Sebastian, the flashy, sleek, powerful and smooth aerialist who woos the heroine, Miss Hutton.

DeMille's greatest problem in tackling the *Greatest Show* was finding a story suitable for a movie plot.

"Do you know that there have been no great circus stories?" he asked. "Biographies, yes. Reminiscences, yes. But story, no. I worked for months with my writers. I took my little granddaughter and a trailer and traveled for months with the circus. A couple of writers and my secretary went along. We played big cities and cross-roads communities. I slept and ate with the circus and talked to hundreds of performers."

DeMille always wanted, he said, to do "a stream of civilization story centering in a railroad station, where great drama passes in review every day." That idea never jelled into a story for him, but the circus idea finally evolved into somewhat the same kind of story.

"The circus," said the 70-year-old producer, dreamily, "is a great magician leading children of all ages from six to 60 across the border of reality into a tinsel and spun-candy world of reckless beauty and mounting laughter and whirling thrills—but behind all this lies a massive machine whose very life depends on discipline, motion and speed—a mechanized army on wheels that rolls over any obstacle in its path."

The Greatest Show attempts to show the personal triumphs and tragedies of the circus performers, to recapture their one-night, split-second, death-defying world. The climax of the story is the big circus train wreck for which DeMille brought up a lot of wrecked railroad cars, wrecked many others and enlisted the services of approximately 80,000 citizens of Sarasota, Fla., where most of the picture was filmed and neighboring towns.

The business district of Sarasota was roped off for the scene. DeMille, old master of the catastrophe, is said to be at his finest in the train wreck as it finally comes off.

According to the story, the first section of the Ringling train is stopped by robbers. A second section plunges into the standing train in a smashing impact of shattering steel and wood, with the cries of the injured and the screams of released animals filling the air.

DeMille had six cameras going and one thing is certain, for The Greatest Show, the old master has provided the biggest darned train wreck ever staged on any continent.

Yvonne Wants a Southern Husband: Can She Find Him in Atlanta?

January 27, 1952

Does anybody here want to marry Yvonne DeCarlo?

Miss DeCarlo is looking for a Southern husband!

In fact, the sultry cinema beauty who usually plays bosomy bad girls who are redeemed in the last 10 minutes of every movie by the love of a good man, confided to me in Hollywood recently that there is such a great, gnawing shortage of good men in her life she's thinking about launching a husband-hunting expedition to Georgia this winter.

"I've looked everywhere else," said Miss DeCarlo, sighing wistfully over her hot roast beef sandwich and Coca-Cola. "I've been all over Europe and just recently to the Holy Land. I've looked in New York and Los Angeles, the mountains and the desert. But I haven't been South yet. Tell me, do Rhett Butler and Ashley Wilkes still live?"

A loyal magnolia blossom to the last, I said staunchly "Of co'se. The cotton fields are full of them!"

So Miss DeCarlo, 117 pounds of spectacularly placed curves, may step in her low-slung Cadillac convertible and come driving down the old post road the minute her present Universal International picture, *Scarlett Angel,* is finished.

She plans to stop off in New Orleans, scene of her career as a honky-tonk girl in *Scarlett Angel,* and then she is committed to come to Atlanta for a blind date with a newspaperman (I HAD to get him first chance, boys. He's one of my bosses.)

But all Southern gentlemen who are thinking about donning their courting clothes might as well know that the requirements are tough and the obstacle course has thrown many another good man. The beauteous Yvonne, she of the smoky blue eyes and the husky voice, likes handsome men as well as the next girl, but they've got to be better than good looking, they've also got to be good.

"Worthwhile," Miss DeCarlo specified, lazily eating a wedge of hot mince pie with hard sauce. "I'll never marry until I can find a man I can respect. To tell you the truth, I wish I could find somebody like Joel McCrae—only younger. You know, a big rugged outdoor man who has a job he is crazy about—like being a rancher, for instance. I've nothing against actors, but I'm not particularly for actors either. I just haven't seen one I wanted to marry."

This spinsterish attitude has not kept Miss DeCarlo from having a good time in Hollywood. Even at the old age of 25 years—and 25 is almost as old in Hollywood as it used to be in the Tennessee hills—she gets around to all the night spots, sees every play, goes to every concert and never misses a performance by the ballet, her first love among the arts.

She would like a husband to be interested in such things. (She speaks French, reads Shakespeare and Greek mythology, has a fine symphony and opera record collection and rides a horse so well she has won rodeo prizes.)

But what she really wants to do is bow to the irresistible force of a great, dominant male personality.

"I'd even quit work for the right man," she said dreamily.

"But wouldn't that mean he'd have to be rich?" I put in, flabbergasted.

"Yes," she said, suddenly dreary. "I suppose it would . . . I don't want to be rich but I do like . . . nice things."

For some years now Miss DeCarlo has been able to afford nice things. Born Peggy Yvonne Middleton in Vancouver, British Columbia, Sept. 1, 1924, she was steered toward stardom from the time she was 6 years old by her mother, Marie DeCarlo, a frustrated dancer. Yvonne too started as a dancer and went to Universal, where executives were looking for a "wolf woman" type to play in a forthcoming horror picture.

"Yvonne," said Joe Lawler of the publicity department, leering at us over his bowl of vegetable soup, "lacked menace."

"Ha!" hooted a passing waiter derisively, and Miss DeCarlo smiled her appreciation.

Anyhow, the dancer didn't get the wolf woman assignment or any other one until Walter Wanger, the agent-shooting husband of Joan Bennett, followed a hunch and had her tested in Technicolor. She turned out to be the best thing to happen to Technicolor since the light bulb was invented.

She has made 14 pictures, all in Technicolor and all of them demonstrating that, wolfish or not, she is a menacing character. In fact, the box office success of all the DeCarlo pictures has been so heartening that the smart young businesswoman was recently emboldened to organize her own production company.

"I've proved that I'm valuable property," she said, grinning a little. "Now I want to pick and produce my own pictures. After *Scarlett Angel,* and one other picture, I hope to do one for my own company, Vancouver Productions. I'm considering a Bible story about Ruth or Esther—I don't know which."

The biblical countries of the Holy Land fascinated Miss DeCarlo, an inveterate traveler, and she has observed that biblical stories, even as DeCarlo curves, have done very well at the box office. Together the two might . . . well, there's no telling.

Anyhow, she might be married and living on Peachtree Street before she even gets around to making another picture. There's just one warning for aspiring suitors. They must be able to work with a chaperon. Yvonne's aunt always travels with her.

"And I'll certainly bring her to Atlanta with me!" said the husband-hunter with a flash of blue lightning from her eyes.

Esther Williams was so pleased with the following profile that she later wired Sibley, writing "Your reportorial awareness and powers of observation are remarkable."

Shapely Esther Is Hollywood's Model Mother

February 17, 1952

Mandeville Canyon Road which winds between the Pacific Palisades and Brentwood sections of Los Angeles is a leisurely, treesy, friendly-looking road that bespeaks with real rural, no-plumbing living or the opposite—platinum-priced real estate and a French provincial decor.

The house where Morgan Hudgens, of Metro-Goldwyn-Mayer's publicity department, turned off, appeared to be neither. It was a smallish, butter-yellow frame house, a story and a half high, built close to the ground with the economy of line and the grace of a north Georgia mountain house. A low fence separated the dooryard from the driveway and boxes and beds were a-blaze with sturdy, old-fashioned country flowers.

The name on the mailbox said "Gage." Morgan, a native Charlestonian who once did a hitch as reporter on the *Atlanta Journal,* noted it in half astonishment, half despair. "Isn't that just like Esther?" he asked. "Movie stars are supposed to shrink from their public after hours. Here Esther puts her name on the mailbox just like any . . . well, anybody!"

"Esther Williams. Occupation: Mrs. Ben Gage," I commented wryly, not much believing it at the time.

Morgan rang the doorbell and a middle-aged white woman answered it and suggested that we go right on out to the backyard where "Mr. and Mrs. Gage have been all day."

The living room door opened into the back yard and we went on through with Morgan yelling ahead: "Esther! Is it all right to come on out?"

Then I saw her—the Esther Williams of the movies, the Esther Williams whose picture rises mermaid-like from the stacks of half the magazines at your corner drugstore, the All-American girl herself. Only here she was running barefoot down the path toward us, flapping a sunbrowned arm, frowning and hissing like a mama adder.

"I SAID . . . ," began Morgan but his hostess cut him short.

"Don't you say another word here!" she hissed menacingly. "You're practically in Benjie's bedroom and you'll wake him up!"

Morgan subsided and we followed her out through a little picket fence to a beautiful blue, kidney-shaped pool. There she turned and we caught the full impact of her brilliant, flashing smile—all white teeth and toast-colored face and warm, friendly eyes. She held out her hand and took mine like Bitsy Grant grasping a new tennis racket.

"I'm glad to see you, Celestine," she said, catching my name on the first go-round. "Please forgive me for yelling at you but Benjie just went to sleep and you know how it is when they wake up too soon?"

I said I knew and she led me to meet what looked like the biggest bath towel extant, but turned out to be a vast terry cloth robe with a blonde, curly head at the top and a pair of big brown feet 6 feet 6 inches to the south. Her husband, Ben, she said proudly and then, swooping up a wriggling, brown infant off the mat, "And this is Kim, my youngest. Isn't he gorgeous?"

Kim, wearing nothing but a thickness of suntan oil and a beatific smile, was in truth gorgeous—almost as gorgeous as his mother and not a whit more natural. For Mrs. Ben Gage wore only a wisp of coffee-colored bathing suit and a smidgen of lipstick. Her short brown hair, streaked here and there with fingers of sunburned gold, was tumbled back from her face in a manner at once unaffected and stunning.

She dropped down on the mat with Kim in her arms and began applying oil to both of them. "Please have off your clothes and let me get you a sun suit," she said. "This sun is so fine, we'd love to share it with you."

I said, "No, thank you," and prepared to get along with the interview, but by the time I'd settled on a chaise lounge beside the pool and dug out a pencil, Mrs. Gage had run over to the little bathhouse on the other side and was helping her husband and two workmen, introduced as "our good friends, Bill and Joe," move a ping pong table.

I thought of a question and waited. In a moment she was back. Marriage versus Career, I decided. That was the tack. "What do you think of marriage?" I asked. But she didn't hear me. She was showing the men where to plant a tree. "How do you combine acting and child-rearing?" I began again, but Benjie awakened and she vanished toward the house.

When she came back Benjie, the eldest son, a tyke of around two years, had to be admired and oiled and sunned and fed at a little table nearby. I suggested as an opener that she seemed pretty experienced at baby-handling.

"No expert," she grinned, wiping papaya off Benjie's chin. "Ben and I just love 'em and spend a lot of time with 'em. I think that's the only way to bring up children. A woman who doesn't have time for her children has no right to have children. They come first with me. A career's nice . . . but only so long as it doesn't interfere with my family!"

The Gages, I learned through catch-as-catch-can interviewing, were having a holiday. Esther between pictures and Ben from his restaurant called The Trails where he has just inaugurated a special blue plate luncheon for Hughes aircraft workers, tailored to fit their 45-minute lunch hour. I also learned that in their six years of marriage Esther has made nine pictures and had three children, losing one, a little girl. They've owned two homes, the first one smaller with a homemade swimming pool. The present one came ready-built but had professionals install the pool, which has a heater to keep the water at 70 to 76 degrees, making it possible for them to swim some every day and for Esther to work out the intricate routines for her pictures.

Esther never expected to be an actress. She was an Olympics quality swimmer and when MGM gave her a one-year contract she was sure it was a fluke so she plunged into every class taught at the studio—dancing and singing and talking and wearing clothes—determined she said to get a finishing school education since she'd had to quit college.

"I knew it couldn't last so I'd better make the most of that year," she grinned. She continues to work as if every year is her last.

Still barefoot and bathing-suited she took us on a tour of her house—the long Early American living room with the big fireplace and bowls of home-grown flowers, the kitchen with its fireplace and baby-proof electric outlets, the boys' rooms and finally her and Ben's upstairs bedroom.

Then she led us back to the pool where she insisted we have a Coke and a swim. I demurred because I knew her suits wouldn't fit me.

"Here's one," she said, holding up a red and white-skirted cotton. "It'll be just right. I wore it when I was pregnant."

Ten minutes later, swimming in the maternity bathing suit, I knew my original idea had been right. Esther Williams. Occupation: Mrs. Ben Gage.

The Truth about Lana Turner

March 2, 1952

A professorial-looking young man with heavy-rimmed glasses and a lecture platform manner was holding forth in a coffee shop in Hollywood, Calif., when I went down to breakfast that morning and the subject of his discourse was one, I found out later, which was destined to replace television in Hollywood bistros and bars for days to come: THE TRUTH ABOUT LANA TURNER.

"The Truth," said the young man earnestly, talking in capitals the way they do in Hollywood, "cannot hurt" Lana Turner.

"Lana Turner," he went on, warming to his subject, "is an old-fashioned kind of movie star. She belongs to the Ermine Era—in type if not age. She's probably the last of the Big Stars, the boys and girls who can get away with doing things in a bold and flashy manner, who marry frequently and spectacularly and who can even survive the breath of scandal.

"I say," he concluded roundly, "that Lana Turner will survive Truth because she has what, for lack of a better word, we call GLAMOUR."

It was not, I thought privately, a very original word and I wasn't sure it would stand Miss Turner in good stead in the face of several startling admissions she had just made in the public prints. (Womanlike, it was hard for me to decide which admission was the more damaging—that her father was a bootlegger and a petty crook who was shot down on a San Francisco street corner after a crap game, or that her eyebrows are not her own but have to be applied daily.)

And then, in one of Metro-Goldwyn-Meyer's old-fashioned, glamorous limousines I went out to Culver City to see Miss

Turner—and what the young man in the coffee shop said might have been spoken by an oracle!

Lana Turner is a genuine, bred-in-the-bone beauty. She could scrub her face with lye water and sand and still emerge looking like one of those little creatures that used to grace the pages of your copy of Hans Christian Andersen fairy tales. She is pink and gold and blue with eyelashes that stick out . . . . to there. She has a waist you could span with a hand and a half, the whitest, evenest teeth in the movies and dimples that are distracting even to carping, female interviewers.

And she hasn't an ounce of pretense about her.

They took me to see her on *The Merry Widow* set and although she looked wickedly feminine in a swooshy black chiffon negligee, she stuck out her hand with the natural friendliness of a small boy. I mentioned that I wanted to talk to her about her sudden venture in Truth.

"You have recently started Telling All about yourself, haven't you Miss Turner?" I asked.

"Yes," she said, nodding soberly, "and it hasn't been easy. People said I'm going to ruin myself with my public—and maybe I am." She paused and stared thoughtfully out of the dressing room door to the balcony set where she was soon to be pictured with her hero, Fernando Lamas.

"Don't they say the truth will make you free?" she asked after a moment. "Well, for years I have pretended to be what I'm not— pretended to be smarter and better. I'm really what I said, a patsy. I've made so many mistakes in my life and I've let people think things that weren't true, hoping what they would think would be better than the truth. I just got tired of it, that's all.

"I had a talk with my agent and I told him I wanted to get the facts straight for once—age, background, lack of education, the way things really happened to me. He agreed with me and we began with a writer he knew, Cameron Shipp, who wrote a first-person story called 'My Private Life' for the *Woman's Home Companion*."

She giggled ruefully. "After it was all down in print, I was stuck with it. And now I'll stick by it. All interviewers get the same—the truth."

The truth, as Miss Turner tells it, is that she was born in Wallace, Mo., February 8, 1921, the daughter of a coal miner who took occasional fliers into bootlegging and often caused his wife and child to pack up and leave town hurriedly—with the police on their heels. They changed their names often but their little girl, formally christened Julia Jean Mildred Frances Turner, was consistently called Judy until she got into the movies. There director Mervyn LeRoy changed her name to Lana—with a broad *A*. But Judy did not become Lana until after her father was killed and her mother, a beauty operator, moved to Southern California. The lass had no flair for scholarship and she was playing hooky from Hollywood High School when she was spotted by a talent scout in a drugstore and launched in the movies.

Her first role was a walk-on bit in *They Won't Forget*. The Turners, mother and daughter, were horrified at Lana's appearance in it. She says she "bounced fore and aft" and on the whole looked like "a blossom waiting to be plucked."

Which may have been what Hollywood thought, too, because after that, success and money and marriage came with dizzying rapidity. Miss Turner admits that she liked the gay nightlife and that her marriage to bandleader Artie Shaw was a spur-of-the-moment thing. She knew him only slightly the night they eloped and when she wired her mother that she was married, her mother assumed she had married Greg Bautzer, the lawyer, whom she knew slightly better. Her marriage to Steve Crane brought her real trouble because she discovered he was still married to somebody else the same day she discovered she was going to have a baby. They got an annulment and remarried later, but that didn't work either and after it was over, Lana insists, she was a "burnt child" who had no intention of ever marrying again.

The millionaire playboy Bob Topping, courted her so pleasantly and persistently, however, she finally gave in, bought herself the most beautiful and flamboyant trousseau imaginable and went off to England on a honeymoon with him.

"I was such a dope," she said. "I didn't know how my arrival with all those suitcases of clothes would look to the British in their austerity era. I got terrible press and I was terribly hurt by it—but today I understand why."

Now Lana lives alone with her only child, Cheryl, the famous Rh-factor baby who was born of her brief and stormy marriage to Steve Crane. She has fallen out with her mother many times but they remain good friends. At the time I talked to her she was vaguely troubled because of her mother's attitude toward her Truth and Consequences spree.

"Mother won't talk to me about it," she said, sighing. "Mother never has been one to talk much about things and I guess she's hurt because I've been so brazen as to air the truth about things she's kept hidden. She's a fine person, though, and I think she'll see it my way."

When I was in Hollywood, Lana's name was being linked with that of the handsome Fernando Lamas who plays opposite her in Franz Lehar's pleasant musical, *The Merry Widow*. They appeared together at the premiere of *Quo Vadis* and later at the Coconut Grove but the actress said firmly that she had "no romance in hand or in mind."

"When this picture is finished," she said, "I'm going abroad—to England and France and Italy. I'm going to see things the way I've always wanted to see them—like a dumb sightseer. Before, when I went with Bob everything was so . . . so plush. This time I'm going to take my car and one suitcase and really do the scenery."

Thinking the title of the picture, *The Merry Widow*, might be prophetic, I asked, "Are you out for a gay and happy time with no honorable intentions?"

She pouted prettily. "I have no intentions, honorable or dishonorable. I guess I'm having a good time—but as for being happy, how many happy people do you know?"

Gloria Swanson Reveals Her Secret of Youth

April 6, 1952

Only people who are bored grow old.

That comes to you on the authority of a woman who flatly refuses to be either old or bored, although the Associated Press's official biography gives her age as 63 years and she admits to 52.

Need you ask? The most glamorous grandma of them all . . . Glorious Gloria Swanson!

Miss Swanson, in Atlanta recently to exploit the charms of $17.95 dresses which she designs for a New York concern, incidentally exploited her own homemade youth secrets.

"If I stopped working," said Miss Swanson, "I'd collapse like an old accordion!"

At that point, the actress, who has a sort of sleek sheen about her, caused by good grooming, cleanliness and an absence of make-up except lipstick and eye shadow, was stretched out on a divan at her suite at the Biltmore like a taut accordion. She uses both hands and both tiny, smartly shod feet when she talks and an interviewer becomes accustomed to seeing Miss Swanson's feet moving through the air as rapidly and as expressively as her hands.

The five-times-married damsel who is said to be contemplating a sixth marriage—this time to her personal representative, young Brandon Brent—fished around in a gold box of a pocketbook and read to me something she had copied down as a recipe for youth.

"Look forward, not backward," she read and then added parenthetically, "my friends have trouble understanding that quality in me but when something is finished, it's finished. I don't look back. The curtain's down!"

She returned her eyes, looking through blue-rimmed spectacle-shaped glasses, to the paper.

"Have variety and interest in your life. Monotony and the lack of mental activity produce age. The ancient Greeks had the formula for youth in a nutshell: learn something new every day."

That, she insists, is her secret but there is, of course, more to Miss Swanson's youth than meets the eye. At a luncheon given for her, 18 or 20 other women ate prettily calorie-laden salads and wound up with a French pastry. The actress ate a vegetable plate, including potatoes, "one of those delicious little muffins with nuts in it" and a fold of toast filled with a cheese mixture.

"I leave off dessert," she said, "but I like bread and potatoes. I like white bread and I need potatoes to give me the energy for the life I lead. Do you want me to give you a story that's never been printed before? I'm going into the bread business!"

Miss Swanson has a theory that the thing that's fat-making about white bread is poor flour and too much shortening. She has evolved a recipe and she plans to have her bread on the market as soon as distribution arrangements can be completed and she can think of a name.

She already designs dresses and from time to time she comes up with an invention that improves the fit of the dress or the appearance of the figure beneath the dress. For stage and screen appearances she has her dresses made boned from bosom to hip to eliminate the necessity of wearing a girdle and to smooth out bulges.

She also has in the mill two of her private complexion secrets—one is a cleanser and the other is the cream that she puts into her skin before she goes out.

"I just clean my face and rub on something—it's a secret!" she added, slanting her blue eyes at me mischievously. "But if the chemist can combine the two, I'm sure other women will buy them. I leave off powder because I like to shine. But some women don't. What I have in mind is a combination that will please everybody."

Then there's the matter of exercise.

Miss Swanson insists that she doesn't exercise, but then went into a quick pantomimic demonstration of how she wrestled, fought and kicked her way to a rip-roaring Broadway success with Jose Ferrer in *Twentieth Century*.

"I was weak and gasping the first week," the actress reported. "After that scene my maid would have to help me off the stage. But after a month I was tough and it became a game with me to really beat Jose. I got a crick in my neck and I went to my osteopath. He was astonished at how hard and muscular I had become.

"Here, hit me here," she said, offering a leg.

I punched at her timidly but under the blue silk of dress, muscle and bone felt like petrified wood.

In the strong light of day Miss Swanson was completely free

from the crinkled lines of age and weariness that bedevil womankind. Her hair was gray but her face looked firm and youthful and her eyes were bright.

Marriage would seem to have been enough to keep Miss Swanson's life free of age-producing monotony. According to the AP record, she has been married to the following men: 1. Wallace Beery, while they were both contract players at Keystone Studios. 2. Herbert K. Somborn, owner of the Brown Derby restaurant and father of her daughter, Gloria Jr., who is now married and has three children. 3. The French nobleman, Marquis de la Falaise de la Coudraye, to whom she was married in 1925 and from whom she divorced in 1931. 4. Michael Framer, the Irish sportsman and father of her 19-year-old daughter, Michelle Bridgit, 5. William Davey, a retired businessman with whom marriage lasted from 1945 to 1946.

While she was married to Mr. Somborn, the actress adopted a son, Joseph, who is studying engineering at Stanford University.

For the last four years since, Miss Swanson returned to the movies to make the sensationally successful *Sunset Boulevard*, she has worked killing hours, traveled great distances, supervised her own wardrobes and handled her own contracts.

"I hope I never stop," she said. "I've just finished one picture, *Three for Bedroom C*, and I'm going out to negotiate another. I've had a television show offered to me and there's a play as well. All I want is more time to do more things.

"I'm crazy about painting and I like to sculpt. I'm a pretty good photographer and then there's a book I want to write . . ."

A reporter who scorned Gloria Swanson pictures in her youth because they were full of "that old love stuff" and a photographer who was in swaddling clothes when Gloria was wowing them in *Zaza* and *The Wages of Virtue,* dragged themselves from the room—two tired old women.

Hollywood's Star Mother . . . Joan Crawford

May 18, 1952

Hollywood husbands and fathers are as amenable to Halloween trick-or-treat pranks as any citizens, but one Beverly Hills householder was slightly jolted last October when he found a full-fledged grown-up witch on his doorstep.

A covey of small spooks had just rung his doorbell and collected their loot when he perceived, riding herd on them from the shadows, a tattered, dusty, droopy haunt of regulation adult size.

"Who are you?" demanded the man of the house nervously. "What are you doing here?"

"I'm these spooks' mother," said the witch with dignity. "Where else would I be?"

She removed her mask, disclosing one of the most famous faces in the world—that of Joan Crawford.

That story was told to me in Hollywood by a man at another studio a few days after I had met Joan Crawford at Warner Brothers. I knew it was true because by that time I had a complete and utter faith in Joan Crawford as a real, honest-to-goodness mother—not Hollywood style but American style. All of Miss Crawford's four children are adopted but, unlike some actresses, she did not acquire the little ones to cast them as supporting players to her role as a pretty and devoted mother.

Joan Crawford loves her children with the fierceness of a

woman who missed out on love in her own childhood. She is rearing them with the rugged, hard-headed good sense that got her to the top of a heart-breaking business and has kept her there for nearly a quarter of a century in spite of cruel handicaps.

I hadn't planned to talk to her about her children when I went over to Warner Brothers about 6 o'clock one evening to interview her in her bungalow dressing room. The evening before I heard the crowd at the *Quo Vadis* premiere go wild with excitement when she walked up to the microphone with that incredible Crawford grace and spoke a few words of greeting. She was an old-timer, easily in her mid-forties although her biography carefully does not say, and yet she retained the lithe figure, the sculptured bone-beauty of face and that special aura that used to be associated with Big Stars. She had won an Academy Award as recently as 1945 and is now starring in *This Woman is Dangerous*. I thought I might try to find how she did it when younger stars age and drop by the wayside.

But from the moment she swept into her dressing room, trailed by her diction coach and a cunning little dog that looked as though he had been bought in a toy shop, Miss Crawford had charge of the interview. The young publicity man with me, a devoted Crawford admirer, too, had warned me.

"Watch her make an entrance," he said. "This woman acts like a Star."

She did, too. She was weighted down with a knitting basket, an armload of books, slim satin evening shoes and a great rustly cocktail dress which she planned to wear to a party. She had on a green slack suit and green suede play shoes and there was a shine about her face and her eyes and her hair.

"I'm SO sorry to be late!" she said breathlessly, dropping her things and holding out a slim, hard little hand. "Here, let me have your coat! What would you like to drink?"

The small living room-dressing room, green-walled with floral print draperies at the window and on the dressing table skirt, came to life. The hostess straightened as she moved about and with practically no pause in conversation at all, had disappeared into her little kitchenette and returned with drinks and a plate of pâté de foie gras and crackers. All around the room were pictures of her children—blonde Christina, 12, Christopher, 10, and the dark little twins, Cathy and Cynthia, who are almost 6.

I made a valiant effort at steering the interview by mentioning her work.

"Work is one of the best things in the world," she said positively. "Inactivity is one of the most unhealthy, degrading things that can happen to a human being! I have my hands full and I'm glad!"

She grinned ruefully. "I just finished firing one cook and now I have to hire another. I had to call home just before I left the set and check to be sure one nurse is not left alone on duty. I'm going to a party and I won't get home until 10 o'clock and I have a rule that one nurse is not enough with four children. One person can sit with them and read to them or watch television, but she can't do all that and hear doorbells and telephones, too."

She sighed and straightened the group picture before her. "They take such care, such love, such firmness. And time, too!"

She has known every child-rearing problem in the books. ("I've had a breath-holder and a non-eater and a non-sleeper and a spit-in-your-facer but we've weathered 'em all with improvement to the children and me, too.") She believed in sending children to public school and even joined the PTA but she found that with her daughter, Christina, public school was not operating like the great democratic institution it is supposed to be.

"Christina was reigning like a queen," she said, wrinkling her pretty nose in disgust. "She had a revolting way of saying, 'I'm Joan Crawford's daughter' and expecting the other children to wait on her. Some of them did and she was getting pretty impossible . . . so I yanked her out of public school and put her in a private school."

She chuckled happily. "You know, the other day she told me she found out there were a lot of important people in the world who had nothing whatever to do with movies! She's even learned that there are some people who don't think being an actress's daughter is very important. It's been good for Christina."

Joan Crawford still has homework problems and although her publicity mentions that she attended Stephens College, she has a lusty way of telling the pure truth.

"Christina said, 'Mother, do you know about math?' and I said, 'I told you I couldn't help you a lick after you got beyond the sixth grade—that's as far as I went in school!'"

She laughed and smudged out a cigarette in an ash tray.

"Christina said, 'Don't you know about a triangle, Mother?' and I said, 'Yes, in movies or in life. But NOT in algebra!'"

Joan Crawford knows quite a lot about life. Born Lucille LeSeuer in San Antonio, Tex., she got into movies by way of the chorus line and she allegedly had the rough edges smoothed off by her marriages to such smooth characters as Douglas Fairbanks Jr., Franchot Tone and Phillip Terry.

For those who think that she spends too much time with her youngsters and is too tough on them, requiring them to perform menial household chores when she is amply able to hire servants, Miss Crawford has a ready answer.

"My children may not be able to afford servants, and if they are, they need to know how things should be done. I love them and I want them to have a happy childhood. I had no childhood of my own. But I have to keep this in mind: I'm not raising those kids for myself. I'm raising them for themselves—and for life. And life is not easy."

Corinne Calvet Wages a One-Woman War against Gossip

October 19, 1952

Interviewing Corinne Calvet is somewhat like a trip on a merry-go-round. It's gay. It's musical. You get a lot of scenery for your money. And at the end of the ride you're not sure where you've been or where you were going. In short, it's dizzying.

When I talked to Corinne Calvet over lunch at 20th Century Fox's Beverly Hills studios in California she was in the midst of suing Zsa Zsa Gabor for saying she was not French at all but Cockney. The price Miss Calvet put on this piece of damaging discourse was one million dollars.

"Is it really worth so much to you?" I asked Miss Calvet.

"But yess!" she assured me earnestly. "You say it does not matter what my nationalitee—and perhaps you are right. But gossip is wicked. Untruth is wrong. I sue not for Corinne Calvet alone but for all the people whose lives, whose careers could be ruined by untruth."

She rolled her dessert spoon between her fingers reflectively.

"Hollywood is like a leetle country town. A beeg family, really. We talk and talk and talk. But it will be a moch nicer town without gossip. There are so many wonderful things we might say."

Maybe the nice things, I suggested tentatively, wouldn't be half so interesting as the un-nice ones.

My tawny-haired luncheon companion sat up straight in her chair and pounced like a tiger.

"What kind of a nature you are?" she demanded.

I scrunched down the back of my chef's salad and assured her that I personally did not favor gossip. I was just, er, making conversation.

"You must hate human-i-ty," Miss Calvet said accusingly. And then she went on to tell me that since the Zsa Zsa episode she had forbidden gossip in her home and had requested her friends to keep personalities out of their conversation.

"If I want to make fun," she said, grinning at me provocatively, "I make fun out of me. And why not, I know me better than I know anyone else!"

Knowing Corinne Calvet could be a career in itself. Borne Corinne Dibos, she chose the Calvet off a bottle of Calvet wine after her father, a prosperous businessman, told her he didn't object to her becoming an actress but he would object to having his name besmirched by a mediocre performance.

At that time she wasn't sure what kind of performance she would turn in because she had been an actress only an hour or so. The notion of becoming an actress hit young Corinne at 2 o'clock one morning.

Being thrifty of time, in the French (not Cockney) tradition, she grabbed a phone directory, thumbed through a list of film folk, let her thumb rest on the name of director Marc Allegret—and dialed his number.

The earliness of the hour and the fact that she had never met Allegret didn't trouble her. After all, reasoned Miss Calvet, she was doing him a favor. She would let him star her in a film.

That she actually did the movie industry a favor is now undisputed. Allegret gave her an appointment and promised her a role in his next picture, but Corrine had decided not to waste any more time. So, as she left his office building, she dropped by the office of a neighboring producer and talked him out of a role immediately.

She had made half a dozen French films when producer Hal Wallis spotted her for *Rope of Sand*.

In 1948 Corinne married actor John Bromfield, the "my Johnnee" of hundreds of Calvet interviews. She is so fond of "my Johnnee" she quotes him constantly, sighs dreamily at the mere mention of his name and has been quoted often on her recipes for staying in love though married.

The day I talked to her one of the subjects we discussed was having a family in Hollywood.

"We want three children," she said and then hastily, "but not now. In a few years, maybe. I am not contented to haf my children reared by nurses. This I do myself. And now I need to be just a little more established than I am. I need all the pictures I am making."

Corinne is extremely domestic despite the fact that she'd rather be caught dead than photographed frying an egg or wearing an apron. She is handy with carpentry tools and recently took down and rehung the garden gate beside her English country-type house because she got tired of bumping into it when she climbed out of the car.

She paints pictures and walls—and when she is working, as she is now in a picture called *Powder River,* she prefers to be painting walls.

"That is the better hobby because when I am painting a picture, if I'm not ready to leave it, I won't."

Interior decorating is her primary interest now. She likes what she calls "big, deep and "com-FORT-able" furniture, the kind you can "nest yourself in for the night."

There was a time when, between pictures, Calvet worked hard on her English but no more. Her teachers gave up, she said, because she was "so stubborn." They accused her of hearing the correct pronunciation of a word and repeating it but in her subconscious way of saying, "Oh, ye-ah?"

"To kill the accent, I can't," she sighed. And then added mirthfully, "But now I must go home and practice my Cockney."

Doris Day Is Hollywood's Kid Lucky

January 25, 1953

Doris Day (she was Doris Kappelhoff of Cincinnati, Ohio) was a dancer at the age of 12 with a promising career on the Fanchon and Marco circuit until a car, in which she was riding, hit a train, crippling her badly.

Today she gets more mail than anybody else at Warner Brothers studio, is one of the country's top box-office stars and is so sought after as a singer that her records are snatched up almost as fast as they're finished.

The result of the automobile accident?

If Doris hadn't had her dancing legs put out of commission for 14 months she might never have lifted her voice in song in the first place. She certainly wouldn't have had the leisure to take voice lessons and sing (for free) on a Cincinnati radio show just to gain poise and technique. But mostly Doris Day thinks she's lucky.

"How could I believe any other way?" she demanded. "Here I am a Hollywood actress and the only role I ever played before coming into the business was a duck in a Mother Goose play!"

The day I saw this self-styled "Kid Lucky" was probably the hottest day on record in Hollywood, but on the Warner Brothers sound stage the snow glittered and glistened like a Christmas card. A whole street of two-story frame houses with domes and cupolas and wooden gingerbread trimmings stretched out in front of me. One of the houses seemed to have a front wall missing exposing a colorful and cozy, if gim-cracky reception hall and stairway of early 1900's vintage.

The lights were on in that hall and the camera was trained upon it. In a moment, music started somewhere and a bouncy, pink-cheeked girl in low-heeled slippers and a bright cotton dress appeared on the second floor with a feather duster in her hands.

"Roll 'em," said the director. "Rolling," echoed the cameraman.

The girl with the duster, caught up by the music, cut a little caper and then began descending the stairs, dusting as she came and singing:

In the morning . . . in the evening
Ain't we got fun!

The tune took me back to my childhood, and standing there in the gypsum snow under a make-believe tree, I bobbed my head in time to the music and felt unaccountably happy.

Later, I decided that's the secret of Doris Day's success. It is compounded of equal parts of hard work, nostalgia and an overwhelming desire to make people happy.

We talked about it a little while after that in Doris' Early American style portable dressing room.

She introduced me to her husband, Marty Melcher, who is also her agent, and served me oatmeal cookies made by her mother, Mrs. Alma Kappelhoff, called "Nana" by everybody on the Warner Brothers set and by all her daughter's friends.

"I'll talk about anything you want to," Doris assured me sunnily, "except two things: politics and bosoms."

I mentioned another actress who even then was making Page One throughout the country with Army-censored photographs of her front elevation.

"Oh, that!" exclaimed Miss Day scornfully. "That's freak publicity. Success built on that kind of thing is no good. People read and comment and go to see her pictures for awhile but you can't build a following on that kind of stuff. The girl must be nuts . . ." Abruptly she interrupted herself to shoot an inquiring look at her husband.

"Huh?" she said. "What are you trying to tell me?"

The handsome, dark-haired Marty Melcher was smiling and writing something on the dressing room mirror with his finger.

"C-r-i-t," read Doris aloud and then she laughed. "Oh, criticism!" she said. "We promised each other we wouldn't criticize other people and I forget. I'm sorry, dear."

Melcher smiled at her approvingly and switched the conversation back to the picture, *By the Light of the Silvery Moon,* which is to be a sequel to the Gus Kahn story, *I'll See You in My Dreams.*

That, they both said, is Doris' kind of picture. She built her success on sentimental, nostalgic music and pictures. (Her first record success of any proportion was "Sentimental Journey," sung with Les Brown.) They both agree that although Doris has demonstrated her ability to handle straight dramatic roles, as in *The Winning Team* and *Storm Warning,* her greatest asset is her naturalness, her ability to make people laugh and join her in singing.

Melcher is Doris' third husband. She was married briefly to Al Jorden, trombonist in Jimmie Dorsey's orchestra and father of her 11-year-old son, Terry. Her second husband was musician George Weidler, brother of the child actress, Virginia Weidler.

It was Weidler who brought Doris to Hollywood. He had a date to play there and she followed him, keeping house in a trailer in West Los Angeles until a year later when they were separated. She got night club engagements and was spotted by director Michael Curtiz.

Doris recalls that she wept throughout her interview in Curtiz' office.

"My personal unhappiness was too much for me and the dam just sort of burst," she said.

In spite of the tears Curtiz hired her, and her climb to stardom was almost instantaneous. She and her husband, her mother and her child dwell in one of the unpretentious houses near the studio and her personal life seems to have smoothed out.

"I'm in the midst of decorating my house," she told me. "But you can't call that trouble. For a woman it's natural—and you can't beat naturalness!"

Did She Kill Her Husband? Olivia Keeps the Secret as My Cousin Rachel in Hollywood

February 1, 1953

She sat there in her velvet dress looking for all the world like Melanie of *Gone With the Wind*—and all the time the cameramen, the crew, her maid and even the publicity department were trying to get her to tell if, as Daphne Du Maurier's *My Cousin Rachel,* she had killed a man.

"Well, did you?" I asked

And Olivia de Havilland smiled a sweet, gentle, mysterious smile and shook her shining dark head.

"I'm not telling," she said.

When Olivia de Havilland takes a role in a movie—a thing she has assiduously avoided since 1948 until 20th Century Fox came up with the Du Maurier story—she plays it all the way. That's why some people will always think of her as Margaret Mitchell's lovely Melanie. It's also why a few people still regard her as a graduate of a mental institution, as in *The Snake Pit*.

Olivia de Havilland has a way of becoming the person she portrays. She reaches deep for the key to that person's character and, good or bad, pleasant or unpleasant, she does not stop until she is that person.

When I went by the *My Cousin Rachel* set to see her she had just returned to Hollywood with her small son to begin a picture and get a divorce. She got the first decree while I was still in Hollywood. She wept as she described her difficulties with Marcus Goodrich, but at work she was outwardly calm and happy. I saw her two or three other times, lunching with women friends, and she always wore the serenity of a Melanie on her smooth fair brow.

She made a small face when I mentioned it.

"All of this," she said, "upsets my nature deeply. I like to see something build up. Tearing down a marriage—or anything—is not easy for me."

But the making of a picture like *My Cousin Rachel* was a help, Miss de Havilland said. Twice winner of Academy Awards for *The Heiress* and *To Each His Own*, the actress was nominated for her GWTW role, *Hold Back the Dawn,* and *The Snake Pit*. She also won the unanimous New York Critics' Award for *The Snake Pit*.

She had been away from the screen since 1948, living with her author-husband, Goodrich, in New England and winnowing mixed reviews by playing Shakespeare on the New York stage.

"And I'd rather be forgotten than come back in a poor picture," she said. *My Cousin Rachel,* she is convinced, is easily in a class with her other quality pictures and she was happily diverted by the twist of plot which leaves to the individual the decision on whether or not Rachel killed her husband, Ambrose Ashley.

"I know," she told me firmly. "Miss Du Maurier doesn't say in her story—and the script doesn't say. Philip Ashley (played by young British actor Richard Burton) thinks so, but he's in love with me and doesn't know. I'm trying to play the role so the audience will know—but I'll never tell!"

The handsome clothes she wears as the young—and probably deadly—widow in the film was a great boon to Miss de Havilland's morale.

"In time of trouble, something pretty to wear always helps," she assured me. She also found working with Richard Burton exciting—describing him as having "a frightening amount of talent."

"He has an immense ability," she said. "He is a violent, moody type—and I shudder to think how fast he's going to be hurtled to success when American audiences get a look at him."

Burton himself, blonde, 25 years old, and full of humor, is not at all frightened by the prospect of being successful. Married to British actress Sibyl Williams, he thinks it might be "really ghastly" to be the idol of too many women but might also further his hobby of "acquiring fast, powerful, low-slung cars, you know."

"The chief thing about acting in films is a kind of mounting frustration," Burton said. "I think I'll take off when this one's done. There's no possible point in my earning vast sums of money—except the fast, powerful, low-slung cars, you know. I can do without fast, powerful, low-slung women!"

Burton, graduate of five years of movie-making with Alexander Korda in England, was imported by 20th Century Fox to play the impetuous young Philip Ashley who suspects his uncle's widow of murdering him and then falls in love with her himself.

While working on *My Cousin Rachel,* Miss de Havilland lived in a hotel with her little boy. He had previously traveled with her during the road tour of *Romeo and Juliet* and she recommends that all actress mothers who can manage it take the youngsters along.

"I think a child is safe and secure as long as the people around him remain the same. Environment can change, but the people should be the same—steady and unchanged.

"Of course, I worry about being a working mother. All of us do. I love my child—and I can cause him unspeakable unhappiness by being the wrong kind of mother. I'm always conscious of that. But we'll make a good life together now . . . I'm sure."

The little boy goes to play school from 9 A.M. to 4 P.M. daily to give him association with other children. He often visits his mother at the studio and so far he has had her evenings free of other masculine attention.

As I left, she asked to be remembered by Atlanta and the friends she met here. She chuckled reminiscently over the picture of General Sherman at the Cyclorama which shows him as a disheveled, dissipated character instead of a trim fighting man—and neither of us mentioned that the last time she saw it she was on her honeymoon with Marcus Goodrich.

New Italian Beauty and Bogart <u>Beat the Devil</u>

February 26, 1954

Hollywood's reigning beauties have a crow to pick with John Huston.

An Italian crow.

The star-gazers tell us this is the season of the Italian movie actress. The dark-eyed damsels of Roberto Rosselini's homeland are being loudly hailed as queens of the foreign film market, an area which the local, or Hollywood, ladies would give them—and welcome.

Now comes Mr. Huston, the famous writer, director and producer, whose pictures always cop critical acclaim and/or Academy Awards, and puts an Italian beauty in his latest picture, *Beat the Devil*. Not only that, but the Italian girl is one whose physical structure is so highly regarded that she is said to have had her bosom insured for $50,000!

Where will this Italian trend lead?, asks Hollywood, What queens are to be deposed now?

John Huston, maker of *The Red Badge of Courage* and *The African Queen,* would be the last to care about the dethronement of Hollywood queens, but he is concerned that *Beat the Devil* be quality entertainment. And if a little beauty with the unpronounceable name of Lollobrigida contributes to that quality it suits him fine.

Gina Lollobrigida was no unknown when Huston cast her in his new picture, but she had never played an English-speaking role before. Huston, described by another star in the picture, Humphrey Bogart, as "a crazy, mixed-up genius," saw her and visualized her as Maria, wife of Bogart in a taut, adventure-thriller about uranium hunters. By happy coincidence he employed Miss Lollobrigida and shot the entire picture in her native Italy.

To uphold the prestige of the Hollywood girls, the movie has Miss Jennifer Jones playing a blonde for the first time in her career and a siren who entices Mr. Bogart away from Miss Lollobrigida, at least temporarily.

Actually *Beat the Devil* has a great many things with which to fulfill the Huston dream of topflight entertainment. Truman Capote collaborated with Huston on the script and Peter Lorre, Robert Morley, Edward Underdown and Ivor Barnard are present in the cast of fortune hunters and cut throats.

The story was a best-selling novel by James Helvick and involved the struggle of Bogart, the two women and a gang of bad men for Africa's richest uranium claim.

When I talked to Bogart in Hollywood he had recently worked with Huston in *The African Queen*.

"What a guy!" he muttered. "He's one for the outdoors, you know. All that tramping around forests and mountains when he could be sitting around 21!"

Bogart swore he was through following Huston to faraway places, but after the success of *The African Queen* brought the star an Oscar "to put on my liquor cabinet" he couldn't hold back when Huston picked Italy for *Beat the Devil*.

Aside from owning part of the Santana-Romulus company, which made the picture, there was the yen to work with Huston again.

"He had me in the beautiful Mediterranean—with all my clothes on," remarked Bogart. "He had me running up and down a cliff and riding around on a mule which was even more stubborn than Baby . . . my wife. But I'll say this for our Italian caper: it wasn't all bad. We had a motley crew that made for a few laughs, the cool Jennifer, the hot Gina, the staid Robert Morley. Since Santana happens to be my company I am mainly interested in the artistic success of the picture, you understand, not money."

More thoughtfully, Mr. Bogart advanced the theory that the best thing for him would be to get no money and no Oscars out of *Beat the Devil*. Then he'll be more cagey about following Huston off into the out-of-doors, he thinks.

As for the Italian star, Miss Lollobrigida, Hollywood has already seen her and beckoned. She is said to be slated for several other pictures, all of them American-made.

The Other Woman in Marilyn Monroe's Life

March 11, 1954

It was toward the end of a working day in Hollywood. Over on one of those big, draughty, dim sound stages at 20th Century-Fox studios, a bunch of us stood around watching Marilyn Monroe undress.

The first half-dozen times Miss Monroe flounced into a little tent and began to reach for her zipper and shake her shoulders and her tights-encased legs free of the mess of ruffles that passed for her dress, I was not there and can't say what the effect was on the watchers.

But by the time I had tiptoed in and found a seat on a stool back of the director everybody was beginning to be testy and tired. For one thing, Miss Monroe never quite got the dress off. She either hung a hook in her tights and had to stop for repairs or the zipper got caught or she paused and kissed Rory Calhoun at the wrong point in her lines.

All the difficulties were mysterious and incomprehensible to me. But the director Otto Preminger, thought they were important and he kept making them do the scene over. At one point he slapped his forehead and cried out in a tone of mock anguish: "When I was a painter I had a canvas, some paints, a landscape. And if I didn't like it I didn't paint it. No boss, no budget—just fresh air. Now what have I got? Thousands of dollars, big house, Cadillac . . . Marilyn Monroe! Isn't this mizzible?"

We all laughed but there was a crowy, exuberant quality in the crew's laughter. They knew that Marilyn Monroe was the greatest thing that had happened to their studio since the days of Will Rogers and Shirley Temple. And one person in the shadows back of the camera didn't laugh at all.

She stood there looking thoughtful and while lights were shifted and wardrobe people worked on the zipper, she went forward to talk to the star. I watched Marilyn Monroe's face and I was surprised at the intent, respectful way she listened and nodded as the plain, dark little woman with the thin face and graying hair talked.

"Who's that?" I whispered to my guide from the publicity office.

"Natasha Lytess," he said. "Marilyn's coach."

He didn't say more because a bell rang and they were ready to shoot the scene again but I watched and from then on I saw Marilyn Monroe was getting her signals from the plain middle-aged woman in the shadows.

Could it be true that the motion pictures' sex queen, like the beauteous Trilby of George du Maurier's story, had a Svengali? Could it be that a plain, smart woman whose plain, sensible dress molded no fabulous curves, whose dark, intelligent face was lined and tired and not in the least likely to provoke a wolf call anywhere . . . could it be this woman was the author of the Marilyn Monroe legend?

I believe now it is true. I believe that Natasha Lytess, who fled to this country from Germany when Hitler came into power, holds the key to Marilyn Monroe's fabulous success.

While they were shooting the rest of the scene from *River of No Return,* a thriller of the Great Northwest in 1875, in which Miss Monroe shares honors with Rory Calhoun and Robert Mitchum,

I talked with Miss Lytess. She doesn't take much credit for Marilyn's success, but some things are undeniable. They met six years ago when Marilyn was under contract at Columbia and Miss Lytess was coaching people like Jennifer Jones and Teresa Wright.

"Never have I met anyone with such an earnest desire to learn," said Miss Lytess. "I'll never forget the day she came to see me to break the news that her option had been dropped by Columbia. True, it's a wrenching moment for any young actress but not often have I seen a human so dispirited as Marilyn was. She tried to be brave but couldn't. I told her, 'You can be an actress if you work at it.'"

Marilyn was broke but Natasha Lytess continued to coach her. Some believe that she advanced Marilyn money and kept her plugging when the girl might have given up and drifted into other work or marriage. Marilyn insists that she always walked "that way," but the fact is she didn't. Lytess probably taught her. Certainly the open-mouthed look is Lytess' work and at least some of the throatiness of Marilyn's voice. (The first time I interviewed her I was amazed to find that she had the high childish voice of a 12-year-old.)

Lytess instilled in Marilyn a consuming passion for her work—a thing which even her critics don't deny she possesses. She tries to be an actress and has tried all along. The purchase of annotated books from the Max Reinhardt collection was no publicity stunt, although people laughed and laughed when they learned the books were printed in German.

Marilyn doesn't read German but it's Natasha Lytess' native tongue.

Anyhow, Marilyn went from obscurity to a bit in *Asphalt Jungle* and then headed swiftly for stardom—and Natasha Lytess has been right beside her all along. Her role isn't an easy one. As I observed, Marilyn looks to Lytess, not to her current director, for instruction. Directors are jealous of their authority and Lytess, being interested in Marilyn alone, always encourages the star to do what is best for her which may not be what is best for the picture as a whole.

"When I hear people talk of Marilyn merely on the basis of sex appeal, I wonder how they can be so wrong," Miss Lytess said. "Her soul doesn't belong to her body. Her beauty is deceptive. I know she has unusual gifts and great depths."

At that time Marilyn was just talking dreamily about Joe DiMaggio—"We visited his folks last weekend in San Francisco," she told me confidingly. She has since married him, been suspended by the studio and gone off to Japan on a honeymoon. It has been rumored that the bridegroom and Natasha Lytess do not get on too well together.

It is a three-cornered drama Hollywood is watching with more than passing interest.

Judy Garland Comes Back to the Movie Big Time

May 2, 1954

If I were Mrs. James Mason, I don't mind admitting my husband would make me nervous. He can become a drunkard too easily!

I saw it happen.

One moment the handsome British star was standing there in the sunlight on the Warner Brothers back lot looking bright-eyed and acute and very much like the gentleman who was selected as the best actor of 1953 by the National Board of Review of Motion Pictures.

The next moment, director George Cukor had said "Action," cameras were turning and Mr. Mason was in a delicately balanced state of inebriation. He was not falling down drunk (any clown can play that), he was smoothly, gracefully, ingratiatingly lit. He didn't stumble. He did nothing so obvious as to slur his words or talk with the lush's thick tongue. Swiftly, and yet subtly, he had put on the lopsided charm of a man who is drinking himself to death and thinks it's his personal secret.

The scene which Mason played was a very small one. He was a big-name movie star being visited on the set by the head of his studio (played by the handsome heavy of a decade of movies, Charles Bickford).

And yet that bit of action brought no smiles to the faces of the crew and the visitors like me who witnessed the lightning transformation. I think it may be that most of the people present recognized Mason's performance for what it was—the portrayal of The Hollywood Tragedy. He was playing the big star who was destroyed by drink.

Because of the poignancy of his role and his own highly skilled handling of it, James Mason may be the main interest in what started out to be Judy Garland's triumphant return to the movie Big Time. If Mason should overshadow the gusty little singer it would be very ironical because a remake of *A Star Is Born* has been a long-time dream of Judy Garland.

"I can't tell you how long I've wanted to play Esther Blodgett," she said. "You know the story's history. It was great when Janet Gaynor and Fredric March made in 1937 and I had an idea that if it were brought up to today—with songs and music—it would be just as wonderful. I wanted to do it even while I was at MGM . . . and then Sid . . ."

She paused and everybody laughed.

"Sid is a very tenacious fellow," someone remarked and Judy nodded her head sagely.

"He got the story and . . . we got married!"

Sid Luft is head of the producing company which is making *A Star Is Born* for Judy's return to the screen after more than a three-year absence. During that time, she had her personal troubles, culminating in a suicide attempt and then she had her triumphs including a fabulously successful personal-appearance tour of London and a comeback in vaudeville at the Palace.

Now she is playing Esther Blodgett, the little star-struck girl Janet Gaynor played so winningly in 1937. The first go-around, the picture came in with Academy Awards for the authors of the original story and six nominations, including those for best picture, best screenplay, best actor and best actress.

Dorothy Parker and her then-husband, Alan Campbell, collaborated on the screenplay for the first version and Moss Hart has rewritten the story to suit the particular talents of the singing Miss Garland. Ira Gershwin and Harold Arlen have turned out some songs which are hoped to pleasantly divert Miss Garland's following from their all-time favorite, "Somewhere Over the Rainbow." These include such titles as "The Man That Got Away," "Gotta Have Me Go With You," "Here's What I'm Here For," "Long Face" and two or three others.

In this version, Miss Garland is a singer with a band when she meets Mason, the big movie star. She befriends him at a benefit at the Shrine Auditorium, where he shows up drunk, and he insists upon launching her in the movies. Of course, sober and at work, he forgets where he left her and she has her troubles until he returns and gets Charles Bickford, playing the studio head, to hear her singing.

Their romance and marriage is as much the story as the grooming of a young girl for stardom. Esther Blodgett becomes Vicki
Lester and a star and her husband, Norman Maine, becomes less
and less of an actor and more and more of a drunk.

The picture is a true tragedy, ending in a way that a whole generation remembers feelingly, although a man's sacrifice of his life
for his wife's career might not strike people outside Hollywood
as valid or necessary heroism.

Jack Carson has an important role in *A Star Is Born,* playing
Matt Libby, the studio publicity director, who hates Maine and
unwittingly contributes to his downfall.

Judy Garland took a whole year to do *A Star Is Born.* Actual
shooting took only five months, but because of her feeling about
the picture, the personal opportunity it affords her as well as the
fact that she and her husband have a financial interest in it, she
spent seven months working out the songs and planning her role.

She is a tiny girl, much smaller than you'd expect from seeing
her on the screen, and according to Mary Ann Nyberg, who de-
signed her clothes, she has a figure that is close to perfect after
much dieting and exercise.

Chapter Five

In Court

Overleaf: Sibley and other members of the press at the John Wallace murder trial in Newnan, Ga., in 1948.

Jail—Wife's Tears—Tots with Measles: A Story of a Bogged-Down Love, and How It Flourishes Anew

May 27, 1948

From where the jaded attachés of Criminal Court of Fulton County were sitting, it was just another war-time romance that had bogged down in dreary domesticity. There was even a sameness about the details: weeping wife, wandering husband, two children at home with the measles, another due in September, not enough money for bills . . .

The clerk yawned, the judge said 12 months—and suddenly the romance which had flowered in war-time England between a pink-cheeked British nurse and a handsome, spoiled American GI became a living, flourishing force in the musty old courtroom!

Twenty-one-year-old Maureen Newby Veal, the British girl who had come to court to complain that her Georgia-born husband had abandoned her and his children, was unaccountably in his arms. Tears streamed down her face and she clung to him. He buried his face in her dark hair and swallowed hard.

The Sheriff moved forward to separate them, and then he seemed to be having trouble with something in his eye. He turned away and left them together. Bailiffs stared tactfully out the window. In the office, the judge was putting on his hat to go to lunch.

Suddenly the young wife straightened up and wiped her face. "I must speak to the judge," she said purposefully. "Please," she turned tear-drenched blue eyes on the Sheriff and her British voice was clear and controlled, "please, will you ask him if I may see him?"

The Sheriff asked, the judge took off his hat and the courageous little Britisher who once asked—and succeeded in getting—President Truman to intercede for her husband in a minor Army jam, marched into the judge's chambers.

That is how Ex-Sgt. Robert Veal, of 215 Georgia Ave., S.W., under 12-month sentence for abandonment of his minor children, happens to have the promise of Judge Jesse M. Wood that his case will be investigated and reconsidered within a few days.

And on that promise the two young people and all those who saw their parting at Fulton Tower are building a hope that this one war-time romance will prove stronger than the adversities besetting it.

"Jail!" wailed the young wife, "I cannot be the one to send him to jail! Oh, dear, I love him!"

"And I love her," a greatly chastened ex-GI muttered behind bars. "I was a fool. I told the judge I was thinking about going to Hollywood to develop my talent as a singer and he clapped this sentence on me before I could explain I wouldn't desert my family. I've got a pretty fair baritone voice, I reckon, but if I can just get back my job as a salesman . . ."

Pending final passage of sentence, the clerk has the Veal case filed under "vs. Star-Crossed Lovers, Et Al."

But Landlord Took a Dim View: Tenant Let a Little Sunshine In

June 8, 1948

They had a tearing good time at the home of Mr. and Mrs. Homer Hardigree "the night before the last big freeze."

That's when Joe Coggins, the Hardigree's tenant, allegedly started tearing the roof off the house.

The Hardigrees brought in such of the neighbors as had their lights on between midnight and 1 A.M. to witness the deroofing of their home and then they called the police.

"He'd been up there once before," explained buxom Mrs. Nora Hardigree, mother of six, "and I called the police. They told me if I seen him on it again to shoot him off like a rabbit."

But Mrs. Hardigree didn't shoot. She took out a warrant charging Coggins with malicious mischief—and that's what Judge Jesse Wood found him guilty of Monday. He will be sentenced today.

Coggins, a cab driver, protested he had been a law-abiding citizen and a renter in Atlanta for 34 years and he accused the Hardigrees of manufacturing the roofing episode in an organized effort to get him out and up the rent of his apartment from $8.50 to $30 a month.

"I was sweeping my front steps and he spit on my head and dropped a flower pot on me," declared Mrs. Hardigree, who lives at 225 Estoria St., S.E.

"She cut off the water in our apartment and we had to call the health authorities to get it back on," put in Coggins.

Court attachés seemed greatly relieved to hear that Coggins has bought a place of his own and is all set to move June 9. It's the fifth time he and the Hardigrees have been to court since "the night before the last big freeze," as Mr. Hardigree fixed a date, variously referred to by the others as March 5 to April 12.

The John Wallace murder trial would become one of the most celebrated cases of Sibley's career. The quirky case, a Midnight in the Garden of Good and Evil *of its time, concerned Wallace, a wealthy Georgia landowner accused of murdering one of his farm-hands, William Turner, and later burning the body. An eccentric fortune teller, Miss Mayhaley Lancaster, became the star of the trial. After her riveting testimony, Sibley took off after Lancaster for an interview. The trial resulted in a trip to the electric chair for Wallace and later served as the source material for author Margaret Ann Barnes'* Murder in Coweta County *and a TV film starring Johnny Cash, June Carter and Andy Griffith. Predictably, Sibley said she favored the book over the television production.*

Seer Says Wallace Threatened to Kill Turner: 'Body in Well, I Told Him'

June 15, 1948

Newnan, June 14—An aging countrywoman with one good eye, a flower-bedecked beanie that kept skidding down over her left ear and the firm conviction that she is "the oracle of the age" bogged down in a morass of mysticism the murder trial of John Wallace here today.

The seer, Miss Mayhayley Lancaster, Heard County's well-patronized teller of fortunes and reader of signs, gaunt, rheumy-eyed was an opening-day sensation as the widely followed "burned bones" murder case began a probable week-long run before Superior Judge Samuel J. Boykin and a 12-man jury.

She told John Wallace where to find the cows (the registered stock allegedly stolen by William H. Turner alias Wilson H. Turner alias Wilson Turner, the slaying victim). She heard Wallace threaten to track Turner down and kill him "agin all laws of the land," and then in a third séance with the balding, bull-necked Meriwether farmer, she prophesied the hiding place of Turner's body and its condition.

That is what Miss Lancaster, with an air of modesty and frequent tugs at her skidding bonnet, told a predominantly farmer jury shortly before the recess.

"John Wallace came to see me three times," testified Miss

Lancaster. "He told me he had lost two cows valued at $3,200 and he wanted me to tell him where he could find them—one a milker and one dry. I told him in a pasture where they were carried in a truck, and he informed me he was going to Carroll County that night, and if he found the cows and Turner he was going to kill him. I said, 'Don't say that. That is a violation of the law.'"

Later Wallace returned and wanted to know something about finding "a dead body somewhere named Turner and wanted to know if the body would ever be found," Miss Lancaster testified. Fixing her good eye on the jury she gave them a graphic account of her reply. "I told him it was in a well with green flies around it."

A.L. Henson, Atlanta attorney and co-counsel for Wallace, tried to pin Miss Lancaster down on the source of her information and its accuracy. She drew herself up haughtily and declared, "We were born this way. We were born not like schoolteachers. Through the inspiration of the all-wise God it came to me."

"The all-wise God has not dispensed that information to very many of us," commented Henson dryly.

The Court interrupted in a spirited give-and-take between the lawyer and witness on whether or not she was wiser than the officers of the Court but not before Henson asked Miss Lancaster if she could "focus your information-finder" and foretell his future.

"You may get what Turner got," the mystic prophesied darkly.

Moving with unprecedented speed for a murder trial expected to last a week or 10 days, attorneys agreed within 45 minutes on a jury which included eight farmers, and the prosecution rapidly began marshaling witnesses against the shining-pated Wallace.

By midafternoon a procession of half a dozen witnesses, led by slender, 23-year-year-old Julia Windom Turner, widow of the slain man, had passed before the jury and Superior Court Judge Samuel J. Boykin to testify:

1. That Wallace and Turner were "in the whiskey business together."

2. That Turner was in mortal fear of Wallace and "being ganged up on" in Meriwether County.

3. That Wallace had Turner arrested in Carrollton for theft of a cow and brought Sheriff Hardy Collier from Meriwether County to remove him to Greenville jail at 3 A.M. without a warrant.

4. That a car driven by Herring Sivell and a car driven by Henry Mobley were seen chasing a pickup truck driven by Turner on the highway near the Sunset Tourist Camp the day of Turner's disappearance.

Wallace definitely planned to kill Turner and would have killed him "on one occasion where he met him in the road but Turner's wife was along and she looked so pitiful he couldn't go through with it," Earl Lucas, investigator for the Alcohol Tax Unit in Atlanta, told the jury. He testified that he went to Meriwether County on a call which came from Gus Huddleston, Wallace's attorney, to "break up the whiskey business on Wallace's place."

Under cross-examination by A.L. Henson of Atlanta, also counsel for Wallace, Lucas stoutly maintained that he did not know whether Wallace was making the whiskey or Turner was making the whiskey. He said since Wallace's arrest Internal Revenue agents have brought charges of conspiracy against him.

Mrs. Turner, coming into the courtroom late and unaccompanied, testified briefly to the effect that Wilson Turner and William H. Turner were the same man, her husband.

Among other witnesses at the afternoon session was E.R.

Threadgill, Chief of Police of the City of Carrollton, who testified he arrested Turner for the theft of Wallace's cow and subsequently turned him over to Sheriff Collier with the understanding that Collier had a warrant for his arrest. Chief Threadgill said
he gave a verbal release over the phone in a conversation with
Wallace at 3 A.M. but had never seen the warrant.

Archie Hodgins, an itinerant cotton mill worker who happened
to be in Carroll County jail at the time of Turner's arrest, testified he heard Turner beg not to take him back to Meriwether
County because "they would gang up on him and kill him there."

Killed Turner in Next County—Wallace

June 18, 1948

Newnan, June 17—John Wallace told a Coweta County jury this
afternoon that he "accidentally shot" William H. (alias Wilson)
Turner while trying to "bluff him into telling me where my stolen cows were."

In a dramatic climax to six and a half hours of almost unbroken testimony, Wallace said Turner suffered only a cut ear at the
Coweta County tourist camp where the State alleged he was
killed.

Death came some time later, Wallace told the jury, when he
took Turner to the scene of Turner's alleged cow-stealing crime
in an effort to get a confession from him. Wallace said only his
uncle, Tom Strickland witnessed the shooting and he completely
exonerated Herring Sivell and Henry Mobley.

Wallace said he stood five feet from Turner beside an old well
in the cow pasture when "I heard somebody holler down by my
right . . . I turned my head in the direction of the hollering and
transferred the shotgun from my right hand and laid it in the bend

of my left arm. At that instant, the gun fired. I didn't see Turner when it fired. I didn't see his face. I had no control over the gun. It blew off the top of his scalp, and when I looked, the man was lying full length with the top of his scalp torn off."

Wallace made it clear that the shooting occurred on the farm of the Chattahoochee Valley Lumber Company in Meriwether County. He said he changed Turner from Sivell's car when Sivell had a flat tire en route from the Sunset Tourist Camp.

Turner, Wallace said, was fully conscious, got out of Sivell's car "under his own steam and sat down in the foot of Henry Mobley's car at my instruction."

On the way to the well side where the shooting occurred, Turner smoked two cigarettes and chatted about the way the dust sifted in through the fittings around the doors of the new cars, Wallace said. He said they left Sivell with his car and the flat tire, and when they reached the old farm, he told Mobley to "go on home."

"Mobley never left his car, never placed his hand on Turner that day," Wallace said.

Tom Strickland and Turner got out of the car with him, Wallace said, and followed him off into the woods.

"I led the way," he said. "I didn't know where I was going or what developments were coming up." He said he took Turner back to the scene where his first cows were stolen "with the same idea in mind that Sheriff A. Lamar Potts, of Coweta County, had when he took Sivell back home to get a confession from him.

"He had a prisoner and he wanted a confession from him," Wallace said. "I had a prisoner and I wanted a confession from him."

Wallace did not mention the disposal of the body, but made a final plea to the jury to believe in the truth of his statement and to allow him to go back home to his family.

GBI Agent J.P. Hillian, who headed the investigation of the Turner murder, said Wallace's dramatic confession would make no difference in the State's case against him. He said the prosecution undoubtedly would proceed with its final arguments tomorrow as planned and "leave it up to the jury to give its verdict."

If the jury should believe Wallace's story of death occurring in Meriwether County, it could either find him "not guilty," in which case Wallace could not be tried again anywhere on the same charge, or it could declare a mistrial.

If the jury's deliberations result in a mistrial, it is understood Wallace could be retried in Coweta County or in Meriwether County, depending upon the jury's recommendation.

Spl. Prosecutor Meyer Goldberg said the State was prepared to put five or six rebuttal witnesses on the stand tomorrow in an effort to disprove "some of the details of Wallace's testimony."

Earlier in the day, Wallace had urged the jury to believe in all of his testimony, but added "if you find I am not telling you the truth in one thing, I don't ask you to believe anything I am telling you."

Indications are the State will re-introduce Dr. Herman Jones, Chief Rader Threadgill of the Carrollton City Police and Sheriff Potts.

The case is expected to reach the jury today. Although defense attorneys did not formally rest the case this afternoon, they indicated Wallace would be their only witness.

In his seven-hour statement, Wallace quoted Turner as telling him, "Put me in the well and let me stay three or four hours, and then I'll move back to your place and work for you."

Wallace said he did not know why Turner said that, he had not even thought about putting Turner in the well.

"I just looked at the well and looked at Turner," he said.

In the longest statement ever made by a defendant in the

Coweta Circuit in 56 years, Wallace made an impassioned plea to the jury to understand his position as a hard-working farmer, who, he said, struggled for two years against Turner's houndings "as a lawbreaker and cattle thief."

"I'm not afraid to die," cried Wallace, striking the witness box with his doubled fist.

"If it means my death to tell the truth, I'll die telling you the truth. I didn't intend to kill Wilson Turner. I'm an average church-going man and I love my God like you love your God. Your God is my God. I'm not a cold-blooded headhunter."

After talking five and a half hours, the hoarse, perspiring man had traced his entire acquaintance with the slain Turner and reached a point where he and three neighbors, Tom Strickland, Herring Sivell and Henry Mobley had set out for Meriwether County jail to see Turner.

Wallace said: "I wanted to talk to Turner, but I didn't mean to talk to him in jail. It wasn't the first time a man was taken out and talked to.

"I had a shotgun in that car. I'm not going to lie to you gentlemen. I didn't take that gun to kill anybody with. I had no idea of killing anybody. I didn't leave my home with murder in my heart."

Wallace's testimony, delivered calmly and with dramatic pauses for emphasis, was expected to be his only defense. Last-minute refusal of Herring Sivell and Henry Mobley to take the stand "left me here a stranger in a strange land with nobody to help me, but God's help in telling you gentlemen the truth," Wallace said.

Wallace's attorneys said they did not know until five minutes before they began the presentation of their case today that Sivell and Mobley would not testify in the trial. Pierre Howard, attorney for the other two defendants, announced to the court he had advised them of their constitutional right to refuse to give any testimony that would incriminate themselves. Gus Huddleston, of Greenville, attorney for Wallace, insisted that Mobley say himself whether or not he wanted to testify.

"I can't talk without incriminating myself," Mobley said, and was allowed to leave the courtroom. Huddleston accepted their attorney's word that Sivell would say the same thing.

Wallace Given July 30 Death Chair Sentence

June 19, 1948

Newnan, June 18—John Wallace, prominent Meriwether County farmer, today was found guilty of murder in the "burned bones" slaying of William H. (alias Wilson) Turner and sentenced to die in the electric chair July 30.

A Coweta County jury arrived at a verdict of guilty at 5:10 P.M. after deliberating an hour and 10 minutes and listening to testimony and arguments five days. Judge Samuel J. Boykin of Carrollton, passed sentence immediately.

Coatless, wearing rumpled gabardine trousers and a shirt, Wallace stood before the bench between his attorneys to hear the death sentence. Judge Boykin asked if he had anything to say and Wallace turned to Gus Huddleston, a member of his counsel from Greenville, and whispered: "Should I say anything!"

Huddleston shook his head and Judge Boykin passed sentence. Later Huddleston reiterated his intention of filing a motion for a new trial. Other defendants indicted jointly with Wallace for the April 20 slaying of Turner will go to trial at 10 A.M. Monday. They include Herring Sivell, Tom Strickland, Wallace's cousin, Henry Mobley and two Negroes who testified against Wallace, Robert Lee Cates and Albert Brooks.

Although the courtroom was crowded, a dead silence greeted the reading of the verdict. Judge Boykin had previously warned against demonstrations of any kind but even after he left the bench the crowds surged sluggishly and without any apparent emotion around the rail. Wallace sat quietly for a moment, talking with his attorneys and chewing gum.

Asked if he had any statement to make, "Not just now. This is a serious time. Maybe later."

As he was leaving the courtroom, a little, gray-haired woman tugged at his coat sleeve and said, "If there's anything we can do John. . . ." He smiled at her and said, "Thank you, I'll let you know."

Since Wallace in his talking marathon of more than six hours of Thursday completely exonerated the other defendants in the case, Coweta County citizens are speculating as to whether the three white men will go to trial on murder charges or be allowed to enter pleas of guilty to lesser offenses. Wallace admitted shooting Turner "accidentally" at an old abandoned well the afternoon of April 20, after a more than five-hour build-up in which he emphasized his fear that Turner would "get me in trouble with his whiskey-making" and charged the young man with "stealing my cows and threatening my security."

Wallace emphatically denied that Turner died from blows received about the head at a Coweta tourist camp and he did not touch upon the grisly details of the recovery of Turner's body from a well and cremation on a pyre in the swamp.

"My mind went blank," Wallace said.

Courthouse attachés confidently expected Wallace's attorneys to seek a change of venue on the ground that Turner was slain in Meriwether County and Judge Boykin instructed the jury to decide that issue first. Venue, he said, was a "material allegation" in the indictment and unless that was proven it was the jury's duty to acquit. The court's charge left only three verdicts open to the jury: guilty, guilty with a recommendation for mercy, or not guilty.

Huddleston, who with A.L. Henson of Atlanta, served as leading counsel for Wallace, described the case as "attracting more attention in this State than any trial since the Leo Frank case." Henson accused the State of making the trial a "Hollywood scenario come to life" and attacked both expert testimony and the testimony of eye witnesses, who, he said, had prejudice "popping out on them like fleas on a dog."

Sol. Gen. Luther M. Wyatt bolstered the State's contention that Turner was actually killed in Coweta County with the testimony of rebuttal witnesses who said there was no evidence of blood or brain tissue on the ground around the old well and the position of the body in the well indicated it had been dead for some time before it was placed in there. Special Prosecutor Meyer Goldberg asked for the death penalty. Turning to Wallace, he thundered, "If you want to keep your trial in your county, Wallace, you keep your devilment, you keep your murder in your county."

Miss Mayhayley Got There First: Sorcery or Science—Coweta Asks Which Solved Slaying of Turner

June 21, 1948

Newnan, June 20—Did sorcery or science solve the fantastic slaying of William H. (alias Wilson) Turner?

Were microscopes or magic the more efficacious in bringing to trial the man who later confessed to the slaying?

Which was of the most value in convicting John Wallace—the

university-bred wisdom of Dr. Herman D. Jones or the "in-born" witchcraft of Mayhayley Lancaster?

The truth may never be known but as far as many citizens of Coweta County are concerned, this much is irrefutable:

"Miss Mayhayley" got there first!

The old lady of the strangely musical name, the outlandish appearance and the unusual background, was in the Turner case telling John Wallace where his cows were, visualizing the body of the murder victim—first "in a grave with green flies around it" and then "taking a trip on horseback"—long before there was evidence available to submit to Dr. Jones, the toxicologist. It was she who assured Wallace the body would be found, according to testimony in the case. And it was after a visit to her house that Wallace, according to the same testimony, moved and burned Turner's body.

"I see," said Miss Mayhayley peering with her one good eye at the handful of cards spread before her on a piano stool in the windowless gloom of her sister's cabin. "I see either life or the electric chair for John Wallace."

Her friends remembered "Miss Mayhayley's" prophesy Friday afternoon when Wallace walked out of the courtroom under death sentence.

In the trial Miss Mayhayley had thought A.L. Hanson, one of Wallace's lawyers was "guying" her about her artificial eye when he asked her how she "saw" her wonders.

"Some folks have got eyes to see," she snapped, "and other folks are like crawfish—with their eyes in their tail!"

Miss Mayhayley is the favorite legend of citizens of this part of Georgia. She lives, as she explained in court, "ten miles measured" from Franklin in a tumble-down house beside a well-worn clay road. She and her sister, "Miss Sally" Hull, cultivate a few acres in corn and cotton, plowing with their own oxen and mule, but allow most of their estimated 1,000 acres to lie fallow.

"We can't farm like we used to before Mayhayley got so busy giving readings," remarked "Miss Sally" in her high, sweet voice, gently shooing a passel of little biddies from under Mayhayley's long skirts and back into the kitchen. "Young married folks are the worst. They come to Mayhayley more'n anybody."

Miss Mayhayley, busy scribbling little notes on minute scraps of paper, cackled happily, "Fifteen, you all make, today. There's six waiting under the tree in the yard—and then them people from Heflin, Ala., in the car."

Heard County's famed soothsayer was born on the farm her English parents homesteaded "no telling how many years ago." The hand-hewn log part of the house is believed to have been built in 1830. The newer part, including a porch and several rooms, is now falling down. Miss Mayhayley has thriftily patched the roof with swatches of worn-out linoleum and bricks until it will take no more and now even she has abandoned it.

At night they lock up the chickens in the kitchen, make fast the shutters and the doors and take their five assorted dogs up the road to the home of some cousins. "The law won't let us sleep here—for fear of our lives," explained Miss Mayhayley. "Robbers came and robbed us of $3,000—and nary a trace of it has been found. We daren't sleep here!"

Although Miss Mayhayley is renowned as a finder of lost articles for her customers she has difficulty keeping up with her own property, including the stolen $3,000.

But her customers swear she is sure-fire in turning up their property. She not only can tell you the name of the man who picked up your lost pocketbook, but what he did with the money in it and when, if ever, you'll see it again. That's what they say about Mayhayley Lancaster—and she modestly admits it.

"It's not a learned gift," she says, "it's a borned gift. I've got some learning—I taught school. I passed the bar in Carroll County and could practice law. But seeing the future is my art."

At least one man left without even hearing his fortune, according to local legend. Miss Mayhayley stubbornly refused to tell him anything about his future. He was killed on the way home in an automobile accident.

Judge Samuel J. Boykin, the Wallace trial judge, remembered Miss Mayhayley and greeted her with a nod and a smile. Years ago in Carrollton it was his unpleasant legal duty to sell a piano at a foreclosure sale. The seer of Heard County bought it and asked to be allowed until 2 P.M. to pay for it.

Knowing her reputation for great wealth, Barrister Boykin granted her the time. A few minutes later he saw her busy in the commissioner's meeting room telling fortunes. By noon she was over at the jail in the sheriff's parlor telling fortunes.

At 2 P.M. she was back at the Courthouse with $199 in crumpled $1, $2 and $5 bills—ready to claim her piano. She had made it all that day.

As Miss Mayhayley's house disintegrates, her fame, given fresh publicity with the Wallace trial, is growing and her clientele is growing. Defense attorneys made many humorous cracks about the presence of a soothsayer and witch doctor as a prosecution witness but Sol. Gen. Luther Wyatt closed the subject effectively.

"Call her a soothsayer," he said before the jury. "Call her anything you like. But her testimony went into the record, undenied by anybody."

South Fulton Wife Is Judged Insane
after Charge of 'Extreme Filth' in Home

April 26, 1949

A South Fulton County husband, who was accused of keeping his mentally ill wife a virtual prisoner in an isolated shack three miles south of Adamsville in conditions of extreme filth, yesterday offered to put his care of her up against the kind provided the insane at Milledgeville State Hospital.

He was overruled by a three-man sanity commission, who held 29-year-old Mrs. Vivian Gray to be of unsound mind and ordered her committed to the State institution.

"When this case is threshed out before God they'll come to me for advice on the care of mental cases!" cried Henry Gray, State Highway Department employee.

Gray, through his attorney, A.L. Henson, introduced everything from her sewing to her poetry to prove his wife was improving under care, which police officers testified, was so bad they removed the 300-odd-pound Mrs. Gray to Grady Hospital on complaint of neighbors and formal petition of her mother, Mrs. Irene Withers.

A notebook containing scores of her verses was placed in the hands of her physician, Dr. C.H. Paine, who was put on the stand as Gray's witness. Counsel asked the middle-aged, graying physician to read aloud two poems which, Henson contended, reflected the "natural attitude of an affectionate, home-loving wife."

Soberly, the physician took the book, cleared his throat and began: "Gitchie, gitchie, gitchie goo to you . . ."

He hesitated.

"Go on," directed Henson.

"Read it aloud?" asked Dr. Paine.

"Please," said Henson.

The doctor resumed: "Just a cutey ootie, ootie oo, it's you, Wancha pitcha little itty bitty woo tonight, baby, with me."

Red to the roots of his hair, a few verses later, Dr. Paine closed the book without comment.

"Now, doctor," said Henson, "if you and I went back about 40 years, wouldn't you say that would be a normal expression of a woman in love with her husband?"

"No," said Dr. Paine. "Not to me, it wouldn't!"

"Well, I said, 'going back 40 years,'" Henson said and hastily removed his witness from the stand.

Witnesses placed on the stand by Russell Turner, attorney for Mrs. Withers, the ill woman's mother, testified Mrs. Gray had spent eight months in the Milledgeville State Hospital and had once attempted to commit suicide while home on leave from the institution. Police officers told of going through a window to reach Mrs. Gray April 4, when she allegedly was locked in the house and left alone by her husband. They told of finding scraps of bread and filth on the floor and no cooking or sanitary facilities. Fulton Detectives C.L. Hughes, M.H. Williams, Capt. J.D. Ragsdale and Lt. J.W. Gilbert; Dr. R.W. McGee, County physician; Mrs. Gray's mother and her brother Oscar Withers were principal witnesses against Gray.

Gray, who took the stand to plead for the return of his wife, exhibited a suitcase full of clothing which he said she made and broke down when attorneys asked him if he considered his wife was improving under his care.

"If I weren't sure of that, before God I wouldn't be fighting this thing!" he said chokily.

Atty. Henson said he would appeal the Commission's decision to Superior Court within four days.

The trial of Judge Robert Carpenter didn't become a national
sensation like the Coweta County case and is largely forgotten today.
In 1949, however, Atlantans hung on every word as the sordid details
emerged in testimony.

"It wasn't a murder case but it had everything Celestine loved in a
trial," former Newsweek *Atlanta bureau chief William A. Emerson*
Jr. recalls. "Anytime you have a judge chasing down a lawyer on
Peachtree Street in his bed clothes in the middle of the night while
firing shots at him over a woman, you're due for a hair-raising
trial."

Carpenter was later acquitted.

Carpenter Said Unfaithful, Gambler, by Lockwood at Opening of Shooting Trial

September 14, 1949

The story of alleged fast living and extra-marital loves of a Fulton
County jurist, as related by the man he is accused of shooting,
became the property of a standing-room-only crowd of avid spectators in Superior Court yesterday as Judge Robert Carpenter
went to trial charged with assault with intent to murder.

John Lockwood, the judge's victim in a predawn shooting on
Peachtree Street July 27, testified Judge Carpenter drank, gambled,
announced he wanted to get rid of his wife so he could "have all
the women he wanted" and was caught in a New York hotel with
one woman who "didn't have on anything but a blanket."

Judge Carpenter's counsel retaliated by asking penetrating
questions about Lockwood's trip to Florida with Mrs. Carpenter,
his registry at tourist camps with her and a visit to her home in
the early hours of the morning.

Judge Virlyn B. Moore, presiding at the trial, which opened shortly before noon yesterday, frequently had to rap for order and at one point he ordered the Sheriff to arrest immediately any spectator caught laughing.

That point came after a heated exchange between Defense Atty. Ellis Barrett and the witness Lockwood.

"Isn't it a fact that you have made life impossible for this child, Barbara?" demanded Barrett, pointing to Mrs. Carpenter's daughter, who sat beside her foster father, Judge Carpenter.

Sol. Gen. Paul Webb, who is conducting the prosecution assisted by Special Prosecutor Elbert Tuttle and Asst. Sol. Ogden Doremus, objected to the question and Judge Moore sustained the objection.

"Well, I'll put it this way," said Barrett. "Isn't it true that you went out to Mrs. Carpenter's home at 1:30 A.M. and Mrs. Carpenter was drinking heavily and you ran this child out of her mother's bedroom?"

"No," said Lockwood. "It's not true."

"Then what time did you go there?" demanded Barrett.

"Twelve-thirty," replied Lockwood.

Laughter swept the courtroom and Judge Moore warned spectators he would sentence them to "sit in the detention cell awhile" if they were found guilty of contempt of court. Frequently during the progress of the trial the judge himself complained that attorneys were wandering afield from the Peachtree Street shooting.

"We're trying to try something about a shooting out here," Judge Moore said. "Now we're getting 'way down there in Florida."

Subsequently, Lockwood explained that he went to Mrs. Carpenter's apartment at the request of her mother and found her in bed suffering from a overdose of heart tonic. He said he went "as her attorney" and stayed only 15 minutes during which time both Mrs. Minnie Sullivan, Mrs. Carpenter's mother, and Barbara, were in and out of the room.

Attorney Barrett told the court he had not planned to call Barbara as a witness but had changed his mind and asked to be permitted to send her to the witness room.

Asst. Sol. Ogden Doremus, making the prosecution's opening statement to the jury, said the State would prove that Judge Carpenter's financial obligations to Lockwood were at least a part of his motive in the alleged attempt to murder. He said the State would prove that Judge Carpenter stalked Lockwood and his wife, Mrs. Helen Carpenter, while they, in turn, were attempting to catch the Judge and Mrs. Estelle Manful together in a cabin at Bishop's Lake.

Doremus said the State would not attempt to try the domestic relations court case of the Carpenters or the Lockwoods but he said he would prove Carpenter "laid in wait for a woman that he had forsaken for another woman" with the "premeditated design of shooting a defenseless person."

On direct examination by Atty. Elbert Tuttle, special prosecutor working with Webb and Doremus, Lockwood testified lengthily about his financial arrangements with Carpenter. He said he lent the Judge $30,000, which was subsequently repaid him at seven percent interest, and later sums of $3,000 on three occasions and $6,000 on one occasion.

He said he did some tax work for Carpenter and offered to write off the $6,700 which the Judge owed him for that if Carpenter would get Mrs. Manful out of the Imperial Hotel.

Relating what defense attorneys derisively labeled a "fatherly talk," Lockwood said he told Carpenter: "Bob, I understand you're having trouble with your wife. Is there anything I can do to help?" He said the judge told him part of his trouble was financial, and he offered to cancel Carpenter's tax work indebtedness to him "if you will get rid of that woman upstairs." He said Carpenter promised to have Mrs. Manful out of the Imperial Hotel by the following Saturday but failed to do so.

The witness said he heard that Judge Carpenter had threatened to break his neck if he did not stop interfering with his affair with Mrs. Manful and when he faced Carpenter with the rumors, Lockwood said Carpenter "put his hand on my back and said, 'John, if I said that to anybody but you, I must have been stupidly drunk.'"

Lockwood said he replied, "Well, you're stupidly drunk too often."

Defense attorneys maintained that Lockwood acted for Mrs. Carpenter while retained to represent the judge. Lockwood said from the first he told Judge Carpenter, "If this is going to be a court case, I'm representing your wife."

He admitted, however, that Judge Carpenter gave him a power-of-attorney with a line blank, the name to be filled in another state where Lockwood said, the judge wanted his wife to get a divorce without publicity.

The witness said he accompanied Mrs. Carpenter and her mother to Florida to see if a divorce could be legally obtained there and they stayed in a tourist court where reservations had been made for them by Juddie Johnson, manager of the Copa Caprice night club in the Imperial Hotel.

He denied that he and Mrs. Carpenter occupied the same room or were caught drinking together or wandering around the grounds holding hands.

"Didn't Mr. Bishop (proprietor of the tourist court) come and catch you and Mrs. Carpenter in a room together?" asked Barrett.

"No," cried Lockwood, "and I'd like to tell you what I think of that question!"

In answer to questions about his drinking with Mrs. Carpenter, Lockwood answered, "How would I know whether I had a drink or not, unless I kept a diary?"

Asked if he had ever spent the night with Mrs. Carpenter at any tourist court, Lockwood replied, "No, never. Mrs. Carpenter is a very decent woman!"

"That's a conclusion, your honor!" cried Defense Atty. William Boyd, leaping to his feet.

Lockwood was the only witness interrogated during the day. He will resume the stand at 9:30 A.M. today for further cross-examination and rebuttal questions.

Judge Moore expressed hope the trial would be terminated by tomorrow at the latest. At the opening of the trial Judge Moore ordered all spectators to check their firearms, if any, with the clerk. He invoked an old English law, requiring even officers of the court to leave their guns outside the courtroom.

A rifle and three pistols, taken from Lockwood and his sons on subpoenas duces tecum, were turned over to the clerk for safekeeping, along with permits and other documentary evidence which is expected to be introduced by defense attorneys later.

Lockwood, talking quietly, but frequently in a belligerent tone, when answering a question put to him under cross-examination said he and Mrs. Carpenter had spent the evening before he was shot driving out the Marietta highway. He said Mrs. Carpenter was ill and asked him to get her some whiskey and later they ate and then spent "about three hours" parked by a side road, waiting to see Carpenter and Mrs. Manful drive by.

He said the shooting had resulted in the loss of the sight of one of his eyes and left him suffering back and neck injuries.

Mrs. Carpenter did not appear in court. Sol. Gen. Webb answered for her when she was called and pointed out that she could not be required to testify against her husband, under Georgia law.

Carpenter Questions Witness in Own Defense; Will Take Stand Today

September 16, 1949

Judge Robert Carpenter, holding a four-leaf clover between his fingers as a talisman for luck, boldly took the lead in his own defense yesterday as his trial for assault with intent to murder moved swiftly toward a climax in Fulton Superior Court.

Rising from his place at the defense table, the handsome 44-year-old jurist set what amounts to a precedent in Superior Court by examining a witness himself.

Today, he and his adopted stepdaughter, Barbara, are expected to be the final and most eagerly awaited witnesses in the trial, which has packed lunch-toting, sensation-hungry spectators into Judge Virlyn B. Moore's courtroom for three days.

Glenn Loudermilk, vice-president and general manager of the Imperial Hotel, formerly employed by Carpenter and brought to the court as a prosecution witness but not called, was the witness Judge Carpenter elected to interrogate.

Atty. Ellis Barrett announced that the defendant would like to examine Loudermilk himself because of the complicated nature of financial testimony he might give. Judge Moore said the request was unusual but all right, adding, "He's a member of the bar. He has a right to represent himself."

Carpenter questioned Loudermilk carefully about his association with Lockwood, bringing out that the witness was Lockwood's partner in the Imperial Operating Company, that he was indebted to Lockwood financially and that he had been summoned to court by the prosecution.

Then he moved on to details of his wife's alleged relationship with John Lockwood. Only once did he falter and that was when Loudermilk testified he remembered hearing Lockwood ask Mrs. Carpenter if she was willing to "go back to the Judge and try again."

Leaning against the rail to the jury box, Carpenter looked down at a small calendar containing a pressed four-leaf clover, which he had taken out of his pocket to check a date, and then he said slowly: "What . . . was her reply?"

"She said she was not willing," Loudermilk replied.

Carpenter flung his head back and lit into Loudermilk with questions which drew the following testimony:

1. Mrs. Carpenter was not employed at the hotel and was there in no official capacity beyond "writing some letters for us."

2. That she drew no salary but occupied up to five rooms at the hotel and has thus far not been billed for them.

3. That Lockwood was with her when she selected the rooms she would occupy on the fifth floor. (The prosecution subsequently brought out that when Mrs. Carpenter moved to the hotel, Lockwood had moved out of his fifth-floor room.)

4. That Lockwood and Mrs. Carpenter sometimes drank together in the office and that he had seen them enter the elevator together.

5. That Mrs. Carpenter and Lockwood frequently left the hotel together and Loudermilk sometimes drove for them.

"When you drive for them, do they sit in the front seat or the back?" demanded Carpenter.

"Sometimes they sit in the front, sometimes in the back," Loudermilk replied.

"What's the reason they can't sit with you in the front seat?" demanded Carpenter.

"I don't know," said Loudermilk, "unless there's more room in the back."

Loudermilk also testified that Lockwood made threats to him against Judge Carpenter, telling him on one occasion to get Andy George to warn Judge Carpenter that Lockwood would shoot him "if he ever saw him coming in the door."

On cross-examination, Loudermilk said he had seen Judge Carpenter in the room of glamorous Mrs. Estelle Manful "two or three times" but added that he was there himself and "others were present."

"The time you were there did you see anything improper?" asked Judge Carpenter getting to his feet again.

"No sir," said Loudermilk.

Andy George, who preceded Loudermilk on the stand, testified that he went with Mrs. Manful himself and added a new sensation to the day's startling testimony by declaring: "Mrs. Manful told me she had to move from the hotel because Mr. Lockwood kept annoying her and trying to come up to her room."

George also repeated threats which he said Lockwood made against Carpenter. He said he was in front of the Imperial Hotel, preparing to go out to eat with Loudermilk, and Lockwood came out and announced that he had given Carpenter "one hour to bring the paper he stole but the yellow [   ] won't come because he knows I'll kill him."

"Did you convey that message to Judge Carpenter?" asked Barrett.

"In about two seconds," George testified.

He said Lockwood had also told him, "Bob Carpenter was ruining his life and he was going to kill him." George said he "talked to Helen (Mrs. Carpenter) and asked her if she wouldn't go back to Bob and she said Bob wanted to be single so long she was going to make him single."

He said she added when Carpenter did become single "he was going to be drug through the mud so deep."

R.C. Bishop, South Jacksonville tourist camp operator, testified that Mrs. Carpenter and Lockwood were sent to his place in May by "my former uncle," Juddie Johnson, ex-Atlanta night club operator. He demonstrated to the jury how the couple allegedly walked about the ground of his place with their arms around each other and testified that they asked him to "fix" his registration book to show that Mrs. Carpenter had been there 90 days previously.

He testified they attempted to reserve the same adjoining cabins for other weekends but his testimony that he refused to make a reservation "because I didn't want people like that at my place" was stricken from the record as inadmissible.

Bishop said Lockwood and Mrs. Carpenter were referred to him by Juddie Johnson, former operator of the Copa Caprice in the Imperial Hotel. He said they were accompanied to Jacksonville by Mrs. Minnie Sullivan, Mrs. Carpenter's mother, but he denied that he saw Mrs. Sullivan with them after they had registered and moved into connecting cabins in the rear of his court.

Testifying that they invited him to come to their cabin for a talk, Bishop said he walked to the cabin about an hour later, found the door ajar and went in to find "Mrs. Carpenter flaying across the bed and Mr. Lockwood rising from where he was sitting on the bed."

He said there were "a couple or three" quarts of whiskey on the dresser. He said Mrs. Carpenter's skirt was wrinkled and her hair was tangled and she excused herself and went in to the adjoining room. He said he told Lockwood the doors between the cabins could be locked but Lockwood instructed him to leave them open.

"Mr. Lockwood asked me if I could rearrange my books so Mrs. Carpenter could establish a residence to get a divorce," the witness testified.

"Did he tell you he'd give you anything for that?" asked Barrett.

"He said I'd be well taken care of," Bishop said. "I told him I was not interested."

Johnson, now living in Memphis, was the final witness placed on the stand by the prosecution before the State rested its case shortly after noon.

Johnson testified he had seen Judge Carpenter drunk on numerous occasions and had seen him in the company of Mrs. Manful in the Copa Caprice and about the hotel. He said he had overheard an argument between Mrs. Carpenter and the judge and at his request, Lockwood had led them from the dance floor where they were attracting attention of other patrons.

He said he was in the office of the hotel using the adding machine and he overheard the judge tell Lockwood to "take Mrs. Carpenter somewhere and get her a divorce because he was tired of supporting two women."

Two physicians were placed on the stand early in the day—Dr. W.F. Durden of Grady Hospital, who testified he removed a fragment of metal from the area above Lockwood's eye after the shooting, and Dr. W.T. Edwards, eye specialist, who testified that Lockwood had lost 75 percent of vision of his right eye "and it will probably get worse." Dr. Edwards said there were many fragments of glass imbedded in Lockwood's eyeball and they will have to be removed from time to time as they work to the surface.

Defense attorneys, training their guns on the State's case against Judge Carpenter, heralded "Lockwood as a Judas Iscariot" and said they would prove he conspired to rob his friend of his money, his wife and his good name.

Judge Carpenter, declared Atty. Barrett, outlining his case to the jury, "is on trial today because it was his good fortune to shoot first."

Carpenter happened to be passing "the home from which he had been driven by Mrs. Carpenter and Lockwood" several hours prior to the shooting and he saw Barbara, "the child he loved as good as his own heart—the child of Mrs. Carpenter he had adopted when he married her—and she was out in the yard in her pajamas crying as if her heart was broken," Barrett told the jury. He said Barbara told her stepfather her mother was out with John Lockwood and told him Lockwood had been to their home in the early hours of the morning and he and her mother had sent her from her mother's bedroom.

Barrett told the jury he would prove Judge Carpenter was upset by his daughter's weeping but he went to the home of his mother and went to bed, where he was awakened at 2 A.M. by an anonymous telephone call to the effect that Lockwood and an unidentified woman had been seen leaving a tourist court on the Marietta highway. He said Carpenter dressed and drove out Peachtree Street in time to see Lockwood and Mrs. Carpenter passing and that he saw Lockwood help Mrs. Carpenter from the car at her door and "embrace her."

Barrett told the jury he would prove that Carpenter only sought to talk to Lockwood and ask him to leave his wife alone "to spare the child, Barbara, more suffering and humiliation," but Lockwood attempted to wreck his car. He said the judge drove alongside Lockwood's car and called, "I want to talk to you," but Lockwood reached for his gun.

"Bob Carpenter is alive today because he happened to shoot first," Barrett concluded.

He said he would prove that the lawsuits brought against Carpenter were part of a scheme "to run Bob Carpenter out of town so they could go their way unmolested" and he promised the jury he would prove that the name of Mrs. Estelle Manful, glamorous so-called "other woman" was "injected into this case for the sole purpose of smearing Judge Carpenter's good name."

Other defense witnesses during the afternoon included: Pauline King, Negro waitress at the Triple A Inn on the Marietta highway, who said she served Mrs. Carpenter and Lockwood the night before the shooting, saw they had a bottle of whiskey, served them only one set-up and saw them leave at closing time, about "a quarter to 10."

E.G. Sammons, former manager of the Blue Room at the Imperial Hotel, who said he saw Mrs. Carpenter and Lockwood together: J.R. Shuttley, engineer, who testified he installed a burglar alarm in Lockwood's office at the hotel and saw the couple sitting in Lockwood's car in the parking lot back of the hotel late at night; Emanuel Loudermilk, hotel parking lot operator, who said he cleaned and "fired out" a gun and delivered it to Lockwood; J.R. Bradshaw, manager of the coffee shop, who said Mrs. Carpenter and Lockwood frequently ate meals together in the coffee shop, sitting on the same side of the bench, and for about a week they had the makings of mint juleps served in their office; Mrs. Fay Bradshaw, who said Mrs. Carpenter and Lockwood sat in the booth together and "talked and looked up at each other and smiled."

Mrs. Bradshaw also testified she saw the couple leaving the hotel together, sitting on the back seat of a car with somebody else driving.

"You saw me in the coffee shop with Mr. Lockwood and Mrs. Carpenter, didn't you?" demanded Asst. Sol. Ogden Doremus.

The witness said she had.

"Well, don't you remember me looking up at Mr. Lockwood and smiling?" asked Doremus acidly.

"No sir, it was the rush hour and I didn't notice," said Mrs. Bradshaw.

Russell Turner, attorney, took the stand in the midst of heated wrangling between Paul Webb and his associate, Elbert Tuttle, to answer a hypothetical question about the duties of lawyers toward their clients. Barrett, propounded a long, involved question about whether it was a lawyer's duty to "ride around at night, drinking whiskey" with his client and Turner answered, "No."

His final witness for the day was John Paul, dry cleaner, who said he delivered three truck loads—one half-ton truck and two three-quarter ton trucks—full of clothing belonging to Mrs. Carpenter to the Imperial Hotel.

He said the clothing had been in storage and he delivered it to the hotel at Mrs. Carpenter's request. He said Lockwood saw it and told him to "set it on the street, he'd take care of it."

Barrett's Male Cast Shows Court 'Love Scenes'

September 16, 1949

Ellis Barrett, veteran criminal lawyer, trod the boards in the best Shakespearean tradition yesterday.

He put on two love scenes in Fulton Superior Court with an all-male cast.

Barrett, chief counsel for Judge Robert Carpenter, is a stocky, gray-haired man with more pretensions to legal talent than to Hollywood glamour—but the fervor with which he flung himself into the role of an affectionate female rocked a full house of sensation-hungry spectators at the trial.

Impresario Barrett was attempting to re-enact for the jury two love scenes which he alleged took place between Judge Carpenter's estranged wife, Helen, and the man he shot—John Lockwood.

For one scene, Barrett enlisted the aid of a lanky, deep-voiced Florida tourist court operator. For the other, a deadpan police reporter.

The tourist court operator, R.C. Bishop of South Jacksonville, told the jury Lockwood and Mrs. Carpenter were sitting and lying, respectively, on a bed in one of his cabins, that they drank whiskey, asked him to "fix" his registration book to help Mrs. Carpenter establish a 90-day residence in Jacksonville and walked around the grounds "holding hands" or with their arms around each other.

"Come on down and show the jury how you saw Mr. Lockwood and Mrs. Carpenter walking," invited Barrett. "Now I'll be Mrs. Carpenter and you be Mr. Lockwood."

"All right," said Bishop, "but you'll have to put your arm around me."

Barrett settled his arm around Bishop's waist and snuggled up cozily while the tall tourist court operator put his arm around Barrett's shoulders. Then the two of them promenaded in front of the jury.

The second performance came when Barrett asked Aubrey Morris, *Atlanta Journal* police reporter to show the jury how Mrs. Carpenter leaned over the wounded Lockwood at Grady Hospital after the shooting.

"Assume that this is the carriage," directed Barrett, grabbing a table directly in front of the witness stand for a prop and flinging himself upon it.

"Now pretend you're Mrs. Carpenter and do what she did."

Morris approached the defense attorney and leaned over him solicitously with his hand on Barrett's chest.

"You want me to say what she said?" asked Morris.

"Say what she said," directed Barrett from his reclining position.

"Darling," murmured Morris unemotionally, peering into the attorney's red face, "you're going to be all right."

The audience was restrained from comment by a stern warning from Judge Virlyn B. Moore—but the criticism of the performance may start coming in today, if prosecution attorneys get to their arguments before court adjourns for the weekend.

In the fall of 1958, Macon restaurant operator Anjette Lyles went on trial charged with the arsenic deaths of two husbands, her mother-in-law and her nine-year-old daughter. From up in the courtroom balcony adorned with a "gleaming brass rail" and 27 other reporters, Sibley covered the spectacle in front of her. "Solemnly we each record details of her dress and coiffure and relay them to the world by telephone, telegraph and teletype—as if by those words we can convey some true picture of this strange woman," Sibley wrote in an Oct. 9, 1958 column.

Forty years later, Sibley assisted Gwinnett County law enforcement employee and author Jaclyn Weldon White as she researched Whisper to the Black Candle: Voodoo, Murder and the Case of Anjette Lyles, *her 1999 book on the case.*

"Anjette was a textbook sociopath," says White. "You would never have a trial like that today. If you had one questionable death like that now, there would be an immediate toxicology screen."

Lyles was sentenced to death and in August of the following year, just before she was to take her final walk, Sibley was the one reporter to whom Lyles granted an interview in her prison cell. "Celestine had established a rapport with her, a bond that the male reporters couldn't manage," says White.

Lyles' life was spared by the parole board and she was sentenced to the state mental hospital in Milledgeville, Ga. Sibley would later note the irony of Lyles' new duties at the facility. The convicted arsenic-

poison murderer was dispatched to the dining room where she served food and baked birthday cakes for the staff and other inmates.

During the trial, Sibley noted how court coverage was changing as she worked elbow to elbow with her new electronic media peers. "Now when you enter the pressroom the air is thick with the deep, rich velvety tones of the radio and television boys reporting to their unseen audiences," she wrote in an Oct. 16, 1958 dispatch. "Each syllable is carefully rounded and slightly caramelized. Things change and I'm not complaining, just noting the change for whatever it's worth. But before the next murder trial I hope I have time for diction lessons. I'm getting self-conscious about my telephone technique."

'Weaker Sex' Will Stand Hours Just to See Anjette

October 12, 1958

Macon, Ga., Oct. 11—"They always told me," said Capt. Bill Adams of the Bibb County police, rubbing his throbbing shin ruefully, "that ladies were the gentler sex."

He glanced toward the door of the Superior Court room and his tone was filled with bafflement and awe: "Oh, those gentle LADIES!" Capt. Adams heads a staff of 12 officers assigned to keep order in the courthouse where Anjette Donovan Lyles is on trial in the most sensational murder case to hit middle Georgia since the famous Woolfolk mass slayings of 1889.

But Capt. Adams wasn't talking about Anjette, a one-time nurse's aide whose ideas of what to do until the doctor arrives, according to prosecution testimony, including spiking her ailing kinfolk's nourishment with arsenic.

Capt. Adams is outside the courtroom—and the women he deals with are the ones who want to SEE Anjette.

"They'll stand three hours at a time," Capt. Adams said. "We tell them there are no more seats in the courtroom and they say that's all right, they just want to SEE her. They'll stand here and wait and when she comes by they don't say anything. They just look at her."

For this dubious satisfaction, hundreds of women, young and old from all parts of Georgia, assemble in the corridors of the Bibb County Courthouse every day. They come in car pools from south Georgia, they come by bus from Atlanta, they even stop off on vacation trips to other states and spend an hour or two listening to the testimony—if they can get in the courtroom—or waiting for a glimpse of the defendant if they can't.

Sweet-faced, smartly clad old ladies have sandwiches in their pocketbooks. Young women have nursing babies at their breasts. Teenagers park their hula hoops outside.

But the ones who fill Capt. Adams and Deputies Jack Haywood and Horace Busbee with a cold terror which almost matches the horror of death by arsenic which witness after witness has been pouring out in the courtroom beyond, are the pregnant ones.

These officers wear guns at their hips. They are obviously reasonably tough and pretty fearless. But they turn pale and break out in a cold sweat at the sight of a 16-year-old mother-to-be!

"A young lady stood right here all day," Officer Haygood replied, wiping his brow at the memory. "She said she was 16 years old and nine months along. I said, 'Little lady, PLEASE go home! You ought to be resting or something, hadn't you? PLEASE go home! But she said, 'No, I'm going to stand right here and see Anjette.'"

With her standing the unhappy officers couldn't enjoy taking a load off their own feet when the trial started and things quieted down in the corridor. They watched her uneasily for three hours, aching with chivalry and acute masculine astonishment at the stern stuff of which frail womanhood is made. The lunch recess came. The courtroom cleared and the crowd in the corridor churned restively. The word came from the bailiffs that there was room for a couple of dozen more spectators in the courtroom and the girls went into action. They boiled forward, pushing at the ropes, squealing in anticipation—ready to fight, hip and thigh and elbow, for a seat.

The young mother-to-be lost her balance and nearly pitched forward. One of the officers caught her and it's an experience he doesn't want to live through again.

"I hope I didn't hurt her," he murmured anxiously.

"I know there's no law to cover it," said another officer, "but I sure wish there was one that prohibited ladies who are in a family way from getting in mobs like this."

If Judge Oscar Long had it within his power to regulate that part of this murder trial, he probably would have done it. He took every step possible to assure order in the courtroom. He allows no standees in the courtroom, no lunch-toters, no comers-and-goers except members of the press who have to duck out frequently to phone in new leads, meet new deadlines. Even chewing gum is forbidden.

"I told one lady who passed me she couldn't take her gum in the courtroom," said Capt. Adams. "She took it out of her mouth, rolled it up in a ball and held it out to me. 'You can chew it till I get back,' she said."

The courtroom itself is fairly small, seating only about 200 persons. Its decor is modern—soft tones of green and brown with no ornamentation except a portrait of a long-ago Superior Court judge on one wall, polished brass rails and a checkerboard wood panel back of the judge's bench. But the atmosphere is almost churchly.

Hymns play at hourly intervals when the courthouse clock

strikes and all of the bailiffs, headed by Deputy Hubert Chapman, are erect, dignified gentlemen of soldierly bearing who seem only to need carnations in their buttonholes to complete the churchly mood.

Some years ago, Maconites say, the sheriff of Bibb County complained of the expenses of using deputies for bailiffs at all trials. The system of engaging retired businessmen for part-time service was inaugurated. The result is that from silver-haired John Eagle, who is an aide in the judge's office, to J.L. McSwain, balcony bailiff, these attachés have an aura of stern and stately propriety about them

When it is time for the trial to resume, Mr. Chapman cues the lawyers on both sides—Special Prosecutors H.T. O'Neal Jr. and Charles Adams and their aide, Chief Investigator Harry Harris; Defense Attorneys William Buffington, Jack J. Gautier and Roy Rhodenhiser. Briefcases in hand, they stride down the middle aisle. The defendant, accompanied by Mr. Chapman's pretty wife, who is acting as matron, and Chief Deputy Billy Murphey, comes down the elevator from the jail and enters the courtroom through a rear door beside the judge's bench.

"Let's have order," says Chief Bailiff Chapman facing the audience and lifting his hands in a gesture commonly used by preachers signaling their congregations to stand.

Obediently the audience stands and Judge Long—a slender, gray-haired man—walks swiftly in and takes his place in the leather chair back of the big, pulpit-high bench.

The trial resumes.

Outside in the corridor the standees sag and some of them ease off their shoes. It will be hours before Anjette comes by again. But there are things to discuss. Her clothes.

She has worn a different costume every day, beginning with a severe black costume on Monday, including a taupe dress, a violet cotton, a white knitted suit and a baby blue twin-sweater set worn with a dark skirt. (Her mother, Mrs. Jetta Donovan, also varies her costume daily and on the day Anjette wore her white knitted suit, her mother was wearing one very similar. Blythe McKay, woman's editor of the *Macon Telegraph,* recorded it thus: "Jetta and Anjette wore mother-and-daughter outfits.")

Witnesses pass going to Sol. Gen. William West's office to await their turn on the stand. Sometimes these are homefolks and stop to talk. There was a contingent of kinfolks of the late Mrs. Ben F. Lyles Sr. from Cochran, Ga. Sometimes they are glamorous or entertaining experts—Dr. Richard Ford, the deep-voiced, caustic poisoning expert from Boston; Dr. Larry B. Howard of the Georgia Crime Lab, Mrs. Mary Beacom, the chatty school-teacherish handwriting expert who talks of forgeries ranging from the days of Anjette to Jezebel.

The standees have plenty to occupy them all right. But what puzzles Capt. Adams and his staff is who's feeding Georgia's menfolks these days.

Mrs. Lyles Sentenced to Die in Chair

October 14, 1958

Macon—A Bibb County jury found Anjette Donovan Lyles guilty of murder without a recommendation for mercy at 10 P.M. Monday. She was immediately sentenced to die in the electric chair between the hours of 10 A.M. and 2 P.M. on Dec. 5.

The jury deliberated an hour and 35 minutes before returning a death verdict for the silver-haired Macon restaurant operator, on trial in the arsenic slaying of her 9-year-old daughter.

She is also indicted in three other deaths, but prosecutors had indicated they would not press those charges if she were given the supreme penalty.

Bit Her Lips

Mrs. Lyles received the verdict without any visible sign of emotion except to bite her lips and flush slightly as Special Prosecutor Charles Adams read the verdict aloud.

Defense attorneys asked that the jury be polled.

Immediately after receiving the sentence, Anjette followed the sheriff from the courtroom to return to the jail on the fifth floor of the courthouse. Her mother, Mrs. Jetta Donovan, who has sat beside her throughout the seven-day trial, wept quietly.

By strange coincidence, the defendant, an admitted follower of voodoo and the occult, received her death sentence on the 13th of the month, and a jury of 13 men, including one alternate who did not join in the deliberations, heard the evidence.

New Trial Motion

Defense counsel filed a motion for a new trial. Hearing on the motion was tentatively set for Dec. 12 which will mean an automatic stay in the electrocution.

Special Prosecutor H.P. O'Neal called the crime unparalleled in "all of the long dark story of human crime." He said the beautiful-faced but heavy-bodied Anjette had killed an insane man in Ben H. Lyles Jr., a blind man in Joe Neal Gabbert, a crippled woman in her mother-in-law Mrs. Ben F. Lyles Sr., and a baby in her daughter Marcia.

The defense based its case for Anjette solely on her testimony in an hour and 18 minute statement in which she said she was not guilty.

"I did not kill my child. I did not kill anybody. I loved Marcy and I miss her," the defendant reiterated in a rambling unsworn statement.

Final arguments in the case ended at 6:30 P.M. and Judge Oscar Long sent the jury to supper. They returned at 8 P.M. and received a 25-minute charge.

The defense rested at noon without any witnesses other than the defendant.

Throughout the afternoon, Anjette, who has remained calm, even engaging in lighthearted conversation with her lawyers and family, cried quietly into her handkerchief. She again wore the severe black dress which she had on the day the trial opened.

Attorneys for the defense contended that the state's case was simply a web of circumstantial evidence, presented in an overly dramatic manner.

Lauds Investigators

Prosecutor O'Neal and his associate, Charles Adams, contended that the case, built upon the testimony of 52 witnesses, was more than circumstantial and amounted to "the most powerful case of which there is a record." Adams paid tribute to the investigating staff, which was able to gather evidence against what he called a "shifty and cagey" woman operating from motives of malice and greed.

Adams sarcastically called arsenic "truly a wonder drug—just a drop here and there—not bad tasting, no odor, delayed reaction and one man will lose his mind, another will become a running sore, another will become a cripple like Mrs. Lyles and another will die a hideous death like Marcia."

Medical science "beat out its very heart to save this child" but could not detect the poisoning without "this," the prosecutor said,

waving a Terro Ant Bane bottle at the jury, and "cutting out the
liver of a dead person!"

"I didn't kill my child, I didn't poison her. I haven't given poison to little Ben, Miss Julia or Buddy Gabbert, and I certainly
haven't given any poison to my child."

Many Denials

That denial, reiterated many times, was the backbone of the
rambling, unsworn statement delivered in a bright, social voice
by the black-clad Anjette as she took the stand shortly before
11 A.M.

The 33-year-old restaurant operator smiled frequently, occasionally frowned and studied her typewritten notes thoughtfully,
paused twice for a drink of water and after she left the stand she
buried her face in her handkerchief and burst into tears.

"Gentlemen of the jury, I have not killed anyone," she began
in a clear and carrying voice. "I wanted to tell you the truth about
this at this time."

Tells of Devotion

And then followed an account in which she described her
struggles to make a living for her two little girls and her devotion to and tender care of all four of the persons she is charged
with having slain with arsenic—two husbands, Lyles and Gabbert,
her mother-in-law and the 9-year-old daughter.

She devoted some minutes to candidly, almost humorously,
defending her belief in "root doctors, spiritual advisers and fortune tellers," declaring: "I've been burning candles a long time. I
believe in them. I went to root doctors. I went to fortune tellers.
I went to spiritual advisers . . . I talked to one every day, I believed
in it, and I liked it. I'll tell the truth about it."

For Luck and Love

She said she burned a long, green candle for luck and money, a red one for love, a white one for peace, an orange one "to keep down talk" and a black one to break up Bob Franks and his other girlfriend. She said she sprinkled salt in four corners of her restaurant to make business good and in her house to bring luck and love to it. She put green garlic, she said, under the rug in her house in the confident belief that it would "bring back anybody who walked on it" and that she put Bob Franks' picture in a sock under her bed and in a stocking in "the north corner of my dresser drawer to bring him back."

"That's what it was supposed to do and that's what I believed it would do," she said. "There are certain roots if you put them in your mouth when you talk to people you can get them to do what you want them to do."

She said she talked to candles as they burned and that her mother-in-law shared this enthusiasm with her, joining her at the candle burnings at night. She said she saved the wax to have it interpreted by one of her "advisers" and that she used Adam and Eve root to "rub on your forehead. Do your hand over your head three times before the morning sun and you'll get what you want."

She demonstrated by lifting her arms over her head and then she added, smiling: "I did it. I believe it."

"It may be crazy to believe in these things," she continued, "but I believe in the predictions of spiritual advisers and fortune tellers."

Quiet about Will

Although she ignored many phases of the charges against her, most conspicuously those having to do with the alleged forgery of her mother-in-law's will, leaving her control of an estate esti-

mated at between $80,000 and $90,000, she denied putting Terro
Ant Poison in any food or drink for her relatives or benefitting
by Marcia's or her first husband's death.

"Little Ben," she said, drank and neglected the restaurant, eventually selling it without her knowledge at a price far less than its
value, leaving her "with 10 cents in my purse the day he died."
She said she worked long hours to make a living for her children,
taking Marcia to the restaurant with her and keeping her in a
carriage in a corner when she was a baby. She said she borrowed
money to buy the restaurant back—and her mother-in-law
worked with her to make a go of it.

They "Got Along"

"You hear that two women can't get along under the same roof,"
she said, "Well, Mrs. Lyles and I got along. I'd say things she didn't
like and she'd say things I didn't like sometimes, but we'd work
it out, and we got along."

She said Mrs. Lyles lived with her at the home of her mother,
Mrs. Jetta Donovan on Vineville Avenue, and later moved in with
her when she acquired a home of her own after Gabbert's death.
She said she had to call the doctor to Mrs. Lyles without the older
woman's knowledge and that she nursed her devotedly, taking her
buttermilk at her request and sleeping on a cot by her bed at night
"because she was scared."

"She said I was the only one that could fix a pillow to her back,"
Anjette testified. "Two times I went home at night and she had
the nurse call me to come back. . . . I tried to help her, I didn't
hurt her."

Met Gabbert

She said she met Gabbert, the Capitol Airlines pilot, the day she
acquired and reopened the restaurant, April 4, 1955, when he sent

a steak back to the kitchen. She said she recooked it and delivered it to him herself, they started talking and before he left he said, "Brown-eyes, I'm going to marry you."

"I had my first date with Buddy in May of 1955," the defendant related. "Every time I saw him he asked me to marry him."

She said she went to Texas at his urging to meet his family and was talked into marrying him at Carlsbad, N.M., in a night ceremony. She said she had already noticed that he had a "red rugged face" and on their honeymoon she observed the rash on his body and made him promise to see a doctor when they got back to Macon (medical witnesses for the state said the severe, "weeping" rash was a symptom of arsenic poisoning). She said the $10,000 life insurance policy he took out was his idea and he would have taken a $20,000 policy but she persuaded him that they couldn't afford it.

"Held Ill Child"

Anjette's voice broke briefly when she talked of her love of Marcia, whose death is the only one of the four for which she was tried this time. She admitted laughing when Marcia had hallucinations but attributed it to "a nervous habit I've had all my life. I've done that instead of crying."

"The nurses told you I laughed," she said, "but they didn't tell you about the times I held her in my arms and tried to quiet her."

She said far from putting arsenic in her child's lemonade in the restaurant bathroom, she was gargling salt water for a sore throat. She said she believed the child was going to die because both her "spiritual advisors" and doctors told her so. She called Bob Franks, the airline pilot she was dating, because "Marcia kept talking about him—both children loved him—and I wanted to ask him to call her the next day.

"It wasn't that I was concerned about hearing from him my-self—it was for Marcy."

Mrs. Lyles said after Marcia's funeral she was resting at home and saw her younger child, Carla, now 7, come down the stairs with a collection of bottles she had found in the bathroom medicine chest, on her way to play "doctor" and "hospital" with the Jones twins who were waiting for her in the yard. She said the collection included two Terro Ant Poison bottles and Carla told her "Marcy drank some—it was sweet and she liked it—and I'm going to take some, too."

She said she was upset and took Carla to the doctor "because if I lost her, too, I didn't know what I'd do." She made no references to the testimony of state's witnesses indicating that she pretended to call the mother of Carla's playmates from the doctor's office but had called her own maid instead.

"I loved Marcy," she said. "I still love her and miss her and I miss my other child, too, which I haven't seen for six months." (Carla has been in the custody of the Juvenile Court since her mother's arrest.)

Crowds, which have increased daily in the seven-day run of the sensation under trial, stood silently in the corridors as Anjette, her heels clicking on the floor, ran toward the elevator to the jail after her testimony.

Anjette Waits in Death Row, Vows to Expose 'Real Slayer'

August 7, 1959

Reidsville—Anjette Donovan Lyles, sentenced to die Aug. 17 in the arsenic-poisoning of her daughter, swung her legs from her bunk in death row at Georgia State Prison Thursday and, smiling, cheerfully promised to do two things if her efforts to avoid the electric chair fail.

"I'm going to see my child Carla before I die and I'm going to talk plenty about some people I've been protecting in this thing," the silver-haired, blue pajama-clad prisoner said.

Mrs. Lyles, who was convicted Oct. 13 in Bibb County Superior Court of the murder of her daughter, Marcia Elaine Lyles, 9, said she had not seen her younger daughter, Carla, now 8, in 15 months and she vowed she would not die without setting eyes on the child once more.

The former Macon restaurant operator, who is under indictment for three other arsenic deaths, including those of two husbands and her mother-in-law, appeared talkative and good-humored as she reviewed events leading up to her incarceration in the death cell.

"I didn't kill those four people," Anjette declared. "Somebody else did. I didn't say anything about it at the time of the trial because I was protecting somebody, but Sheriff Jim Woods knows about it and I hope he will find out the truth. I wouldn't walk in that room and die with a lie on my lips for anything in this world."

The plump prisoner who says she lost 30 pounds as a result of a bout with pneumonia last winter, appeared in good health and high spirits, laughing frequently and continuing to dimple becomingly as she spoke of her faith in God and warned Christians everywhere against the evils of whiskey and night clubs.

"How I got where I am today, I don't know," the dark-eyed young woman mused. "I pray and trust in God and I don't worry about what's going to happen to me. I pray that God's will be done."

Mrs. Lyles said that although she had been a member of the

Mulberry Street Methodist Church in Macon most of her life, she was not a real Christian until after her arrest for murder.

"Six weeks after I went to the Bibb County jail I fell on my knees," Mrs. Lyles said. "I didn't know God when I went in but I found Him. He helped me there and He's helping me here. He will see me through."

Mrs. Lyles said in addition to her intention to see her little girl and to "tell the truth" about the multiple arsenic poisonings, she had but one desire to fulfill before the date set for her electrocution.

"There's one other person I want to see," she said demurely. She declined to name that person, shaking her pony tail girlishly and closing her eyes. "It's somebody in Macon—that's all I'll say."

The 32-year-old mother said relatives had kept Carla from her, ostensibly for the child's own good. She said Bibb County juvenile court authorities kept her posted on Carla's life and she knew the child to be happy and well cared for "but they promised me I could see her this summer and I haven't seen her. I think about her all the time."

Loved Husbands

Touching on the other three relatives in whose deaths she has been charged but not tried, Anjette said, "I loved my first husband (Ben F. Lyles Jr.) better than anything in this world and I wouldn't have done anything to hurt him. I loved Joel Neal Gabbart but we didn't have a chance. We lived with my mother and Mrs. Lyles was with us all the time, too. I loved Mrs. Lyles (Mrs. Ben F. Lyles, Sr.) and I never spoke a disrespectful word to her in all the years we were married. Mrs. Lyles loved me too. She didn't think I could do any wrong."

Did Wrong

Anjette's face, free from make-up, clouded momentarily and in a moment she added, "I admit I was wrong about Mrs. Lyles' will. While she was in the hospital I got mad at her—I admit I had something to drink at the time—and two people egging me on, so I got it signed."

Anjette did not say specifically that she forged Mrs. Lyles' name to a will leaving her complete control of the older woman's property, but she recalled that a handwriting expert testified during the trial that the signature on the will had been traced. Officers also testified during the trial that they found tracing paper bearing an imprint of the signature in Anjette's bedroom.

"I admit I did wrong. I'm glad I told it and got it off my chest," Anjette said.

Mrs. Lyles, who could be the first white woman to die in the electric chair in Georgia if her efforts to get her sentence commuted fail, spends her days in cheerful conversation with two nurses who take turns watching over her on the fifth floor of Tattnall Prison. She is not allowed to have any clothes in her cell except the blue Indianhead shorty pajamas which were made in the prison sewing room to fit her. And she was under the impression that she could not keep make-up with her. However, when Warden R.P. Balkcom Jr. told her that she could have a lipstick she graciously accepted one from a newspaper reporter and applied color to her lips before posing for her photograph.

She was emphatic in her refusal to be photographed behind bars. But she was gay and cooperative about taking directions from the photographer when he assured her he could shoot the picture around the bars.

Likes the Food

"The food in here is so good, well-cooked and well-seasoned that I eat all the time, and they laugh and tell me I may be too big to get through these doors when they come and get me for the electric chair," Anjette said, laughing heartily at the joke. She said she spent her time sleeping and praying, eating and talking and insisted, "I'm not depressed, not blue. I've always been able to take anything that comes and I guess I still can."

In May, 1960, Sibley was sent to Darien, Georgia, to cover the messy divorce of tobacco heir Richard J. Reynolds and his wife Muriel. Mrs. Reynolds was seeking a six-million-dollar alimony settlement.

By May 3, the second session of the 10-day trial, neither party in the case had yet put in an appearance. He had eight attorneys representing his interests while she had five. Mr. Reynolds, suffering from emphysema, stayed in seclusion at his Sapelo Island mansion. Mrs. Reynolds was tracked by local authorities and served with a subpoena in her Florida hotel room.

Meanwhile, Sibley, the Journal's *Gordon Roberts and other reporters covering the case were housed at the Fort King George Motel and took turns sitting in the motel's office, calling in their copy on the facility's single phone as a cranky myna bird frequently interrupted their dictation efforts by screeching "Hell-ooh, babee!"*

In the courtroom, as Mr. Reynolds's attorneys threatened to "pound Muriel Reynolds to pieces in this courtroom and throw her out the window," she finally arrived in court (via station wagon) on May 12 to testify to her husband's frequent drunkenness. She stated that he "barely had a sober moment" from April 1953 to December 1954 and recounted how on one yachting trip in Bermuda she had been forced dive into the ocean in her evening clothes to fetch her husband after he "stripped to his BVDs" to go for a late-night swim.

Sibley took down every juicy piece of testimony, later wryly writing that "one of the remarkable things about the R.J. Reynolds divorce trial is how quickly it has inured most of us to contemplating great sums of money. . . . The truth of the matter is that I'm traveling in such a fast league here, I've gone plumb out of my mind and think nothing of paying 85 cents for a sandwich and grandly ordering up pie à la mode any time it occurs to me."

Later, as Mrs. Reynolds' purchase of a $35,000 pair of diamond earrings came up in testimony, Sibley was inspired to dig "around in my pocketbook to try and find the mate to the pair of gold (washed) earrings I bought for $1 in a fit of extravagance some weeks ago. But it was no use, earrings have some diabolical personality of their own, and one always vanishes. . . . Now when Mrs. Reynolds loses an earring—and surely she does—I imagine they call out everybody from the Coast Guard to the FBI."

After an appeal, Mrs. Reynolds eventually ended up with a two-million-dollar settlement.

Reynolds Labels Wife a 'Nagging Salem Witch'

May 6, 1960

Darien, Ga.—Richard J. Reynolds, Sapelo Island tobacco millionaire, launched in absentia his fight for divorce from the dark-eyed Canadian divorcée Muriel Reynolds Thursday by picturing her as a knife-packing, hard-drinking, hard-cursing woman who woke him up in the middle of the night to nag him and desired only to hasten his death and collect his estate.

Neither Reynolds nor Mrs. Reynolds appeared in court again

but volatile Savannah attorney Aaron Kravitch read the husband's written complaints against his wife with such fire and feeling that her counsel asked the court to call him down. "She was more than a scold, she was what I would call a Salem witch," Reynolds said of his wife in a long written interrogatory which is to substitute for his appearance in court. "She was very, very domineering.

"She believed in voodoo and witchcraft and had a way of shuffling the cards. I kept my bedroom locked at night to keep her out.

"When she was drinking she would talk about her underworld connections who would do her bidding. She said she was a gypsy and told fortunes. She never told me what my future was but she acted like it wasn't good." Defense attorneys, whose inning will not come up until later in the trial, got such licks as they could on cross-examination by emphasizing that Reynolds wrote his wife letters and sent her gifts during the time she was in Europe shortly before he filed suit for divorce. They bore down again on the same "buck rabbit" to "doe" love letters which he allegedly wrote Mrs. Reynolds but claimed in the interrogatory that he merely penned at her insistence to keep her from nagging him.

The most sensational testimony of the day came in Reynolds' interrogatory, but five witnesses did take the stand during the day. Two of these were physicians, both of whom testified that Reynolds is gravely ill and unable to leave the island and come to court. Three were character witnesses.

Dr. Harry E. Rollins, Savannah internist, stayed on the stand for nearly two hours testifying as to Reynold's physical condition and his observation of his relationship with his wife. The doctor denied that he had anything to do with the estrangement of the Reynoldses but said that Mrs. Reynolds had twice called him up, abused him violently, accusing him of trying to break up her home and threatening to ruin him economically, professionally and destroy his marriage.

The young physician testified that on Christmas Eve, 1959, Mrs. Reynolds called him up and told him she had dreamed some commandos had attacked him and described the various acts of torture and death so horrible that he said he could not repeat her language in front of ladies. "She said she was going to see that dream come true," Dr. Rollins said. "She said she was going to see my marriage broken up just like hers had been."

Dr. Rollins said Mrs. Reynolds later called back and attempted to speak to his wife and he would not call her to the telephone. Sometime later, he said, she called back and apologized for the threat, said she was living in a 15-by-15 room in New York, was "very unhappy" and asked him to use his influence to get Reynolds to effect a settlement.

Dr. Rollins described in detail Reynolds' condition which he described as chronic pulmonary emphysema, a malady of the lungs which leaves them limp and rubbery, full of moisture and unable to draw in oxygen.

Sibley made two trips to Memphis to cover the trial of accused Martin Luther King Jr. assassin James Earl Ray. Constitution publisher Ralph McGill accompanied her there in Nov. 1968 but Ray switched lawyers and the trial was delayed until March of 1969. (Three weeks before she returned to Memphis, Sibley mournfully covered McGill's funeral for the Constitution.)

The only woman among the international press corps to cover the Ray proceedings, Sibley noted the tight security. She wrote: "The press . . . marched single file through the search area, signed an agreement to be searched, relinquished their valuables to be held in sealed envelopes outside the courtroom, were photographed, had their voices recorded and were frisked. A woman deputy searched the only woman reporter present (this writer). Shoes were removed and searched and pocketbooks were tagged and stored outside the court-room."

The Constitution *scribe* also recorded the ever-evolving mechanics of covering a murder trial. "For instance, there was the matter of a little speech Judge Preston Battle made after the sentencing," she wrote in a March 11, 1969 column. "It was an exercise in public relations, of course, a frank defense of another nowadays word—the 'image' of Memphis. Judge Battle cut loose and quoted Shakespeare, which is not something a judge does every day in the week and we all scribbled furiously."

Ray Gets 99-Year Term after King Guilty Plea—No Plot Found in Slaying

March 11, 1969

Memphis, Tenn.—James Earl Ray, who has seen a lot of prisons and escaped the last with a vow never to return, Monday chose the longest jail sentence of all—99 years—rather than stand trial for the slaying of Atlanta civil rights leader Dr. Martin Luther King Jr.

Defense attorney Percy Foreman told a hastily impaneled jury that Ray's choice represented "the extreme penalty short of one—death," and he expressed the opinion that there is "no punishment at all in death except for the moment it comes."

Under Tennessee law Ray will have to serve 33 years of the 99 years before he will be eligible for parole. If the sentence had been life imprisonment, he could have applied for parole in 13 years.

Sheriff William Morris said Ray will be transferred to the state penitentiary in Nashville "anytime now, as soon as the governor says he is ready for him." The penitentiary is understood to be installing super security precautions similar to the ones under which Ray has been incarcerated in Shelby County Jail.

Shelby Criminal Court Judge W. Preston Battle passed sentence on Ray at 12:10 P.M. at the end of what had promised to be one of the most sensational murder trials of the decade and turned out to be one of the most anticlimactic. The verdict and the sentence were agreed upon before court opened but Tennessee law requires that the jury hear enough evidence to confirm both.

The jury of men, two of them Negroes, agreed to accept both the plea of guilty and the 99-year sentence before they were sworn in. Then they heard the testimony of four witnesses—two of them friends of Dr. King and eyewitnesses to his slaying last April 4; the county medical examiner, a city detective and an FBI agent.

The rest of the details of Ray's cross-continent wanderings before and after the shooting of King, his abandonment of a white Mustang automobile in Atlanta, his flight from Canada and subsequent arrest in London were summarized to the jury in a narrative of stipulations agreed to by attorneys from both sides.

Ray spoke only half a dozen times during the trial. "Yes sir . . . yes sir . . . yes sir!" he said over and over in answer to Judge Battle's questions as to whether he entered his guilty plea "with free will and full understanding of its meaning and consequences."

Once when Judge Battle asked if he had acted out of pressure or desire to protect someone else, Ray replied shortly, "I'm pleading guilty!"

'Not Agreeing'

Later, when his attorney told the jury that he, Foreman, was convinced that Ray had acted alone and not in a conspiracy to kill

King, Ray stood up and mumbled that he wanted to "add" something about "not agreeing with" Atty. Gen. Ramsey Clark and FBI chief J. Edgar Hoover.

Foreman and Judge Battle looked puzzled and both again asked him if he still wanted to plead guilty.

"Yes sir, yes sir," said Ray, sitting down.

Atty. Gen. Phil Canale told the jury that despite rumors that Ray was "a dupe, a fall guy," in a plan to kill Dr. King, "we have no proof other than that Dr. Martin Luther King was killed by James Earl Ray and James Earl Ray alone."

In Washington, the Justice Department said Monday it would continue its investigation into a possible conspiracy in the King assassination even though federal officials do not have evidence to show Ray was hired to kill King.

"The investigation into the conspiracy allegation is still open," a Justice Department spokesman said.

Ray, who made a career of looking inconspicuous, was the least conspicuous thing in a courtroom filled with reporters from all parts of the world and tremendous sheet-covered mockups of the Lorraine Motel where Dr. King was killed, the rooming house from which Ray allegedly fired the fatal bullet and the surrounding neighborhood. He came into the courtroom at 9:44 A.M., wearing a blue suit with a faint gray stripe, a white shirt and tie.

Brothers There

Ray apparently took no notice of his brothers John and Gerald, who sat in the small section reserved for the public. Neither Mrs. Coretta King, widow of Dr. King, nor his father were present.

Throughout the proceedings and afterward emphasis seemed to be on the theory that Ray acted alone. The only motives suggested came from Atty. Gen. Canale during a press conference after the trial when he said, "I think race had a lot to do with it. Several things on race were in the background."

Among the things he mentioned were a map of Atlanta found in Ray's room at a boarding house. Dr. King's residence, church and the headquarters of the Southern Christian Leadership Conference were circled.

Canale told reporters he felt they had sufficient evidence to show that Ray earned money running contraband drugs "and perhaps jewelry" between the United States, Mexico and Canada. He said Ray had saved a substantial sum in the Missouri Penitentiary which he sent out before he escaped, and that he had been linked with possibly two bank robberies in Montreal, Canada, and one in London.

"I am satisfied he had sufficient income to live the life he was living," Canale said.

Judge Battle made a point of emphasizing that there is "not in possession enough evidence to indict anyone as a co-conspirator in this case."

"Of course, this is not conclusive evidence that there was no conspiracy," Judge Battle said in a statement before he adjourned court and after he had passed sentence on Ray.

"It merely means that as of this time, there is not sufficient evidence available to make out a case of probable cause," the judge said. "However, if this defendant was a member of a conspiracy to kill the decedent, no member of such conspiracy can ever live in peace or security or lie down to pleasant dreams, because in this state there is no statute of limitations in capital cases such as this. And while it is not always the case, my 35 years in these criminal courts have convinced me that in the great majority of cases, Hamlet was right when he said 'for murder though it have no tongue, will speak with most miraculous organ.'"

Judge Battle took a little time to defend Memphis' reputation and praise all those who had anything to do with bringing the case to a "just conclusion." He paid tribute to "Tennessee, Southern, America, West Free World, justice and security," the FBI, the U.S. Department of Justice and law enforcement agencies and Canada, Mexico, Portugal, England, and the Shelby County officers and attorney general, adding, "I wish to thank them all officially and personally and if I have overlooked anyone I want to especially thank them too."

He said that Memphis had been blamed for the death of Dr. King —"to me wrongfully and irrationally." He said neither Dr. King nor his killer lived here. "Their orbits merely intersected here."

The man under 99-year sentence was still in the courtroom when Judge Battle summed up with, "I submit that up till now, we have not done too badly for a 'decadent river town!'" Then he paraphrased Winston Churchill's defiant reply to the Axis threat to wring England's neck like a chicken: "Some chicken, some neck."

'Some Town'

"I would like to reply to our Memphis critics," Judge Battle said, "Some river, some town."

He concluded by telling the jury that he understood that lunch was ready and "you've spent a long morning, but you'll get lunch out of it anyway."

The Rev. Samuel D. Kyles, pastor of the Monumental Baptist Church of Memphis and a longtime friend of Dr. King, said he had gone by the motel to pick up the civil rights leader and take him to his home for some "soul food" about 6 P.M. April 4, during the time Dr. King was leading a demonstration on behalf of Memphis striking garbage collectors. Dr. Kyles said he was standing by Dr. King on the balcony and had turned and walked five or six steps away when he heard his friend fall.

He demonstrated to the jury the position he saw Dr. King lying in and said he saw a gaping hole in his neck. The witness' voice dropped and he apparently choked up when asked to identify photographs of the slain King.

Chauncey Eskridge, Negro attorney from Chicago, who said he represented Dr. King, told the jury he was standing in the courtyard below the motel balcony also waiting for King and watched the Negro leader walk out putting on his coat.

"A sound coming at my right ear said 'zing!'" the witness said. "I turned to see where it came from and then I turned back and saw Dr. King had fallen."

Both friends testified that they attended Dr. King's funeral in Atlanta.

Dr. Jerry Francisco, Shelby County medical examiner, said he performed an autopsy and attributed death to a gunshot wound which went into the side of Dr. King's face, passed through his jaw into his neck, severing the spinal cord. He said death resulted "shortly." Dr. Francisco identified a bullet he removed from the body and demonstrated with a pointer and the mockup of the buildings the angle he believed the bullet to have traveled from the upstairs window of the rooming house to the balcony of the motel.

N.E. Zachry, Memphis inspector of police in charge of the homicide bureau, identified an array of physical evidence he said he collected outside the rooming house after Ray is believed to have fired and fled. This included a rifle, binoculars, a transistor radio, pliers and hammer, cartridges in a pasteboard box, two tins of beer, toilet articles and underwear. All of these things were turned over to the FBI, he said, and the stipulation later read said they had been found to contain either fingerprints or hair or bits of fiber linking them to Ray.

Got Mustang

FBI Special Agent Robert G. Jensen, in charge of the Memphis office of the FBI, said that he had been present in Atlanta to claim the white Mustang abandoned in Capitol Homes and identified it and most of the physical evidence as being definitely Ray's property.

All of Ray's travels to and from New Orleans, Los Angeles, Mexico and Canada were admitted in the stipulations along with the aliases Raymond George Sneyd, Paul Bridgeman, Eric Starvo Galt and the names which Ray allegedly borrowed from several highly respected Toronto citizens.

Ray's brothers showed no sign of emotion as they watched their brother enter his plea and accept his sentence. When reporters asked them during a recess if they knew about the plea, Gerald replied, "I had an idea," and added, "I ain't surprised at nothing."

First Approach

Canale told reporters Foreman first approached him with the word that Ray was considering pleading guilty last Feb. 22. Foreman told the jury, the first 12 men in the box, that the Memphis system of having to confirm such a verdict was old and "Anglo-Saxon jurisprudence." Then he polled each one individually, calling him by name and asking if he was willing to accept the plea and the sentence.

"I've covered many a murder trial," Sibley wrote in June 1971 from her motel room in Humboldt, Tenn., "but never one involving a writer. The irony of Jesse Hill Ford's situation is endlessly engrossing to the reporters covering his trial. Here he is, a liberal author who probed, with some sympathy and bitter humor, the mores of the Southern conservative and laid bare the suffering, the humiliation of the Southern Negro. And here he is on trial for killing a Negro. 'Both whites and blacks are mad at him,' they will tell you in Humboldt. 'How could they be? He understood so much,' a reader will say. 'Oh, they didn't read the book,' comes the answer.

"The other great irony is that this trial, as hard as it must be on the author, has stimulated a great surge of interest in his books. Reporters who haven't read or who read and forgot The Liberation of Lord Byron Jones *rushed to libraries and got it out." The jury later found Ford innocent of the charges.*

Girl Testifies: Victim in Ford Case Said Partly Disrobed

July 2, 1971

Humbolt, Tenn.—The young soldier which novelist Jesse Hill Ford is on trial for slaying was naked from the waist to the knees and barefooted at the time he died, witnesses testified Thursday.

Miss Allie V. Andrews, companion of Pvt. George H. Doaks the night he was fatally shot in a car in Ford's driveway, was the principal witness introduced during the first day of testimony.

The state rested its case against Ford after introducing 14 witnesses. Principal witness at the trial is expected to be the defendant, 42-year-old Ford.

Miss Andrews, a slim black girl with a large Afro hairdo, told the jury she and Doaks had gotten lost after a trip to a dairy bar and she did not know why he stopped and turned off the lights and the engine in Ford's driveway.

The young girl in a barely audible voice denied on cross-examination that she knew Doaks was disrobed until after the shooting when she fled from the scene, taking with her the four-year-old child with whom she was baby-sitting.

Defense attorney John Kaizer unsuccessfully attempted to bring out a possible vengeance motive for the black visitors to Ford's property by asking her if she was related to Mrs. Dorothy Claybrook.

The witness said, "She is my second cousin."

"Isn't she the wife of the undertaker they found dead in Crockett County a while back?" Kaizer asked. "She considered herself Emma in the . . ."

District Attorney General W.R. Kinton interrupted with a swift objection which Judge Dick Jerman sustained.

(The character Emma in Ford's novel *The Liberation of Lord Byron Jones* is the wife of a rich Negro mortician whose portrayal Humbolt blacks are said to resent bitterly. The jacket of the book describes her as a "slut.")

Doaks' mother, Mrs. Rudolph Doaks, 56, a portly black woman dressed all in white, testified that her son left home the night of Nov. 16, saying he planned to catch a bus back to Ft. Leonard Wood, Mo.

She said she was "cleaning chitterlings" in the kitchen of their home when he left and she did not know if he walked out then because he did not like the smell of chitterlings.

"The last time I heard from my son," Mrs. Doaks testified, "someone called and told my husband he had been shot. The next time I saw him was at the wake."

Mrs. Doaks said her son came home about two weeks before

his death and was married to the mother of his baby daughter who was born on Sept. 6. She identified his companion Allie Andrews, as a second cousin and said that the families had been "close" but the young people had not known each other until a week or two before the shooting.

Miss Andrews testified that Doaks came by her house to tell her good-bye and she asked him to take her and the little girl with whom she was baby-sitting to a dairy bar for a "derby," a concoction she identified as ice cream covered with chocolate.

She said when they got there she found the weather so cold she decided against the ice cream, and Doaks bought a small hamburger for the little girl, Linda.

Defense attorneys attempted unsuccessfully to get her to trace her and Doak's travels on a Humbolt street map which they set up on an easel before the jury.

She said she could not identify the streets and under cross-examination admitted that she and Doak had not talked much about being lost. She said they did not know that Ford's driveway was a private road because there is a street sign there. But when they got toward the end of it and saw lights on in his house, they turned around and started out, she said.

Doaks pulled over to the side of the driveway, turned off the ignition and the lights and after about two minutes, she said her attention was attracted to the back by her charge, Linda, who called out to her, calling her "Punkin."

When she turned she said she saw a man at the rear of the car and heard somebody hit the rear end of the car.

"All I know, he was white," she said. "I didn't see well enough to recognize him. I think I recognize his coat. He had a gun in his hand."

Later, she struck the side of the rail on the witness stand to demonstrate how Ford struck the parked car and quoted him as saying, "Get out of my driveway!"

She said almost immediately she heard a gunshot and hid on the floor until she felt blood on her head and shoulders. Asked if Doaks made any noise, she said, "a moan."

The girl said she took her charge out of the car and ran down the driveway until she came to the home of Mrs. and Mrs. James Teague, a white couple whose house is near the entrance.

The Teagues later took the stand as state witnesses and testified that they heard a shot and went out in the yard in time to see Miss Andrews and the little girl running toward them.

Both husband and wife denied under defense cross-examination that they heard more than one shot.

Ford testified at a preliminary hearing that he fired one warning shot into the air before he shot into Doak's car.

Later in the day Thursday, sheriff's officers said they found two spent cartridges near the driveway and one round of ammunition near the house. Deputy Sheriff Harry Coble identified a .30 caliber Enfield rifle as the death weapon and said it was surrendered to him by Ford when he visited the house shortly after the shooting.

Evan E. Hodge, an FBI agent and firearms identification specialist, testified that the unfired cartridge came from Ford's gun.

Last witness of the day was the Rev. George Henry Doaks Sr., father of the soldier, who burst into tears as he mounted the witness stand and told that the last time he saw his son he was dead from a bullet wound through the head.

During cross-examination he denied knowing that his son was AWOL from the Army.

A Hollywood screenwriter, Stirling Silliphant, who worked with Ford on the movie version of *The Liberation of Lord Byron Jones* and did the script for *In the Heat of the Night*, was understood to be flying to Tennessee Thursday night to appear on Ford's behalf.

Sally Ford, wife of the author, who has stayed by him throughout the trial was missing from the courtroom Thursday because she is expected to testify Friday. His son, Charles, who was indirectly involved in the shooting in that Ford feared for the boy's safety when he heard the automobile in his driveway, is also slated to testify and did not appear in the courtroom Thursday.

The author's other children, Jay, 19, and Sara, 16, were by his side and his mother and sister had seats in the press section.

The courtroom was crowded with new arrivals from the press and a large number of local Negroes who laughed frequently during the testimony.

The heat pressed down on the city hall roof. The air conditioning labored and gave up. And the big ceiling fans, which were used in former years, were turned on but had to be cut off when it was found that they interfered with the court reporter's recorder.

Judge Jerman rapped for order mildly a few times but drew laughter himself when the attorney general asked him to excuse the FBI agent so he could get back to Washington.

"We need somebody up there," Judge Jerman said, calling a recess just as laughter and some applause broke out in the courtroom.

Both Mr. and Mrs. Teague, with whom the Fords have apparently had disputes over dogs, testified that Ford had asked them not to cooperate with the authorities in the investigation of the shooting. He told them, Mrs. Teague stated, that he wasn't "just charged with manslaughter, it was first-degree murder."

Defense attorney James Senter, cross-examining her, asked her if she had not had some dogs killed.

"Un-huh," Mrs. Teague said heatedly. "But that's not got nothing to do with this!"

Her husband, James Teague, said that Ford stopped at the mailbox in front of his house one day and asked him not to "cooperate. It would cause him to lose everything he had."

Both the Teagues said Ford's driveway was not designated as a private drive at that time. They indicated they felt reflector signs further down the driveway warning against trespassing were inconspicuous.

In the summer of 1972, Sibley was on assignment in Maryland for Arthur Bremer's trial. Bremer was accused of the attempted assassination of Alabama Governor George Wallace. Sibley, separated from her familiar Southern colleagues, grew uneasy covering the young man prosecutors claimed was "programmed to fail" since birth.

Security at the trial was extreme and the typically engaging reporter couldn't even persuade an Upper Marlboro police officer to give her directions in the sleepy town known for its tobacco exports.

"The courthouse itself has a bed in the center of the front lawn featuring a stately row of tobacco plants," Sibley reported on Aug. 1, 1972. "It happens those tobacco plants were the only thing the officer patrolling the front of the courthouse would talk to me about on the eve of the Bremer trial. 'Those are tobacco plants, aren't they?' I asked an officer. 'Yes ma'am, they are.' 'Pretty,' I offered. 'Yes ma'am, they are.' 'The courtroom here is on the second floor, isn't it?' I asked. 'I can't say, ma'am,' he said. Then he looked embarrassed. 'I know,' he amended. 'But they told us not to say anything. Tight security.' I said I understood and turned away. 'But the tobacco plants are pretty,' I added."

Filing copy to a newsroom 700 miles away was also a challenge. A trip to a Western Union operator turned into "a wild goose chase," Sibley wrote. "Her little house was set back in the woods, and the telegraph office was a telephone on the desk in her living room. When she saw I had a sheath of typewritten pages in my hand instead of a one- or two-line message, her face fell. She was going to have to read it over the phone to an operator in some distant place and we both realized I had made a mistake in coming."

Bremer was sentenced to 63 years in prison.

'I Have To Kill Somebody'—Bremer

August 4, 1972

Upper Marlboro, Md.—Aspiring political assassin Arthur Bremer decided to give Alabama Gov. George Wallace "the honor" of dying at his hands only after deciding not to shoot Sen. George McGovern and failing six times to get President Richard Nixon, Bremer's diary revealed Thursday.

Defense attorney Benjamin Lipsitz read further portions of Bremer's diary to a Prince Georges County jury, chronicling two months of frustration for the defendant, who is charged with gunning down Wallace May 15 during a rally at a Laurel, Md. shopping center.

At one point, the diary described Bremer's failure to shoot Nixon after the President's limousine left an airport in Ottawa, Canada. "A dark silhouette rushed by in a black car," Bremer wrote. "All over. I had missed it. The best chance to get him was over."

Alternating between exclamations of despair over his repeated failure to kill anybody and hope that he would finally "do a bang-up job" and get people to know him, Bremer's diary was a fumbling, troubleprone blueprint for attempted assassination.

Six times he thwarted himself in his effort to kill President Nixon, complaining, "You can't kill Nixie boy if you can't get close to him."

He decided to give Wallace "the honor" of dying instead of

Nixon, and then worried that the killing of the Alabama governor would rate but three minutes of network television and
that a newspaper would write at the bottom of the front page:
"Wallace Dead. Who Cares?"

"It seems I would have done better by myself if I had killed
old G-man Hoover," Bremer wrote, and then a bit later added, "I
hope my death makes more sense than my life."

He also considered killing Sen. George McGovern, he said. He
speculated that he would spend his life in jail if he did, and when
the guards asked him why he had done it, he would say, "I
don't know. Nothing else to do. Why not? I have to kill somebody."

"I am one sick assassin," he wrote, detailing the symptoms of
an ache in his back "behind my heart" and adding, "I'd really feel
better if Michigan had a death penalty. . . . I've found something
to do with my $10 Confederate flag, wipe the dust off my shoes.
It's too thin to polish with, just right to wipe dust. Bang! I'm going
to get convicted. . . . It's going to be another Sirhan."

Bremer thought his diary might be "the best-read pages since
those scrolls in the caves," but he admitted that he got tired of
writing about his failures—which were many.

He followed President Nixon to Ottawa, missed him there repeatedly, went back home to wait out the chief executive's trip
to Moscow, and then drove to Washington where he got lost in
traffic and had difficulty getting close enough.

He returned to Milwaukee and then read a newspaper story
that led him to write: "You know something? Our great leader
made an appearance in front of the White House to shake hands
with tourists that day after I left. Man, he was right there, so close
I tore the paper to bits. I could have killed him for that alone!"

Bremer, who was at an eating establishment when he read the

story, wrote that he was so angry at his failure to get Nixon he left the waitress a two-cent tip—two Canadian cents.

The first half of his diary, numbering 241 pages, has not been brought to court—Bremer wrote that it was buried somewhere. He vacillated between hopes that it would be found and make him famous, and obscene exclamations of disgust with it and his life.

"I only hope somebody other than peace officers, judge or jury reads this. I don't know . . . I don't know. I still don't know if it's jail or prison for me or bye-bye brains."

Throughout his diary he expressed disgust that he had not died earlier, ostensibly after completing a newsmaking assassination. He thought he might go to Hollywood and then, evidently remembering that he got a traffic ticket in New York, he wrote: "I might make a fortune on the silver screen just like I was going to—300 of New York's finest.

"Hey world," he wrote, "Come here. I want to talk to you. One of the reasons I write is I want money."

He said kidnapping had been fashionable earlier in the century, then hijacking airplanes came along, "and I'm going to start the next crime binge, ha! ha!"

One of the reasons Bremer thought he had failed to "get" President Nixon in Canada was that he took the trouble to go back to the motel and brush his teeth, change his suit and take an aspirin. He said he "was ashamed to say" he had taken this detour, and compared himself unfavorably to Sirhan Sirhan. .

"I want to shock the [   ] out of the SS (Secret Service) men with my calmness. Something to be remembered," he wrote.

In a crowd of hippies where he stood out because he was proudly clean-shaven and "nicely suited," he said he had to be careful not to let anybody "press next to my coat pocket and feel the outline of my noisemaker." The President went to a white-tie concert that night, and Bremer hung around the concert hall, observing later, "To wear white tie and tails and get Nixon . . . Boy, wow. To get him in a sweaty tee shirt would lack glamour."

He went to the White House press room in Ottawa and copied down the President's schedule for the next day, which he said was more detailed than the schedule he had been getting from newspapers and television.

He hung around in front of the American embassy, and Nixon "passed me again and I even thought of killing as many SS men as I could—something to show for my effort.

"I didn't want to get in prison or be killed for an unsuccessful attempt. I couldn't take that chance. All my efforts—nothing."

When he compared his manuscript to the Dead Sea Scrolls, he added: "I want something to happen. My fuse is about to burn. There's going to be an explosion soon. I'd just like to take some of them with me and Nixon. All my efforts and nothing!"

And he gave the next full page to these words: "Just another goddam failure!"

Chapter Six

Politics

Overleaf: Sibley with State Representative John Greer, *left,* and House Speaker Tom Murphy, *right,* at the Georgia legislature in the 1970s.

*Of Georgia's infamous multiple governor incident, Sibley once wrote:
"When [Georgia Governor-elect] Eugene Talmadge, at the age of 62
years, slipped from a coma into death at old Piedmont Hospital four
days before Christmas in 1946, he set off what until Watergate was
rated by observers as 'the biggest and oddest political row in U.S.
history.'"*

Supporters of the ailing Talmadge knew of his deteriorating
health when they went to the polls that November and scratched out
his name and wrote in his son Herman's name, hoping to keep the
office in the family. Out-going Governor Ellis Arnall refused to give
up the office. The lieutenant governor-elect, Melvin E. Thompson,
meanwhile assumed he was the legal successor. Herman Talmadge
got himself sworn in and changed the locks to the governor's office.
That's about the time Sibley filed this story.

Talmadge remained in office for 63 days until the Supreme Court
ruled that Thompson was indeed Georgia's governor. Talmadge won
the office in 1948 and served until 1955.

'Aroused Citizens' Organize, Bolster Suit

January 28, 1947

With the fiery oratory of a dozen speakers ringing in their ears
and pledging them to "eternal vigilance, the price of liberty,"
between 500 and 700 Aroused Citizens of Georgia went home
Monday night, fully organized for a fight to "restore Constitutional government to our state."

In a day-long meeting here at the Ansley Hotel, approximately
375 official delegates from 58 counties had accomplished:

   1. The retention of Dr. Paul E. Bryan, professor of law
   at Emory University, as legal counsel to represent them

before the Supreme Court in litigation to remove Herman Talmadge as Governor.

2. Passage of resolutions calling on the General Assembly to adjourn until the courts act and asking Talmadge and M.E. Thompson, claimants to the office, to "do everything in their power to speed a decision by the courts on the merits of the issues involved."

3. Perfected plans for a State-wide organization and named as officers Judge Blanton Forison of Athens, Chairman; Mayor Harvey E. Kennedy, of Barnesville, Co-Chairman; Mrs. Evelyn Bush, of Barnesville, Secretary; and S.C. Candler, of Madison, Treasurer.

Funds to carry on the work of the organization began pouring on the speakers' table before the meeting adjourned. Shortly before adjournment, Edwin Fortson, of Barnesville, a cousin of Judge Fortson and Chairman of the Nominating Committee, reported the Senate had declined to adjourn.

"That just proves," Chairman Fortson said, "we still have our work ahead of us."

John Atkinson, of Greenville, lawyer son of former Gov. Atkinson, characterized the fight as "the same battle our great-great-great-great grandfathers fought 125 years ago" when the people first took the right of electing the Governor from the General Assembly.

Dr. Bryan was the principal speaker at the morning session, introduced by John Sammons Bell, Macon attorney and veteran. The professor, a member of the Emory faculty for 27 years and described by Bell as the State's foremost authority on constitutional law, said he believed Atty. Gen. Eugene Cook was correct in his ruling that Ellis Arnall could have held office for a second term as the result of Gov.-elect Eugene Talmadge's death. He said

Herman Talmadge's interpretation of the Constitution "distorted it beyond all recognition" and described the write-in election of Talmadge as being done through "trickery, chicanery" and as "utterly lacking in good faith."

The assembly gave Mayor Kennedy, of Barnesville, organizer of the Aroused Citizens, a rising vote of appreciation. Other speakers heard were Charles C. Mathias, an Atlanta veteran, who said, "We entrusted our democracy to the legislators and they misused it."

Mrs. Grace Connally, Talmadge-ite, was ousted from the meeting shortly after it opened when she interrupted speeches with cries of "Save the white primary!"

"My heroine" is how Sibley described former First Lady Eleanor Roosevelt in a 1960 column. Decades after this story ran, she would continue to reflect on sitting beside Roosevelt during her 1949 visit to Atlanta's Wesley Memorial Church. Roosevelt, noticing splotches of yellow and green paint on Sibley's arms, easily engaged her in conversation about Sibley's basement woodwork-painting project. A photo of the women together at the meeting remained on the wall of her Constitution office until Sibley's death.

Must Sell Democracy to World—Mrs. FDR

September 9, 1949

Nearly 2,000 Southerners, some of whom had come from points as far away as Texas to hear her, applauded Mrs. Eleanor Roosevelt warmly last night when she placed the responsibility for World Democracy squarely on their shoulders.

Bringing to a close her two-day visit here to participate in a human rights workshop staged by the church women of 10 Southern states, Mrs. Roosevelt told her audience Communism has lost its hope of immediate domination of Europe and is now awaiting world revolution which Americans can help or hinder.

"Time is on their side," Mrs. Roosevelt declared of the Russians. "They are willing to wait—and the down-trodden peoples of Europe and Asia are the ones they are waiting on. They are the people we in America have to convince that Democracy has more to offer them than Communism.

"If we believe in the Christian religion, we have an obligation to face the responsibility that lies on each of us in this nation."

Americans who believe in the individual's dignity and human rights, Americans who say they believe and live their beliefs are the country's safeguard against Communism, the former First Lady declared.

Weary from a full day of speaking, Mrs. Roosevelt delayed her return to New York until today, although she had originally planned to leave last night. Her son, Elliott Roosevelt, is expected to drive her home at 5 A.M. today.

Mrs. Roosevelt spoke intermittently throughout the day. She delivered two formally scheduled addresses and talked informally at a luncheon meeting, a press conference and with members of the Atlanta Junior Chamber of Commerce who sought a brief interview during the afternoon. She participated in two panel discussions and unhesitatingly got to her feet and answered any questions directed at her by the audience.

Pink-cheeked and blue-eyed, the former First Lady spoke in a soft, rather high-pitched but carrying voice. She interspersed her reports with wry humor, particularly on the subject of the Russian delegate's delay-dissent policy. She concluded with a passionately sincere appeal to Americans to believe that the spiritual and moral qualities in the hearts of individuals will be the telling factor in the Battle for Democracy.

"The things that go on in your small town, in your country community, are the things that Russia knows about—and will use if possible," Mrs. Roosevelt declared. "Many times they pick up the news of unpleasant happenings before I have heard it and they greet me in committee meeting by reciting it before representatives of 59 countries. Then they will ask, 'Is this Democracy?'"

Mrs. Roosevelt said the Russians' propaganda system was perhaps the best in the world and the United States was probably the worst principally due to the fact that Americans generally do not feel it necessary to propagandize.

"We have no Iron Curtain," she said. "The world is free to see us as we are. We are the most read-about, the most pictured, the most listened-to country in the world."

Mrs. Roosevelt referred to the graft and petty political evils which *Constitution* editor Ralph McGill discussed in a preceding talk on some Georgia counties at the morning session.

"I couldn't help thinking," she said gently, "of the years my husband besought New York to consolidate its counties—or if not its counties, its townships. The same things Mr. McGill said of some Georgia counties are true of some of our counties in New York. So much he said would be pertinent in any audience in any part of the country."

Mrs. Roosevelt came to Atlanta at the invitation of Mrs. M.E. Tilly.

There's No Law Segregating Gallery, Sheepish House Told

February 9, 1960

Redfaced members of the Georgia House admitted Monday they have been enforcing a non-existent state law when they barred—

with some commotion and once with abusive language—white and Negro spectators from sitting in the same section in the House gallery.

At the same time a hasty check of law books by legal aides to the speaker of the House disclosed there is no state law against either integrated public meetings or integrated eating places in Georgia.

"Well, we used to have such a law," declared Speaker George Smith II, a prominent Swainsboro lawyer, grinning sheepishly. "Ellis Arnall must have taken it out of the constitution when he was governor."

(The state constitution was rewritten during the Arnall administration.)

Later Speaker Smith rallied and invoked another law: "The old, old law of Georgia custom."

He said he will continue to enforce separation of whites and Negroes in the gallery under House rule 13, which gives the speaker the right to clear the gallery "in case of disturbance or disorderly conduct therein."

"I think it would be right to rule it a disturbance if it violates our sacred custom," Smith said.

The search for the House rule or state law against mixed seating was precipitated when a reporter questioned the House doorkeeper, Robert J. Smith of Nahunta, about removal of two small white children who sought to sit in the section roped off for Negroes during the speeches of U.S. Senators Talmadge and Russell Monday.

Robert J. Smith, 32-year-old lawyer, who plans to run for the Legislature next September, is the doorkeeper who received nationwide publicity last week when he ejected a white Morehouse

College professor from the gallery for sitting near—not with—two of his Negro students.

"You know as well as I do I have to enforce the rules of the House," the doorkeeper said.

Asked to cite the rule he was enforcing, the doorkeeper said he did not know the number. Speaker George Smith, questioned, said there was no rule but the House operates under state law. He then launched the fruitless search for the law.

Doorkeeper Smith, applauded by members of the House when he ordered Professor Ovid Futch from the gallery with abusive language last week, Monday made two trips to the roped-off Negro section to ask small white children to move. All seats for whites were filled but the Negro section was mostly empty.

No Marriage of Minds on Quickie Bill

February 19, 1960

In one of their more boisterous moods of this session, members of the Georgia House Thursday cheered, applauded, cracked jokes about man-hungry old maids, spoke of hangovers, hummed "Hearts and Flowers" and brought forth a watch-your-language reprimand from the Speaker.

The subject was a new, all-embracing ban on quickie marriages, which the House says it defeated and the Senate says the House passed.

Lack of a marriage of the minds and Senate leaders happened this way: the quickie marriage ban, providing a three-day waiting period for all marriage license applicants instead of just those under 21, was contained in a Senate amendment to a House bill.

The House voted down that amendment on Wednesday but on Thursday morning passed an amendment to the amendment. (This second amendment was a trivial matter concerning the caption.)

Then Rep. Charles Gowen of Glynn County pushed his motion to reconsider the Senate amendment, which brought forth the exuberant debate and resulted in a vote of 90 ayes and 71 nays. Speaker George Smith ruled that the amendment was defeated for lack of a requisite 103 votes and sent the bill back to the Senate to be agreed to without the amendment or put in a conference committee.

In the Senate, Lamont Smith contended that by amending the amendment (this with the trivial caption change) the House had automatically signified its agreement. President Garland Byrd upheld him and the bill was sent back to the House.

"The amendment was defeated in the House," declared Speaker Smith.

"Our records show that it passed the House," said President Byrd.

Whatever the fate of the amendment, which will probably be settled Friday, members of the House were positive in their stands on it. Rep. Gowen and Rep. Edward Brennan of Catham County, spoke for it. Reps. Maddox Hale of Dade, George Bagby of Paulding, John Odom of Camden and James Floyd of Catoosa heatedly opposed it.

Rep. Brennan said the new measure would fix up the present law against quickie marriages, which provides a waiting period for people under 21, and which he said was "gutted" when it was passed two years ago.

"The only fees it will deprive anybody of are those from people who couldn't wait three days to get married," Brennan said. "We are not talking here about a dog license. We're talking about a license for marriage—the most sacred foundation of our society."

In the back somebody hummed "Hearts and Flowers" and Rep. Johnnie Caldwell of Upson County asked what would be gained by a 48-year-old couple waiting three days.

"I'll tell you what's to be gained," said Brennan. "It will give people a chance to recover from their hangovers and think about it, to get home from the road houses where they've been drinking beer all night."

"Does the gentlemen say that only people with hangovers want to get married?" asked Caldwell.

"Don't you think this is unfair to old maids who catch a man while he's willing, ready and able and may lose him if they wait?"

"Yes, but think how it helps the man!" snapped Brennan.

Rep. Floyd said he thought the amendment deprived over-21 individuals of an important right and cited his own experience of coming home from the Army and getting married in one day. He said he and his wife will soon celebrate their 17th wedding anniversary and they have three children.

"And if anybody says that's a quickie marriage they are a bald-faced liar and an S.O.B.—and that doesn't stand for sonny boy!" Floyd cried.

Speaker Smith rapped sharply for order and "respectively requested the gentleman to watch his language."

Rep. Gowen reiterated statements made Wednesday about corrupt license-issuing practices in the border counties. He said they could be documented by court records which show the conviction of a "blood tester" who was arrested with 60 blank Brantley County marriage licenses "in his brand-new Cadillac."

Rep. Odom of Camden cried, "We in Camden County don't condone that kind of thing! I ask you gentlemen to strike down that amendment!"

Session Goes Out with (Gavel) Bang

February 20, 1960

The House got the jump on the Senate Friday in what is probably Georgia's most traditional political close-harmony duet—adjournment.

About two seconds before the hands of the clock showed 4:50 P.M., Speaker George Smith II of Emanuel County intoned the final words, ". . . this House do now adjourn *SINE DIE!*"

The boys in the Big Room rose to their feet in a high-spirited, wahooing, paper-throwing surge. Speaker Smith trotted to the front of the rostrum and, one hand on his mid-section, one on his back, made his traditional little-boy-at-dancing-school bow to the right and then to the left.

And across the hall Lt. Gov. Garland Byrd was just sounding the gavel and the words, ". . . this Senate do now adjourn *SINE DIE!*"

By century-old custom, the two presiding officers face each other across the breadth of the capitol, lift their gavels together and adjourn at the exact instant. But the House may have grabbed the lead in ending the 1960 session of the General Assembly out of sheer schoolboy impatience. The lower chamber had finished all of its real business by noon, including the giving of presents to officials and attachés. The Senate, on the other hand, had several House-passed bills to consider, including the important administration mental health measure on voluntary admission, and the highly controversial fireworks bill.

So the Senate worked and the ebullient House members entered that end-of-session period of giddy shenanigans, which frequently brings out oratorical talents in members who haven't made a speech all session.

One north Georgia legislator left the chamber to make a telephone-radio broadcast over his hometown radio station from the adjoining anteroom.

"I don't know what the folks back home are going to think," he reported dolefully, "The minute I started talking about the important legislation we've accomplished at this session, somebody in here started calling hogs!"

And Hounds Bay . . .

That "somebody" was Rep. D.D. (Sheriff) Hudson of Irwin County. He not only called hogs, he did a full-scale fox hunt, imitating the bugle baying of half a dozen July hounds, and he came back to do an encore by leading the singing of "The Old Time Religion" and a mournful song which ran: "The devil wears a mighty big shoe . . . If you don't mind he'll slip it on you."

The Speaker, the Speaker Pro Tem, the floor leader, the clerk and assorted aides were given gifts of appreciation for their labors, accompanied by speeches of varying degrees of humor and/or floweriness. This is usual in both Houses. So are dozens of resolutions known to old-timers as "He's-a-Great-Man" resolutions.

From Photogs to Orr

But new this year was a gift by press and television cameramen to Rep. Wilbur Orr, of Wilkes County, author of a bill to ban them from courtrooms. Rep. George Bagby, of Paulding, presented a trick camera and a trophy inscribed to a "Champion Bull

Thrower" on behalf of the "misrepresented, misquoted, misguided, misunderstood" boys of the press.

Rep. Orr, who is going to run for solicitor general instead of returning to the House, slightly misquoted Scripture for his thankyou speech. He told the members to fear not when men "revile you and persecute you and say all manner of evil against you but rejoice and be exceeding glad for," waving the phony camera, "GREAT is your reward!"

In the following article, Sibley casually refers to "two Constitution reporters who would have missed the train, except for a rescue squad of friends and Pullman porters who yanked them aboard" as the LBJ whistlestop special pulled out of a Georgia station. The two Constitution reporters happened to be Sibley and political writer Gene Britton.

"That's a rather juiceless interpretation of it," scoffs longtime friend and fellow journalist William A. Emerson Jr. who was already aboard the train that afternoon in 1960. "As the train was pulling out, I was looking behind us and suddenly I saw Celestine running like a racehorse after the train, lugging a portable typewriter with her. As we attempted to pull her aboard, she refused to let go of that goddamn typewriter. She came over the top of the door at an incredible speed and we all landed in a heap inside the car. I still don't know how we managed to get her aboard. In retropsect, it was a damn foolish thing to do. We could have been killed."

Still, Sibley, a life-long lover of trains, was suitably impressed with Johnson's mode of travel. In a column published two days later she wrote: "I'm thinking about running for public office. A whistlestop tour of the nation is the closest thing I can imagine to trouping the world with a circus."

N. Georgia Goes Wild for Johnson

October 12, 1960

En route with Lyndon Johnson, two native delights of the old-time rural South—a political campaign and a railroad train—balled the jack into the hearts of multitudes of light-hearted, leather-lunged north Georgians Tuesday night.

"The LBJ Special," custom-outfitted private train of the president of the Texas & Pacific railroad, brought the Democratic Party's candidate for vice president, Lyndon Johnson, "back where Grandpa started in 1838—the great state of Georgia."

He made whistlestop appearances at Toccoa, Gainesville and Atlanta—the first railroad platform appearances of a major political candidate many Georgians had witnessed since the days of William Jennings Bryan—and they gave it all they had.

In Toccoa they washed down the main railroad crossing at Alexander and Four Acre Streets with a hose, placarded the right-of-way with "All the way with LBJ" and "We Want Jack" posters, called forth their two high school bands to play "Dixie" and went as far as five counties away to bring in senior citizens to "take a look at this boy from Texas."

The "boy from Texas" swept off his white Stetson, introduced his wife Lady Bird and swiftly ingratiated himself with his hosts.

Surprise of the itinerary was a supposedly "blasé big city" —Atlanta. The pros on the campaign train said a crowd of ten people would be pretty good in a big city late at night. Johnson himself told his press conference that big city crowds wouldn't be likely to show up in as great numbers as in small towns and country places.

The train pulled into Terminal Station and a gaudy, bumptious, roaring throng waved banners, shouted, jumped in time to the scarlet-clad Grady High School band's "Yellow Rose of Texas." Television lights flooded the scene. "Georgia Loves Lyndon and Lady Bird!" one placard proclaimed. "Nix On Nixon!" echoed another.

Obviously moved by the hefty, hearty country fair quality of this urban welcome, which Mayor Hartsfield and local Democratic leaders whipped up on one day's notice, Senator Johnson hit his stride as a Southern-style orator. He lampooned Vice President Nixon's travels so humorously the crowd roared its appreciation. And he hit a poignant, near-tears homestretch by telling the story of Sen. John Kennedy's brother's death with a Texas hero in World War II.

Capt. Joe Kennedy and the Texan volunteered for a mission from which they never returned, he said, finishing hoarsely, "No one dared asked those boys who died that you might live, what church they went to that morning!"

A murmur swept the crowd and erupted again and again into applause and loud cheers.

The crowds in Toccoa and Gainesville responded so enthusiastically that one small child, who stumbled on a cross tie, was almost trampled to death and two *Constitution* reporters would have missed the train, except for a rescue squad of friends and Pullman porters who yanked them aboard as the southbound special gathered speed.

Later in a press conference, Sen. Johnson pronounced whistle-stop electioneering "wonderful." He said it was suggested to him by former President Truman, who recommended it as a means of getting to people outside the big cities.

"It was a very excellent recommendation," Sen. Johnson declared. He said he had never ridden a train until he came to Washington in 1951 because there were none in his part of Texas.

"Grandpa moved away from near Austin when the trains came in. He preferred live oak trees to railroads. He must have chosen the terrain well because it's been a hundred years since he moved and we still don't have a railroad in Johnson City."

Faces Reporters

The vice-presidential candidate seated beside Mrs. Johnson, faced a battery of newspaper, radio and television reporters and cameras to sum up his impressions of the campaign so far.

"I would say the South's in better shape than it's been since the Third Term," he replied to a question about its allegiance to the Democratic Party.

"But Senator," protested a reporter, "you said that in New York."

"I'm not prohibited from repeating myself, am I?" countered Johnson.

"But you sounded a little more convincing this time," the reporter continued.

"I always try to sound my convictions," Johnson said crisply. "If I sounded hollow in New York, I apologize."

Won't "Undo"

He said he could not believe the South would have elected Democratic governors, senators and representatives and then "undo" that by failing to elect a Democratic president.

To a question about a "heckling" Nixon sign which appeared in a crowd along the route (not in Georgia), Senator Johnson said he was undisturbed by evidences of difference of opinion.

"I am amazed that there's so little difference of opinion," he said. "I have seen a few Nixon signs. That's not unusual. I have asked our people not to take our signs to other people's meetings and not to waste our signs on Republican cars. I think that's just good manners."

Mrs. Johnson, who was in Georgia last week to crown the Homemaker of the Year, injected another sign into the talk. She said she hoped photographers got a picture of one "up the road apiece" which read: "The Poor Man Has Two Friends—The Good Lord And The Democratic Party."

Another reporter asked her if she saw the one which read: "I Like LBJ Better Than Grits."

Railroad officials in Toccoa said the LBJ Special was the first presidential campaign train they had brought through this part of the state. Franklin D. Roosevelt often passed through on his way to Warm Springs and he spoke in Gainesville on several occasions.

"We went down there to hear him," Cliff Mitchell, 76-year-old justice of the peace of Martin, 10 miles away, explained. He said he was a lifelong Democrat and he expressed confidence that Georgia will go Democratic in this race. "We have a Republican down home," he explained with a wry chuckle. "Man had some children in the Army and he voted for Eisenhower. First time I ever heard of it happening around here."

Mugger Is Slugged by Legislator

March 9, 1973

A state representative used the Golden Gloves boxing experience of his youth to disarm a mugger and break his jaw in downtown Atlanta, the legislator told his House colleagues Thursday.

Rep. Henry Bostick of Tifton, known as "Battling Bostick" in his boxing days, took the floor on a point of personal privilege to decry the lack of law enforcement on Atlanta streets. He said he was the fifth member of the General Assembly to be attacked or threatened on the streets during the current session.

Bostick's complaint spurred the House to adopt unanimously a resolution that said the state Capitol should be moved to Waverly Hall, a small town in Harris County.

During his speech, Bostick flourished the knife he said he had wrested from his assailant.

Bostick said a white man with the knife attacked him as he walked along Peachtree Street two blocks south of the Fox Theater Wednesday night.

"He said, 'Wait, mister,' and he started to pull this knife out of his pocket," said Bostick, showing his colleagues a knife with a blade about four inches long.

"When he did that, I creamed him," Bostick said. "The knife went one way and he went the other."

"The city of Atlanta stinks," Bostick shouted. "I don't want to see you gentlemen give them any more money until they clean up the place.

"We need to clean up those whores, robbers and muggers," he declared.

Among legislators Bostick listed as victims or near-victims of city street assail were Rep. Claude Bray of Manchester, Rep. Ren Jessup of Cochran and Sen. Jay Carroll Cox of Twin Cities.

"If it wasn't for his long legs, Donald Fraser (one of the shorter members of the House) might have been robbed by a prostitute and her boyfriend," Bostick added.

Charging Atlanta leadership with not keeping the city safe for members of the General Assembly who have "done so much for them," Bostick said, "I don't think the state of Georgia ought to give them anything for the city of Atlanta. It's a disgrace to this House."

As a result of Bostick's experience and that of the members he mentioned, Rep. Earl Davis of Columbus and Rep. J. Hoyt Adam of Upatio introduced the successful resolution to move the Capitol and all other functions of state government to Waverly Hall.

Reminding their colleagues that Atlanta was considered an iniquitous place as early as 1877 when there was another effort to move the Capitol, the authors of the resolution recommended Waverly Hall as "a tranquil city of fresh air, clean streets, beautiful homes, good workers, good schools and churches and law-abiding Christian people who would be eternally grateful to have the Georgia state Capitol in their city."

Having never covered a national political convention prior to 1976's Democratic National Convention in New York City and the Republican Convention in Kansas City later that summer, Sibley forever claimed she was nervous about not getting access to key events.

"She was not nervous," says Jim Minter who, as the AJC's managing editor at the time, sent her to the conventions. "That may have been her act, mind you. She was a tough reporter and one of the most-read people on the staff. It was a no-brainer to send her."

The following dispatch from New York details Sibley's alleged apprehensions about gaining access to convention's main players. In the end, she managed to get to everyone, including the presidential nominee's mother, "Miss Lillian" Carter. The matriarch invited "Christine from down-home" to sit with her in her hotel room as Carter anxiously awaited a meeting with the cast members of her favorite TV show, All My Children.

Rambling Reporter Takes
Doormen to the Cleaners: 'V.I.P.'
Pass Opens Convention Doors

July 14, 1976

New York—Who says New Yorkers are tough? Who says Democrats are well-organized?

They're not even observant.

After all *The New York Times* said about the many-colored passes and the pecking order in the press (a red pass being better than a peach one, for instance, and a mauve one being best of all), I've been getting around a full day on a Roswell, Ga., dry cleaner's ticket.

It's pale green and it says in neat-not-gaudy black letters: "V.I.P."

If it hadn't rained the night the convention opened, I wouldn't have known what a treasure I had. But I hauled out my raincoat Tuesday morning and there it was, assuring me in agate type that my old coat (called "this garment") had been given V.I.P. treatment "but the spots remaining cannot be removed without damage to the color or fabric."

Then a bit further down it notes: "We bring this to your attention so that you will know that we did not overlook it."

On the off chance that the dry cleaner's apology (reproach?) might get me in more places than the heavy load of passes issued by Robert S. Strauss, chairman of the Democratic Party, I left the ticket on my coat.

Right away I got into the caucus of Latin delegates. Their doorman saw my green cleaner's ticket, showed all his white teeth and bobbed his head deferentially, "Si si! Com' een!" he cried.

It was a mere technicality that I didn't understand a word they said (I don't understand many words that English-speaking New Yorkers say, so that wasn't surprising). I took copious notes and departed.

In rapid order I was admitted to the bedroom of Averell Harriman's secretary to await an interview with him. He was busy, she said, with interviews lined up for hours to come. Then she glanced at my dry cleaning ticket and added, "But I know he will want to see YOU!"

To do her credit, when I explained to Mrs. Margaret Chapman that I was an impostor, not really a V.I.P. at all, she laughed heartily and made me all the more welcome. I was glad because the atmosphere in Averell Harriman's suite at the Statler Hilton was Old World elegant, bordering on the exotic.

I wasn't surprised at the fresh pink roses in the vase in the living room but the sight of a woman (a maid maybe?) pressing Mrs. Harriman's underwear on a portable ironing board set up in the bedroom was a dizzying view of how the Democratic Party's eldest and perhaps richest and most stylish elder statesman retains a hold on the finer things.

Still called "governor," although he has been many other things in government since the 1930s, including ambassador to Russia and the court of St. James, Secretary of Commerce under President Truman and special envoy to Churchill and Stalin in the World War II years, Gov. Harriman is now at 84 the author of a new book, the Democratic Party's Washington adviser on foreign policy, a New York delegate at large and a whingding of a Jimmy Carter supporter.

"Of course, they are all so different," Harriman said of the candidates of the last 40 years. "Gov. Carter has the unique faculty of understanding people, of talking to his audience. That was a quality Roosevelt had. I think he compares with Roosevelt more than anybody else."

Franklin D. Roosevelt, said the old Democrat, smiling reminiscently, "used to glory in his enemies—and so did Harry Truman in a different kind of way. I don't see that in Carter. He has enormous sympathies with the problems of people and, unlike the Republican who says he wants to force people to work, Carter believes that if the jobs are available the people will take them."

Harriman said he will not be offered a job in the Carter administration and he doesn't want one.

"At 84, I do many things but working 18 hour days, which you have to do in government, is not something I want to do."

Harriman, the wealthy scion of the Union Pacific Railroad family, was, along with Roosevelt, called a "traitor to his class" back in the 1930s. He smiled at the memory, obviously content that the fights and fortunes of the Democratic Party have been worth his energies and support.

Asked who would be the nominee for vice president, he smiled and shook his head. "I'm not going to guess. As I used to say in Roosevelt's time, I never answer iffy questions. I was never hired to be a prophet. And I have no preference."

As a director of the Illinois Central Railroad, which owned the Central of Georgia, Mr. Harriman made many trips to Atlanta early in the century, he said.

"I've seen Atlanta and Georgia develop and know it well," he said. "Therefore, it is no surprise to me that we have a unique man to come out of Georgia. Georgia is a great state. Atlanta is a great city."

My dry cleaning tag and I bowed out on that and left the old governor to a *Newsday* photographer.

The next door I intended to open was that of the Persian Room at the Plaza, where the American Association of Retired Persons was meeting and the candidate's mother, "Miss Lillian," was expected to be in attendance.

Getting to the Plaza from Madison Square Garden might give your ordinary country bumpkin a little trouble. Not one wearing a Roswell dry cleaner's tag.

Policemen bowed and took my arm and escorted me to the entrance of subway stations. Token sellers gasped at the V.I.P. and shouted to me over the roar of the trains exact, if unintelligible, directions for getting to my destination. Other passengers smiled and when I asked for more directions (I always check directions against directions) they asked me politely if I was staying at the Plaza.

I stopped for a sandwich in a health food bar (New York's frozen yogurt may be the best discovery since hog jowl and peas). The proprietor left the backroom and came out and asked me if I knew Carter personally and what kind of man he is. (I gave him a report only his blood kin could beat.) He respectfully sought my opinion on who will be the vice-presidential nominee and I was authoritative as only a V.I.P. can be. Everybody I said, knows it will be Barbara Jordan. He seemed surprised but pleased.

My tag didn't open the door of the Persian Room at the Plaza for me but it wasn't its fault. There was nobody there. No meeting. (John Keasler, the *Miami Herald* columnist said later, "There's a lot of that going around.")

So I headed back toward Madison Square Garden, looking for people to tell, as I promised Georgia's Lamar Plunkett, that *Newsweek* magazine's symposium didn't accurately reflect what the former state senator feels about Carter. He's afraid people will not understand that he "loves, values and admires" Carter and is working very hard for him at this convention.

And now I've got to hurry. There's a hookers' caucus across the street. I wonder if I'm V.I.P. enough to get into that. I have already got the word from demonstrating "lesbian sisters and gay brothers" to "Live Free—Love Freely."

Sibley was a life-long Democrat and ardent supporter of her party. Still, while covering the Republican National Convention in the summer of 1976, the reporter attempted to remain neutral. Knowing Sibley's political affiliation makes the following correspondence even more entertaining. As usual, she had a few exploits to share with readers in her dispatches from Kansas City. While packing for the trip at Sweet Apple, her legendary log cabin home in suburban Atlanta, she was dive-bombed by a swarm of hornets. ("The only explanation I have for their behavior is that they're Republicans and wanted to come with me," she commented.) When she got to Kansas City, there were no taxis available so she accepted a ride from "a fat man in a white plastic cowboy hat" who assumed she was a Republican delegate. Wrote Sibley in the Constitution's *Aug. 17 edition: "People who say politics is a masquerade are a way ahead of me. I'm just finding out that covering politics is a masquerade."*

Media Is Welcome to Watch—Not Eat

August 18, 1976

Kansas City—What is said on the Republican National Convention calendar for Tuesday was "Brunch for Republican Women Leaders. Guests Betty and Susan Ford, Nancy and Maureen Reagan . . . Invitation Only. Open to News Media."

Both Elizabeth Ray and I thought that meant us.

We and about 25 or 30 other reporters and photographers showed at the posh Alameda Plaza Hotel looking for the International Room. You know Elizabeth Ray, a secretary-turned-reporter who doesn't know how to type? Well, she didn't get any closer to the action—or the quiche Lorraine—than I did, despite her other skills.

The Republican Women Leaders didn't mean they WANTED us at their shindig or that they INVITED us. What they meant was that we could come and watch them eat.

Honest. They had one end of the International Ballroom chained off with a plastic ivory chain, and that's where the news media was corralled. Photographers were given a sort of carpeted box to stand on to provide elevation necessary for watching Mrs. Betty Ford chew and record it if they had telephoto lenses. (Nancy Reagan didn't eat a bite as far as I could make out. You don't think she stays bone-thin by eating at all the places she's asked, do you?)

The rest of us sat or stood and watched the cantaloupe go by and then the quiche and the salad and finally some compote-looking dessert and coffee.

Some of the Republicans ladies apparently overslept and didn't get there. (Mrs. Patricia Hutar, president of the National Federation of Republican Women, who was presiding, said it was "their heavy responsibilities" that kept them away.) So there was some cantaloupe left over and a pleasant woman with hospitality responsibilities offered it to the press.

One plump lady who is both a practicing Republican and a reporter for a San Fernando Valley, Calif., paper said cheerfully, "I'm not proud. I'll take it."

Then she turned to the glum crew behind her and said, "Will anybody split it with me?"

Everybody stared stonily ahead, including a girl who had called it a "drunch," and didn't answer. The California lady looked disappointed, but she handed it back.

"I always think it's nice to accept anything if somebody wants to give it to you," she murmured.

I asked the "drunch" girl what she meant, if the meeting had begun with drinks. She pretended not to hear me.

Meanwhile, Elizabeth Ray was stopped somewhere above stairs and didn't even get in the room. Photographers had her so occupied she never even got to see the quiche go by, much less hear the speeches.

It's possible Miss Ray wouldn't have considered the speeches very stirring. They ran heavily to congratulations and counter-congratulations and more congratulations for 1. Being women, 2. Being Republican women.

The way Mrs. Hutar put it, they had "an intrinsic sense of achievement that is felt by every woman here who has set out to do what she wanted to do." (I don't think she had Elizabeth Ray in mind.)

Mrs. Hutar called Mrs. Ford and Mrs. Reagan "campaigners who are teammates of their husbands," and Mrs. Ford, looking sumptuous in a white silk dress with black and yellow trim and every hair in place, stood up to say a few words. (Mrs. Reagan didn't. Apparently she doesn't open her mouth for speeches, any more than for food. She just smiles and looks fragile and luminous and loving.)

Mrs. Ford began by halting the applause with a commanding wave of her hands. (You can tell she was a dancer, she does this so gracefully.)

"I know we are in a hurry and we can't spend too much time on applause," she began. So they applauded again.

And then she got to the congratulations. She was overwhelmed, she said, by the presence of so many accomplishing women and she hoped to see twice that many the next time they get together —women getting into government and becoming leaders.

"Grasp it," she said of leadership, "take it and run with it and more power to you!"

Carla Hills, Secretary of the Department of Housing and Urban Development and the third woman to hold cabinet rank, dispensed a fair number of compliments and congratulations and then hit her main theme—Democratic spending.

"I recommend that you read the Democratic platform," she said, "not for reading pleasure but as an exercise in the occult!"

She said she had checked it out and it proposes to spend $62 billion a year on housing alone—a deficit the national economy cannot sustain. If the Democrats are elected, she promised, federal spending will "drive our country to the wall and usher in an era of bureaucracy from which there might not be any rescue."

The meeting ended with a prayer and I tried to find Elizabeth Ray when I left for outside. I think she had gone to lunch.

A Most American Day:
'Ladies and Gentlemen, the President . . .'

January 21, 1977

Washington, D.C.—There are some combinations of words which make an American citizen come to instant, tingling attention. They said them Thursday about Jimmy Carter.

"Ladies and gentlemen, the President of the United States!"

There was a swift intake of breath by many of the 117,000 Americans sitting on little folding chairs or standing in the snow in front of the gleaming east facade of the U.S. Capitol. There was a sudden, unbidden rush of tears to some eyes.

A dark-eyed 12-year-old from Baltimore clutched his camera and said, "Oh, wow!"

A black woman from Georgia said softly, "Yes, Lord!"

"The President . . . !" An elderly man in stocking cap whispered, "He's in."

Off in the distance, a cannon began booming the traditional 21-gun salute. A security man on the peak of the Capitol roof took the binoculars from his eyes and shifted his stance to a jaunty, assured parade rest.

President Jimmy Carter began speaking.

In his light, earnest-schoolboy voice, he spoke the ancient, majestic words of the Old Testament prophet Micah, and while he spoke, except for the sound of melting snow dripping off the photographers' vanned roof and the blocks-away wail of an ambulance, the quiet of total and intense attention was unbroken.

Six times they stirred to punctuate his speech with a light spattering of applause. Once, when he promised that this country will "fight our wars against poverty, ignorance and injustice," there were cheers.

And when he finished—less than 15 minutes after he had begun—they applauded and then got to their feet with bared heads or hands over their hearts to join their own thin uncertain sopranos and baritones with the strong voice of Cantor Isaac Goodfriend of Atlanta in singing "The Star-Spangled Banner."

"I'm glad I was here," Mrs. Bessie Sutton of Boston said. "I'm 80 years old and it's my first inaugural—the most American of all ceremonies, wouldn't you say?"

It had been a "most American" day for many of us. I began it at 6 A.M. at the Lincoln Memorial, arriving two hours early to avoid the crowd. I avoided it so thoroughly there was nobody there except for some television crews stringing cables across the icy walks, Abraham Lincoln and me. It was dark and so bitterly cold that when the Forest Service men began arriving and setting up oil drums and building fires in them, the heat they generated was barely noticeable, even when you hovered over the drums.

"When you're standing on ice, it takes a heap of heat," a Forest Service man explained.

But gradually they began to arrive for the prayer service. First a young father named James McMann and his 10-year-old son David from Blue Point, Long Island. They had a backpack and a thermos jug, and they had been traveling all night to be sure to get there on time.

They were in time to join me in a lonely little interlude with the gentle, tragic marble man in the chair—the homely, sad-faced Old Abe.

A black man with a rag and soap powder scrubbed at the marble base of Abe's statue, and we stood for a moment looking at him: his plain, squared-toed boots, the big joined hands on the arms of the chair.

Then Davis stood with his back to the statue and his daddy took his picture.

Daniel Wirth of Jackson Heights, N.Y., was the next person to arrive, and we stood together and read the words carved over Old Abe's head: "In this temple, as in the hearts of the people for whom he saved the Union, the memory of Abraham Lincoln is enshrined forever."

The television people were multiplying and their speaker system was pouring out record music, a tune called "Something Stupid" and a commercial for the People's drug stores.

The Washington Monument laid a dark finger against a pale gray sky, and beyond it the Capitol dome lent the dawn a crown of lights.

Then the ushers arrived. The Meditation group from the United Nations—men in pale blue coats and white trousers, women in fragile multicolored saris (they all assured me that they had on long-john underwear and it was not enough).

Three hundred singers from many Washington choirs and the Atlanta Boy Choir came next—wearing a conglomeration of choir robes pieced out with fur coats, army jackets, netted caps and combat boots.

Fletcher Wolfe, director of the little boys from Atlanta, said they all wore long underwear under their robes and plastic sandwich bags on their feet.

They took their positions on the cold stone steps leading to the white-columned gallery housing the statue, and because it was early and the audience had not fully arrived, Norman Scribner, the conductor, led them in what was to be a little warm-up session.

The sun was beginning to rise, staining the tall columns with a rose-colored light and making a path of brightness toward the Washington Monument when opera singer Leontyne Price approached the microphone to warm up her vocal cords.

Instead of singing a few bars, she opened her mouth and gave them the whole, rich, heart-stopping spiritual "He's Got the Whole World in His Hands."

The entire choir broke into spontaneous applause.

Day had come and with it Jimmy Carter's pastor, the Rev. Bruce E. Edwards of Plains, to pray, and Carter's sister, Ruth Carter Stapleton, to read the Scripture.

And there was "Daddy" King, the patriarch of the civil rights movement, the father of Martin Luther King Jr., to preach.

"I stand here with a little bit of reluctance and timidity from these hallowed grounds," the 80-year-old Atlanta minister began. "Fourteen years ago my son stood and delivered his great speech on this green."

He said that he didn't know if the President-elect was there (he wasn't), but "if so, I highly greet him and his family."

The venerable pastor took his text from Jesus' admonition to Simon Peter, "Lovest thou me? Feed my sheep."

"The sheep must be fed," he said. "This is what it is all about. Martin Luther King Jr. gave his life talking, preaching all over the world that the least of these wouldn't be forgotten.

"It's what the President-elect is all about. God grant, God grant that our President will remember always the least of these. We always will have as far as I know, more of the least of these than all the rest."

While he talked, cries of "Amen!" came from the audience. And back of the standing crowd of an estimated 4,000 people, cries of salesmen mingled with a strident voice calling, "The attorney general is a racist."

It was a most American beginning to a most American day. All this and a Washington crowd standing together in the cold, "raising" as Dr. King put it, that old camp meeting hymn, "Amazing Grace."

Administering the oath of office to Vice-President Walter F. Mondale seemed to take longer than it takes to administer the oath to the President.

House Speaker Thomas Peter (Tip) O'Neill began by saying, "Walter F. Mondale, citizen of the state of Minnesota, duly elected vice president, are you ready to take the oath of office?"

"I am," Mondale replied in a strong, carrying voice.

O'Neill then asked if he would take the oath "without mental reservation or the purpose of evasion."

And the vice president-elect said, "I will."

Mondale placed his hand on the Bible his mother gave him a few years ago. Next to it was a Bible used by George Washington when he was administered the same 35-word oath in 1789.

When the inaugural was over and he had lunched with senators, President Carter and his First Lady walked together the length of the parade route from the Capitol to their new home at 1600 Pennsylvania Avenue.

I walked it, too, but a policeman stopped me when I got to 1600 Pennsylvania Avenue.

"It was her idea," Sibley's AJC editor Amanda Miller says of Sibley's final reporting assignment. "She was talking to me about wanting to see this Roosevelt memorial they were dedicating in Washington. She said, 'Do you think the paper would send me?'" Being the AJC's most senior, most respected correspondent had its privileges.

Upon her return, Sibley had the enthusiasm of a cub reporter. "She gave me all the details," says Miller. "She said what really got to her was the depiction of the men in the bread line, how the sculptor was able to capture these really proud men who had been forced to stand in a line for something to eat. She teared up as she talked about it."

A Grateful Nation Honors the Roosevelts

May 3, 1997

Washington, D.C.—They came on crutches and in wheelchairs. They came wearing Gold Star Mothers caps. One old soldier wore a World War I uniform with a line of medals across the pocket. They stood when the Navy band played the "Star-Spangled Banner," held their hands over their hearts when the six flags of the nation's military passed. They applauded the present President of the United States and, because so many of them remembered another President and another day, they cried.

It may have been the most moving celebration Washington has seen in a generation.

A benign sun poured gold over Potomac Park. A cool breeze rippled the waters of the Potomac Basin just beyond a row of cherry trees. Great planes from National Airport roared overhead, and before a platform just in front of a long row of granite structures, an estimated 20,000 people gathered for the dedication of the first big memorial to honor President Franklin D. Roosevelt.

He had not wanted a big memorial, he who dedicated the magnificent memorial to Thomas Jefferson in 1943, but many speakers pointed out that this 7-acre, $48 million monument is a lest-we-forget effort. How will the young remember and value him?

As President Clinton said, "For years, none (no memorial) seemed necessary . . . the America he built was a memorial all around us, from the Golden Gate Bridge to the Grand Coulee Dam, from Social Security to honest financial markets, from an America that has remained the world's indispensable nation to our shared conviction that all Americans must make our journey together, Roosevelt was all around us."

The crowd began gathering in the park hours before the program was slated to begin. And many of them were young parents with babies in strollers, smart young Marines and Air Force men, resplendent in their uniforms, offering their arms to guide distinguished guests and the aged and infirm to folding chairs. The press of the world seemed to have come to the party, and more than 50 television and newspaper photographers filled the loft built over the press section.

Princess Margriet of the Netherlands drew applause with some homey touches. She mentioned she was Roosevelt's godchild, born in Canada, where she and her parents and her grandmother, Queen Wilhelmina, were in exile during World War II.

"President Roosevelt was proud of his Dutch ancestry," she said. "When he was sworn into office, he held his hand on the Dutch family Bible." Because his name meant "field of roses" in Dutch, growers there developed an orange-colored rose to "reflect the close ties between the Roosevelts and the House of Orange."

A great bouquet welcomed visitors at the entrance to the memorial, and the princess presented armloads of the rare orange rose to first lady Hillary Rodham Clinton and Tipper Gore, wife of the vice president.

President Clinton formally received the memorial from Sen. Daniel Inouye, who, with former Sen. Mark Hatfield and FDR grandson David Roosevelt, represented the memorial commission, which spent six years getting the memorial planned and executed. "The United States proudly accepts this Franklin Delano Roosevelt Memorial," Clinton said.

Clinton had a break in his voice when he ended his talk with quotes from a speech Roosevelt was writing when he died at the Little White House at Warm Springs, Ga.

Later, he conducted a tour through the four chambers of memories. Like many of the visitors, I held out my hand to touch the hats of the poor, discouraged men depicted in a bread line.

During the afternoon, the park was filled with visitors, many of whom had their pictures taken with the bread line statues. One plump lady in a running suit posed for a photograph with Eleanor Roosevelt, whose statue was very moving, plain and big. Somebody had anonymously put a bouquet of roses beside one of the statue's big ugly shoes.

The whole monument, in spite of its size and its cost, is very simple. It relies on waterfalls and the inscribed words of Roosevelt in every so-called room.

The blocks of concrete were cool and gray, and many young families sprawled out on benches to rest. I heard a young father say to his 10-year-old son, "Why can't you stop and let me read this to you."

Like an old lady wearing a Gold Star Mothers campaign cap, I felt that I knew every one of those men Mr. Roosevelt lifted out of the bread line—and am kin to some of them.

AFTERWORD

In the early morning hours of Sunday, August 15, 1999, after a lengthy battle with cancer, Celestine Sibley passed away at her beach house on Dog Island, Fla. She was 85.

She had continued to work until the final weeks of her illness, with her last regular *AJC* column appearing on July 25.

By noon, her colleagues had gathered in the eighth floor features department conference room to begin assembling memorial coverage. Reporters set about soliciting quotes from the people who knew Sibley. Responses came in from former presidents, governors, Pulitzer Prize-winning peers, her street friends on Marietta Street and hundreds of her intensely loyal *AJC* readers who had lost a breakfast companion of nearly 60 years.

Sibley's co-workers quietly shuffled in on Monday morning to begin the first work week without her they had ever known. Her cluttered, lively office, usually consisting of Sibley and her assistant Debra Childers congregated near *Constitution* editor Henry Grady's rolltop desk answering reader mail or analyzing the news of the day, was locked and darkened.

Over the years, the reporters stationed on the eighth floor knew the real job perks didn't lie with the dental plans or 401K options the newspaper offers to its employees. It was grabbing that first morning cup of java at the coffee station next to Sibley's office and hearing that gravelly but upbeat voice greet one with: "Come in!" When one complied, that statement invariably would be followed with "Whatcha know?" as her reporter's quizzical eye firmly fixed on her colleague.

Co-workers and readers alike assembled at Sibley's old church, North Avenue Presbyterian, on August 18 to bid her good-bye, some turning up 90 minutes early to insure a seat. WXIA-TV, Atlanta's NBC affiliate, pre-empted its regular programming to cover the memorial service live.

In his eulogy, colleague and friend William A. Emerson Jr. told the capacity crowd, "Just 10 days ago she told me, 'Bill Emerson, get them to stop this legend-talk. You can tell them I'm not a legend.' It is modest and typical that Celestine would say that, *but she is a legend*. There is going to have to be some celestial intervention to edit out all of that legend-talk. There's a scarcity of legends in the journalism business today, and Celestine's death is a serious loss."

After swapping damp tissues and hugs and pimento cheese sandwiches, Sibley's *AJC* admirers eventually surrendered to their impending deadlines and returned to the newsroom. It was there that the buzzing over her *New York Times* obituary began. Former *AJC* editor Bill Kovach was quoted in it remarking, "She was the last voice of the white-glove, tea-and-apple-blossom set that had not a sharp edge on it." Someone in the newsroom read the quote out loud and the air instantly became electric. Sibley's longtime newsroom pal Betty Parham's jaw went slack.

Mimicking her departed friend's gut reaction anytime Sibley felt an injustice had been dealt a loved one, Parham sputtered, "Gimme that phone!"

Sibley's allies gathered around Betty's desk, exhibiting the intensity of the torch-bearing villagers outside the mad scientist's castle in the final reel of *Frankenstein*. Parham perched her bifocals on the tip of her nose and dialed Kovach's office at the

Nieman Foundation for Journalism at Harvard University. Thirty seconds later, she had Kovach on the line.

"Mr. Kovach, I don't know if you remember me or not but this is Betty Parham at the *AJC* in Atlanta," she began politely. "We've just gotten back from seeing Celestine off and we were a little confused by your quote in her *New York Times* obit." Parham then re-read the quote to Kovach and asked if he had been quoted correctly. Kovach replied that he had.

Her voice rising almost imperceptibly, Parham asked, "Did you even *know* her, Mr. Kovach? We're all standing around here at the paper looking a little stunned. We really can't believe you would describe her that way—in the *New York Times*, of all publications— if you had known her at all. She shunned that whole white glove thing. It's just a complete misrepresentation of everything she stood for."

Colleagues standing closest to Parham later claimed they could hear Kovach's necktie tighten through the phone as he graciously backpedaled and then finally conceded the caller's point. Betty then casually suggested that a possible retraction might be in order. Parham thanked him for listening to her thoughts and as she returned her phone to its cradle, a cheer and a standing ovation went up across half the newsroom. Her defenders couldn't shake the feeling that Sibley's spirit was there leading the applause.

Across the room, the door was open and the lights were once again on inside Sibley's office.

SOURCES

Books and Journals

Darnell, Tim. *Southern Yankees: The Story of the Atlanta Crackers.* Atlanta: Self-Published, 1995.

Garrett, Franklin M. *Atlanta and Environs: A Chronicle of Its People and Events,* Vol. 2. Athens, Georgia: University of Georgia Press, 1969.

Martin, Harold H. *Atlanta and Environs: A Chronicle of Its People and Events,* Vol. 3. Athens, Georgia: University of Georgia Press, 1987.

McDonald, R. Robin. *Secrets Never Lie: The Death of Sara Tokars—A Southern Tragedy of Money, Murder and Innocence Betrayed.* New York: Avon, 1998.

Sibley, Celestine. *Peachtree Street, U.S.A.* New York: Doubleday, 1963.

———. *Turned Funny: A Memoir.* New York: Harper & Row, 1988.

White, Jaclyn Weldon. *Whisper to the Black Candle: Voodoo, Murder and the Case of Anjette Lyles.* Macon, Georgia: Mercer University Press, 1999.

Interviews

Sibley, Celestine. Interview by the editor. Tape recording. *Atlanta Journal-Constitution,* 1 April 1999.

Newspapers

Barringer, Felicity. "Celestine Sibley Is Dead at 85; Columnist Embodied the South," *New York Times,* 17 August 1999.

East, Cammie. "Mobilians Remember Celestine Sibley," *Mobile Register,* 17 August 1999.

Emerson, Bo. "She Wrote Her Name on a Region: the South Mourns Celestine Sibley," *Atlanta Journal-Constitution,* 16 August 1999.

Staff of the *Atlanta Journal-Constitution* and Celestine Sibley. "Celebrating Celestine," *Atlanta Journal-Constitution,* 22 August 1999.

ACKNOWLEDGMENTS

Scanning miles and miles of newspapers stored on microfilm for a concentrated period of many months is not an activity that inspires everyone. I cherished every frame. Twelve years after I closed my last college textbook as a journalism major, I never anticipated taking another writing course. Unearthing, scrutinizing and manually inputting every single one of these articles word by word, sentence by sentence, paragraph by paragraph into a computer was just that and more. Work on this project also yielded a rare opportunity to spend more time with a woman who served as a mentor and a beloved newsroom friend, a woman I could only ever refer to in person as *ma'am*.

Attempting to compile a comprehensive selection culled from nearly 70 years of a daily newspaper reporter's work is a daunting task. When that individual is a Southern icon adored by countless readers and someone one has admired since age 16, the stakes are raised even higher. Each time the job threatened to swallow me whole as I worked in my midtown Atlanta study, I would hear through my window the bells chiming from Sibley's old church, North Avenue Presbyterian, two blocks away. It was almost as if she were cheering me on and offering hope.

Other people hugely responsible for this project's positive outcome include Tom Payton, Patrick Allen and Anne Richmond Boston of Hill Street Press; Sibley Fleming; Bill Emerson; Terry Kay; Sam Massell; Barbara Babbit Kaufman; Jaclyn Weldon White; Lee Walburn; Jim Minter; Laura Micham in the Special

Collections Department of the Robert W. Woodruff Library at Emory University; Debby Starnes at the *Mobile Resister*; Charlotte Chamberlain at the Mobile Public Library; Christine McDowell, Lani Suchcicki and Earl Melvin at the *Pensacola News-Journal* and Ginny Everett, Jennifer Ryan, Pam Prouty and Valerie Boyd in the *Atlanta Journal-Constitution* news research services and photo departments.

One of the traits Celestine and I shared was the realization that people are life's most valuable currency. This book would not have been possible without the following treasures in my life: John Schultz; Mary and Palmer Marsh; Charles Chambers; Jim Cassell; Chris Sink and the rest of my family at "The Burkhart's"; Clint Carruth; Mike Fisers; Andrew W.M. Beierle (for 24-hour tech support!); R. Robin McDonald; the Fleitz and Rapin families; Michael Johnson and Rhett and Carolyn Tanner.

Marylin Johnson, Eleanor Ringel Gillespie, Eileen Drennen, Amanda Miller, Carolyn Warmbold, Betty Parham, Lisa Axelberg, Maryn McKenna, Michelle Brooks, Bo Emerson and Maureen Downey all contributed immensely to this project and make going to work at the *AJC* each morning an absolute joy. Special thanks go to *AJC* staff writer and longtime Sibley associate Don O'Briant who mentored this project from its first breath.

My unyielding love, respect and gratitude go to Lee Eldredge and Leslie Ann Eldredge. Ultimately, this book wouldn't exist without former *AJC* editor Krista Reese who dragged a shy but admiring reporter into Celestine Sibley's office on September 22, 1994, and deposited him in front of her for the first time.

This volume is dedicated with much love and respect to the memory of the woman who wrote its words—Celestine Sibley—and to the memory of Barbara Eldredge, the woman who taught me to appreciate Celestine Sibley.